Written by Scott B. Comings
Designed and illustrated by Royal Bruce Montgomery

Published by Royal Bruce Ink, LLC

The Nature of Block Island

Scott B. Comings and Royal Bruce Montgomery

Published in the United States by Royal Bruce Ink, LLC.

Royal Bruce Ink, LLC., Box 1298, Block Island, RI 02807

ISBN #978-0-9718443-1-3

Manufactured in the United States of America

First printing: July 2005

1 3 5 4 2

Scott Comings, as an employee of The Nature Conservancy, wrote many of the initial parts of this book as articles that appeared in the Block Island Times. *While most of the articles have been reworked for this book, his work for The Conservancy had a role in its development and thus, any net profits that he receives will go directly to The Conservancy for its Block Island education program. The written content of this book solely reflects the views of the author, and not necessarily those of The Nature Conservancy.*

The roundest rock on the Block

If you go for a walk on a West Side beach
Where the rocks roll around in the sea,

You might find a rock that's a million years old
And as round as a round rock can be.

But...
If you don't pick it up, and you don't take it home,
You leave it right there where you found 'er,

The very next day, on the very same beach,
You'll find one a little bit rounder.

—RBM

Table of Contents

To my parents William and Margaret Comings,
who have profoundly changed my life by giving me two of the greatest gifts,
a childhood on Block Island and the ability to live here as an adult.

—SBC

To my pal Peglet, the rarest bird I know.

—RBM

An introduction

By Keith Lang

When the Block Island Office of The Nature Conservancy opened in 1991, I received a thoughtful letter from a summer resident. He wrote of his support for the initiative, but he also took the opportunity to express a personal perspective. It was his feeling that we seemed to be more interested in the preservation of a federally endangered insect, while his more pressing concern was what the future held for his young grandson as he observed him digging in the sand of Crescent Beach.

I wrote back to him to say that I was also concerned about his grandson, and, in fact, my own daughter, and that was why I was concerned about the American burying beetle. It was, and continues to be, my belief that all species are interconnected and that when one of us is threatened, it is simply a matter of time before we all will be.

There is so much we can learn from the other species that inhabit our planet, beings that our culture tends to view as existing only for our use and benefit. It is true that many of these plants and animals have benefited us in many ways, but they can only continue to do so if our often thoughtless activities do not cause their ultimate demise.

Block Island is an offshore refuge, a last bastion throughout the state and region for a number of species whose habitats have been destroyed elsewhere. Scott Comings has spent a great deal of time studying the species of Block Island and sharing his thoughts and observations with the readers of the *Block Island Times*. Many of his articles in the paper have been enriched by the wonderful illustrations and design of Bruce Montgomery.

This book brings all their collaborations together and provides the opportunity to see the island through Scott's eyes. In reading about these plants and creatures, we learn more about them and what they require to exist and flourish. At the same time, we learn more about ourselves in that very same regard.

Whether it is a plant located on an isolated hillside, a bird that graces the island sky, or a young child playing by the shore, each is an important part of the whole. Our lives are enriched by the relationships Scott describes. We can learn much from his observations and be inspired to go out and see for ourselves. What could be better than that.

Keith H. Lang *has been a trustee of the Block Island Land Trust and a director of the Block Island Conservancy. Keith was the first State Director for The Nature Conservancy in Rhode Island, and the Block Island Program was initiated during his tenure. He worked for many years for the late United States Senator John H. Chafee, and is now the Executive Director for The Champlin Foundations.*

Spring

Spring is a season of great hope as the Block Island emerges from the doldrums of winter. It is a season that some years returns in April and other years is almost completely bypassed. There is much to be enjoyed during this season including: singing spring peepers, blooming daffodils, mating American woodcocks, migrating songbirds, the shadblow, and the return of many plants and animals that have been dormant all winter long.

At dusk in March when the first peepers start calling, spring is truly here. This little tree frog and its buddies belt out an amazing and sometimes deafening chorus that comes from the many small wetlands around the island. For as loud as this species is, it is quite small and almost impossible to find; as soon as anyone gets near a wetland all the peepers go quiet.

In April, the daffodils start to bloom with their majestic yellows and oranges, which brighten up the drab wilds. This is the time to go to Clay Head and enjoy the thousands of daffodils tirelessly planted and maintained by the Lapham family. This amazing display of flowers is truly uplifting, and will positively benefit your spirits. Please remember not to pick the daffodils so future visitors can enjoy them too.

About the same time the daffodils bloom, the American woodcocks start to call at night. This goofy bird, which is quite difficult to spot, is easily identified by ear. An unmistakable nasal "peent" can be repeatedly heard almost anywhere on Block Island, especially during the full moon.

During the day, songbirds begin to return to the island from their southern adventures, some staying 'til autumn and others just passing through on their way to the northern part of the country or Canada. Birding in the spring is amazing because the males are decked out in their gaudy breeding plumages and are easy to identify. Those who enjoy auditory experiences will be amazed at the many different songs that can be heard only during this season.

Not to be outdone by the daffodils, the shadbushes bloom in early May. When all of the bushes are in bloom it is called a shadblow, and looks like it has snowed. This is truly one of the most beautiful times on Block Island.

By mid-May, animals are very active and plants have leafed out, both telltale signs that summer is near. This is a time when we welcome all of the biota back from their winter sleep or travels, and when Block Island becomes a lush and diverse environment again.

For the people who live on Block Island, the spring season is a time of preparation for the summer, and a time to rejoice that winter is over.

It is a time when residents start to reacquaint themselves with the beauty that is Block Island. Toward the end of spring, there is also a lot of anticipation, both positive and negative, of what the summer season will bring.

Unlike any other season, spring is a magical time on Block Island, when we see or hear unparalleled beauty from amphibian, flower, bird and bush.

The early signs of spring

It is early March, the winds are howling and winter seems as if it will go on forever. The animals disagree. Certain subtle changes in their behavior show that spring is coming. You too, can observe these changes if you know how to look and listen for them.

The return to Block Island of large numbers of American robins is the first sign that winter is winding down. These large flocks of robins go just far enough south (Maryland, Virginia) during the coldest parts of the winter, and then return in late January or early February. In the "pre-spring" they are seen in groups on lawns or in the shrubs that still have fruit. Soon they will be setting up territories and building nests.

In the middle of February, on a warm night, the singing of the American woodcock is first heard. The male woodcock makes a nasal "beezp" and repeats it over and over again. If you are lucky enough to catch a glimpse of this funny-looking animal, it is unmistakable; an 11-inch plump bird, with bulging eyes and an extremely long bill. It is often seen and heard near places that have open fields, mud or shallow standing water.

Red-winged blackbird.

American oystercatcher.

At the end of February, I was taking the high school class on a walk down Payne Road when a familiar sound was heard. At first I thought I had made a mistake because it seemed early, so we stopped and listened. The second time, there was no mistaking the "konk-la-ree" cry of the male red-winged blackbird. This common all-black bird with red and yellow epaulets on its wings disappears from Block Island in November, and then returns toward the end of winter to set up territories for females that will return in mid-March.

In the beginning of March, down at Andy's Way, a loud shrill "pic, pic, pic, kleep" is heard. This signals the return of the American oystercatcher from the shores of the Gulf of Mexico. This tidal flats bird, with its all-orange beak and black head, can be seen scouring flats looking for shellfish and other small organisms to eat.

Sometime in March we can hear the call of a spring peeper, a sure sign that winter is almost over. This tree frog is heard in chorus groups throughout Block Island in bushy areas underlined by water. The sounds from this peeper can be surprisingly loud for an animal that is only 0.75 to 1.25 inches long. It is easily separated from other frogs by its brownish-gray color and an imperfect black "x" on its back.

During your travels around Block Island, keep your eyes and ears peeled for the signs of spring. They will help you enjoy the long-awaited end of winter.

American robin.

Songs of spring

At the beginning of spring, it's been a number of months since the songs of birds have graced our ears, making early March truly wonderful. In your early spring travels, you will undoubtedly notice a number of new sounds coming from the bushes.

It all begins with the return of the American robin. One day there are no robins, the next day, they are everywhere, making their "cheer-up cheerio" song. Like the robin, other birds have just returned from down south, and are now staking their territory by singing. Another example is the red-winged blackbird. This 8¾-inch, glossy black bird with red shoulder patches has a song that is a liquid, gurgling "konk-la-reee." This bird is very common on roadsides and especially near swampy areas.

Another bird that has just returned is the eastern towhee (formally the rufous-sided towhee). This bird has one of the most distinctive calls on Block Island: "Drink, your tea," it seems to say, although this time of year it mostly just says "drink." In this 8½-inch species, the males are black above and the females are brown. They both have reddish-brown on the sides, and white below and in the tail. This species is found on the edges of shrubs and in them. The towhee is often on the ground where it is most comfortable looking for food.

The gray catbird has also returned from a "winter vacation" in the southern part of the country. This bird has a meow-like call, hence the name "catbird." It also has a call that goes "eric, eric, eric." The catbird is like the mockingbird in that it can imitate many different bird songs in addition to the two listed above. This 8½-inch bird is plain dark gray with a black cap and chestnut-colored feathers under the tail. This is one of the most common birds on Block Island and can be seen in and around shrubs.

Gray catbird.

In addition to the songs from birds that have just returned, we are now hearing birds that have been silent all winter. An example of this is the song sparrow, which has a song with three short clear notes and then a trill. This 6¼-inch bird is brown on the back and white below with heavy streaking, and from a distance, it has a brown dot on the breast. This common bird is found in thickets and shrubs.

The Carolina wren is another bird that has started its loud "teakettle, teakettle, teakettle, tea" song. This 5½-inch bird is rusty-brown above and tan below. It also has a call note that sounds like your thumb running down a comb. Look for this bird in the shrubs, but you can hear its loud song anywhere.

At night, keep an ear out for the American woodcock. Its call is a nasal "peent" that is one of the few sounds of the night this time of year. This goofy bird is 11 inches, very chunky, with brown above, tan below, and a long bill. This bird is found in fields and meadows.

This is an exciting time to listen for birds' songs because from March through May, each week you will hear new ones. Even if you don't know the name of the bird that is singing, it is still wonderful to listen to all the varied sounds. So take a walk, and I bet you'll hear a few new bird songs!

Carolina wren.

American woodcock.

Searching for barn owls and their nests

Have you ever seen a barn owl on Block Island? This mysterious species, which is often difficult to see, plays a very important role in the island ecosystem by keeping the Norway rat population down. In fact, this owl, which is found on every continent except Antarctica, is encouraged to nest in many places, because of its rodent-eating ways, by erecting nest boxes.

Over the last eight years, in the spring, I have taken many Block Island School classes searching for barn owls and their nests. Due to this animal's state-endangered status, it is important to document nesting sites each year for this species. Before taking students searching for the elusive barn owl at any of its past nesting areas, it is important for them to be able to identify this animal and know its basic biology.

Owlets in their nest.

This light-colored owl has a dramatic heart-shaped face that separates it from all other owls, a tawny breast, and a rusty-brown back. Measuring 16 inches, it is the largest owl on Block Island in the spring, and at night it makes a raspy, hissing screech, which is truly unmistakable (unlike most owls this species does not hoot). The barn owl is perfectly adapted to night hunting for rodents. The heart-shaped face funnels sound to the ears, which are offset to allow the animal to triangulate (find exact location of) the noise. The large eyes make it easier to see at night, and the feathers are specially designed so that its flight is silent.

Block Island is the only place in Rhode Island where this once-common owl still nests. In a typical year, there are three to four nests on the island. The barn owl likes to nest in the bluffs, and can be found by looking for holes about 5 inches in diameter just below the bluff crest, with whitewash (fecal material) underneath the holes; and by looking for bleached bones of small rodents near the boundary of the bluff and the beach.

After each class learns the barn owl basics, we then go on a field trip to search out this special owl. Mostly we go to Clay Head and take the trail to the beach. Once on the beach we walk north to the clay bluff and start scanning for holes that were caused by rocks falling out of the bluff (owls do not dig their own holes; it would dull their talons).

Usually whitewash running down the bluff is found fairly quickly, but locating what hole it came from is often very difficult. Using binoculars, students investigate each appropriate-sized hole for owl activity. Each potential nest hole is recorded, and students also make a note of it in their field notebooks.

At Pots and Kettles there is an area of bluff dotted with small holes, and above it a large hole with a ledge: pay dirt. For the past five years this large hole has had activity, and with the binoculars sometimes we are even able to see the tip of the female owl's head. What is interesting about the continual use of this hole is that barn owls only live two years on average, meaning that this was probably a different individual or possibly a descendant of the owl that inhabited this nest when it was first identified.

Barn owls will lay between five and 11 pure white eggs that are incubated by the female, who is regularly fed by the male. After about three weeks, the first egg hatches and an owlet, or baby owl, emerges. In eight weeks the owlets fledge the nest. The survival rate of the owlets in the nest depends on food availability, specifically the size of the Norway rat population. If food supplies are good, owls often raise two broods each year, and if they are poor, nesting will not occur.

With further observation of the area, the students often ask, "What are all the small holes around this predator's nest?" These are bank swallow nests which are active from May to July; the birds nest close to the owl nest for protection (barn owls cannot catch bank swallows).

In addition to the one or two nests at Clay Head, the barn owl regularly nests in the bluffs: east of the Southeast Lighthouse, at Black Rock, and at Lewis Farm. One year an owl even nested north of the entrance to Scotch Beach. So they can be anywhere where there are bluffs with large holes.

If you want to search for barn owl nests on your own, go to any clay bluffs and look up from the beach for holes that are of the appropriate size. It is important to use binoculars and view from afar because barn owls can be very aggressive and may surprise you by swooping at your head!

The great seal rescue

On Wednesday, April 2, 2003, The Nature Conservancy received multiple calls that a small seal had been seen on Scotch Beach. While hauling out to rest on the beach for less than 24 hours is a normal behavior, we learned that this seal had been in the same place since the previous day.

We get involved in a seal rescue under any of the following five circumstances: the seal has a major gash and is bleeding profusely; the seal is entangled; the seal is extremely thin (with bones protruding through its skin); the seal is recently deceased; or the seal has been hauled out for more than 24 hours in the same place.

Because it became apparent that this seal had potentially been in the same place for more than 24 hours, we decided to conduct an initial exam of the animal. At 12:30 p.m., we came upon the seal sleeping on its back in the middle of the beach just north of the Scotch Beach entrance. We noted it was a gray seal pup, and it was a little on the skinny side. Upon further inspection, we noticed that its eyes were clean, and as we got closer it started to growl. These are both good signs, suggesting the seal was not that sick. We did notice, however, that its breathing seemed to be a little labored.

We then returned to the office, called Mystic Aquarium in Connecticut, and reported the potential stranding. Lisa Mazzaro, a research scientist at the aquarium, answered the phone and asked me a lot of questions. Armed with this information, she went to speak with the staff veterinarian. At 1:15 p.m., Mazzaro called back to tell us to get the seal and put it on the ferry.

I quickly realized we only had 45 minutes to complete this rescue, because the only ferry to the mainland was leaving at 2 p.m. Luckily, we were prepared for this and grabbed the necessary equipment to perform the rescue: a seal cage (similar to a dog carrier, given to us by Mystic for these type of rescues), and two pieces of plywood measuring 2 feet by 5 feet. We then raced out to the seal.

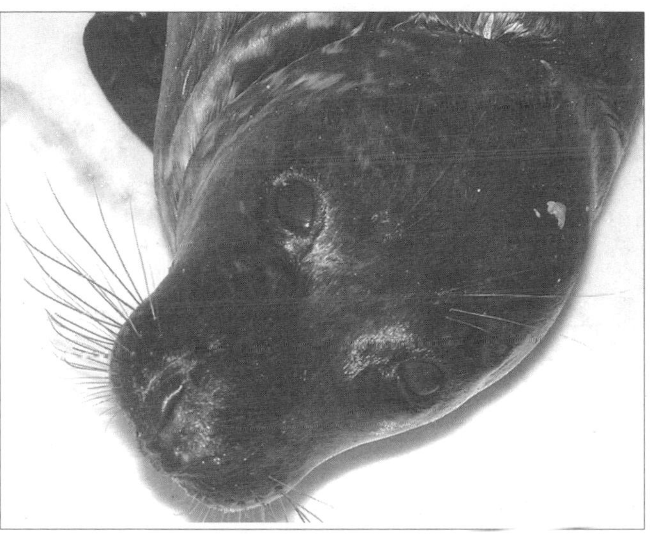

The male gray seal pup at Mystic Aquarium after its rescue from Scotch Beach.

When we reached the seal at 1:25 p.m., an unleashed dog was harassing it. It is important to remember at this time of year that it is common for seals to be on the beach, and dogs (preferably leashed) and people should give them a lot of space. Once the dog was corralled, we went about the rescue.

The cage was set up between the seal and the ocean with the door open. We then used the plywood to create a track to the cage. At this point the seal was agitated and trying to bite us. Gray seals are fairly aggressive and deliver a nasty bite that is prone to infection. Thus, we were very careful as we helped the seal down the track and into the cage. After some initial resistance the seal went right in.

The seal, in its new home, was carried back to the van and transported to the boat. When we reached the ferry, it was 1:35 p.m. As always, with seal and other marine mammal strandings, Interstate Navigation was extremely helpful, bringing a pallet for the caged seal's transport to the mainland. By 1:40 p.m., the seal was on the boat, and we could relax.

The gray seal was picked up by a Mystic volunteer and taken to the aquarium, where it was cleaned and examined. Mazzaro called to tell me "the gray seal was about three to four weeks old and was a male due to its coloration. While it did not have obvious injuries it did have a high white blood cell count (meaning minor infection) and parasites."

The seal was to remain at Mystic until it got better and was eating on its own. It then would be released back into the wild. At the time of the rescue, Mystic Aquarium had seven seals in the Seal Rescue Clinic: three gray seal pups and four yearling harp seals. The aquarium is a non-profit organization that handles marine mammal strandings in Connecticut, Rhode Island and Fisher's Island, N.Y. The Nature Conservancy on Block Island and Mystic Aquarium have been working in partnership since 1991.

Please remember: If you find a seal on the beach, give it plenty of space, because this is how they rest and renew their strength. With the help of many concerned people, this gray seal pup will make a full recovery and be released back into the wild.

****

Postscript

This seal had epilepsy. Two weeks into his care at Mystic, the seal had a seizure and drowned.

Those amazing chimney swifts

One April day, I was out with the sixth grade of the Block Island School at Fresh Pond when we saw a sure sign of spring, a chimney swift flying overhead. This amazing dark brown swift is 5 inches long, has a cigar-shaped body, with a short, stubby tail and long thin wings. It is the only swift that is regularly seen on Block Island (mostly in the spring and fall). The swift is often seen high in the sky and when it is flying, the left and right wing alternate, seemingly rocking back and forth. The swift has a loud chattering call that can be easily heard when the bird is sighted.

Chimney swifts spend the winter in Peru, Chile and Brazil, migrating to the eastern and mid-western United States for the summer breeding season. Although this species nests from Florida to Canada, including mainland Rhode Island, here it is only passing through, and there are no records of the species nesting on Block Island. While here, the swift refuels by catching flying insects in the air. In fact, this is often why you see them make sudden changes in direction.

Once on the breeding grounds, which are usually composed of woodland and open areas near human habitation, swifts nest in chimneys. They make half-saucer nests attached to a chimney wall about 22 inches down from the top. Historically, these nests were made in hollow trees, but now chimneys are the main nesting area. This species greatly benefited by the arrival of European settlers, whose buildings provided an abundance of nesting sites.

Often nesting in colonies, the chimney swift collects nest materials, predominately twigs, in flight. These are then glued to each other and to the chimney wall with saliva. When the nest is near completion, after roughly 18 to 30 days, four to five eggs are laid. The nesting pair is often assisted by a helper, either

male or female, and sometimes two. These birds assist with both feeding and incubation.

Eggs are incubated for 28 days, and the chicks reside in the nest for three weeks. When they are ready to go, the fledglings use their sharp, strong claws to cling and crawl up the vertical wall out of the nest, and then they fly out the top of the chimney. The fledged birds and nonbreeding adults flock together in groups numbering several thousand, and roost together in chimneys. In the late summer, the swifts begin the long trek back to South America.

In April, the chimney swifts return. The students and I observed one swift's amazing aerial acrobatics. We watched this individual catch a few insects, soaring high into the air, and finally disappear. The students made a note and a quick sketch of the swift's unique flying style in their field notebooks. If you are outside on Block Island, be sure to look up for the "cigar with wings" near the end of its amazing journey. What better way is there to show that spring has sprung?

What do you know about bird feet?

Raptor:
Easily distinguished by its long nails, called talons, which are used to swiftly kill its prey.

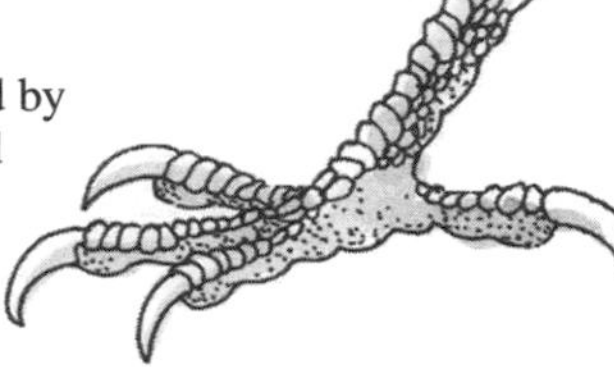

Songbird:
Its foot is ideal for perching or walking on the ground, with three delicate toes in front and one in back.

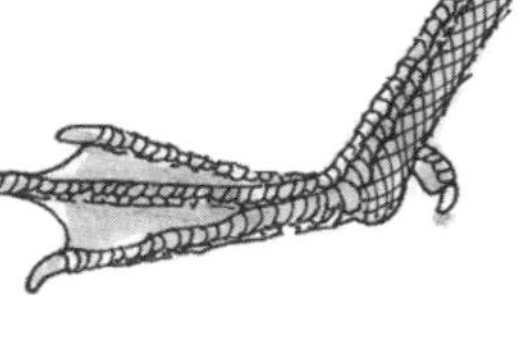

Duck:
The skin that connects its toes helps make the duck an extremely strong swimmer

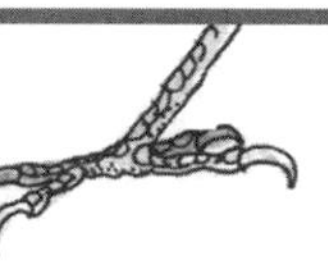

Woodpecker:
The two toes in front and back allow for better gripping on tree trunks.

Owl:
The feathers that completely cover the owl's foot help make it silent when approaching prey.

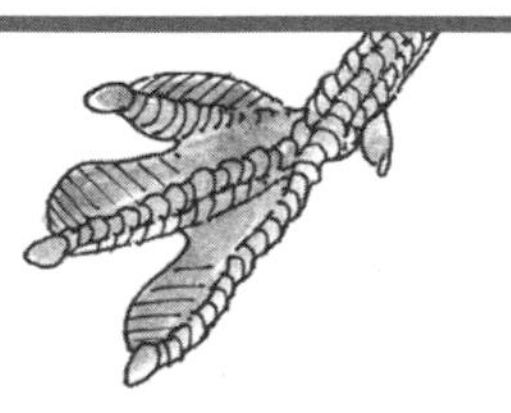

Grebe:
Its paddle-like foot is designed for swimming and diving.

Creatures of the night

In the spring, many creatures of the night make themselves known. In mid-April after dark, near swamps and ponds, the sounds of spring peepers can be deafening. In the fields, the mysterious song of the American woodcock can be heard at dusk and dawn (all night long when the moon is full). The loud call of the barn owl can be heard almost anywhere at night during this time of year, if you stop to listen.

These three animals are the predominant nocturnal animals you will hear and, if you are lucky, see at dusk and into the night. For me, when I start hearing or seeing these animals, it means that spring is really here.

The spring peeper is the most numerous and vocal nighttime animal. This tree frog is heard in chorus groups throughout Block Island in bushy areas underlined by water. The best way to locate this frog is to follow its sound. In some choice areas, the sounds from the peeper can be surprisingly loud for such a small animal.

When approaching a peeper "chorus group," you must be as quiet as possible or else these tricky amphibians will stop singing, and then it is nearly impossible to find them. Once in a peeper area, scan the bushes for a small frog that is only 0.75 to 1.25 inches long. Skin is brown or gray in color, and on its back is an imperfect "x". The Latin name, *Hyla crucifer*, refers to the "x" or cross.

The American woodcock is probably the funniest looking nighttime animal on Block Island. This unmistakable 11-inch plump bird, with bulging eyes and an extremely long bill, can be found throughout the island, especially near places that have open fields, mud, or shallow standing water. The woodcock, using its unusual beak, probes in the mud for earthworms and other "delicious" invertebrates, eating more than its weight every day.

In the spring, the courtship display of the woodcock can be seen between dusk and dawn. The male, with its

wings whistling (the outer wing feathers of the woodcock are modified with a small gap between feathers to produce the whistling sound), flies in widening spirals rising up to 100 feet, circles his highest point, and zigzags to earth like a falling leaf. When it reaches the ground it releases a nasal "peent." This display is repeated many times.

The best way to locate this species is to go to an open field at dusk and listen for the whistling sound. When the sound is heard, look up into the air and you may see the woodcock. A note of caution: walk very slowly and look where you step because woodcocks only flush when they are about to be stepped on, and thus will give you a serious start when they "flush up" right next to you. They are extremely well-camouflaged, nearly invisible during the day.

The barn owl is one of the most elusive nocturnal animals on Block Island. This light-colored owl has a heart-shaped face, rusty-brown back, and measures 16 inches. It is the largest owl on Block Island in the spring. Keep your ear out for a raspy, hissing screech; it is truly unmistakable!

The island is the only place in Rhode Island where this owl still nests. The barn owl likes to nest in the bluffs, and can be found by looking for holes about 5 inches in diameter just below the bluff crest, with whitewash (fecal material) underneath the holes; and by looking for bleached bones of small rodents near the bluff/beach boundary. If you are lucky, you can see the owls from the beach as you look up toward the bluff. Barn owls can be very aggressive and may surprise you by swooping at your head, so you should not get too close!

This raptor hunts at night in open fields and along many of the trails found throughout the island. It eats its prey (favorites being the meadow vole and Norway rat) whole, and then regurgitates a pellet, composed of fur, bones, and other indigestible material. There is a good chance of seeing these pellets on the trails at the Nathan Mott Park and Clay Head Preserve.

If you go for a walk in the spring at night, keep an eye and an ear out for these nighttime creatures. They are all around you.

Vernal ponds

What is a vernal pond? It is a pond that exists in the spring but generally dries up every year during the summer, and then is replenished in the fall or early winter. These ponds are also known as ephemeral ponds. On Block Island, many vernal ponds that are extremely full of water in the spring may be nothing but cracked mud by July.

Because of this drying-up cycle, no fish are found in this type of pond. Thus, many different types of insects, amphibians, and other animals can be found in them because they are not eaten by fish. At this point many people may lose interest; to freshwater aquatic experts, however, vernal ponds are the most interesting thing on Block Island.

Funded by The Nature Conservancy, aquatic expert Mark Chandler from the New England Aquarium studied the ponds of Block Island from 1997-2001. He has surveyed over 100 ponds for plants, animals, and water quality. After reviewing all of the data, Chandler and The Nature Conservancy believe that vernal and fishless ponds are the most important freshwater habitat on Block Island.

Vernal ponds have some really rare animals that are extremely interesting. At one such pond in Nathan Mott Park, a predacious diving beetle was found that measures over 1 inch long and has never been recorded in Rhode Island, and only documented once before in New England. This beetle, dark in color, feeds on other aquatic insects and due to its size is unmistakable.

Fairy shrimp were first recorded in Rhode Island by the Block Island School fifth-grade in 1999 at Payne Farm! They have since been found in five other vernal ponds. This interesting freshwater arthropod, measuring 0.5 inches, has many legs with red gills, swims on its back, and is transparent in color. In Massachusetts, a pond only gets a vernal rating if it contains fairy shrimp. There are 25 species of fairy shrimp in the region and Block Island's are the largest type.

Red-spotted newts, Block Island's only salamander, were found in all of the fishless ponds sampled. This newt has three main life phases: larvae, eft, and adult. The aquatic larvae, which are olive to green in color, have external gills and measure 0.75 to 1.5 inches. They most often live in fishless ponds and after an undetermined amount of time, transform into terrestrial efts (this phase is often bypassed on Block Island), then return to the pond and become an adult. The only constant characteristic throughout the various stages of this animal's life is that it has up to 21 red spots present on its back.

Other amphibians that were found in some of the ponds were spring peepers (a light-brown tree frog, smaller than 1 inch, with an "x" on its back) and green frogs (the only large frog on Block Island). The painted turtle (up to 4 inches in diameter with red and yellow markings).

In addition to the animals mentioned above, countless insects were found that were identified by microscope back in Chandler's laboratory. These insects included mayflies, dragonfly and damselfly larvae, true bugs, caddisflies, and stoneflies.

WET NOW, DRY LATER — This springtime pond, bisected by an old stonewall, is on the lane leading to Heinz Field.

As the water surface shrinks in a vernal pond, it becomes easier to see all of the different animals inhabiting the pond. When the pond is reduced to a puddle there is nothing but activity as animals vie for the limited remaining water. Finally, animals will either go into the mud, become adults and leave the pond, or die. It is a harsh reality but it takes a special animal to live in a vernal pond.

When next you see a small pond that looks like a puddle, treat it with respect by leaving a buffer of vegetation around it, avoid using fertilizer near it, and never introduce fish. Make sure to observe it because you will be amazed at the amount of life in such a small area.

Exploring Fresh Pond Preserve

Fresh Pond Preserve is a wonderful place to visit in the springtime to experience what inland Block Island has to offer. The northern and western sides of Fresh Pond look the way much of Block Island used to with open, rolling fields and stonewalls. The pond itself is the largest freshwater body of water on Block Island. It is also one of the deeper and cleaner ponds on the island.

As you enter the preserve from Lakeside Drive be sure to read the marker that relays the story of the first settlers and their tie to Fresh Pond. The meadow habitat that surrounds the trail is composed mostly of common milkweed, chicory, various goldenrod species, butter-and-eggs, and pasture rose. In this area are many different species of spiders, including crab and grass spiders (both harmless).

As you continue down the trail you will notice two old apple trees that are vegetative signs of the past. Be sure to observe the holes in the trees to see if any bird species are nesting in them. Also look at the trunks of these trees, which are covered by yellow-bellied sapsucker holes from foraging exploits during this bird's migration pit-stops on Block Island.

Venturing down the hill, be sure to stay on the path because there is a lot of poison ivy (leaves of three, let it be). At the base of the hill is a small creek that is fed by Fresh Pond and is often inhabited by green frogs, red-winged blackbirds, and yellow warblers. Deep in the poison ivy is one of the few spots on the island that has orchids.

Across the bridge and to the left is a wonderful spot to look at Fresh Pond. In this area there are lots of lily pads, small fish, and dragonflies. While this looks like a good access spot to go swimming, please remember that there is no swimming in this pond (it is a back-up reservoir for the town). Besides, Fresh Pond is home to some of the largest leeches that are found on Block Island. This is however, an excellent spot to sit for a while taking in the sights and sounds of the pond.

Looking opposite of the pond you will notice Smilin' Thru, once the home of Arthur Penn, a famous songwriter in the 1920s. Picking up the trail again, it starts to get steep. On your left, you will see Phragmities, an invasive, tall reedy grass that grows where there was once an icehouse. This grass only grows in areas where the soil has been disturbed. Continuing the climb, the trail branches; take the left fork, which will lead to a magnificent view of the pond and the plains. This gives an excellent view of the southeastern part of the island.

Rejoining the main trail the habitat changes to coastal shrubs, with shadbush, bayberry, black cherry and arrowwood the most common. This short loop trail is in a small hollow with a globally imperiled morainal grassland site on its west side, which has specialized plants and lichens, including northern blazing star, little bluestem, and switch grass. At the end of the loop if you go right, the adventure continues into Rodman's Hollow, but a left turn takes you back to the trailhead.

Over the past five years, the Fresh Pond preserve has been an inventory site for middle school classes studying biodiversity at the Block Island School. With weekly observations stationed at various parts of the preserve, many plants and animals have been observed and recorded including daring jumping spiders (a spider that lives under rocks with orange spots on its abdomen), isopods (sow bugs), millipedes, centipedes, raptor pellets (regurgitated fur and bones), 50 species of birds, muskrats, many species of aquatic invertebrates and much more. As the years go by the list of species continues to grow.

So on your journey throughout the Fresh Pond Preserve see how many different plant and animal species you can find, or just enjoy the hike and views. This preserve is truly one of the jewels of Block Island!

A waterless hollow

When I lead trips for school groups in Rodman's Hollow, one of the most common questions I get is, "why is there no water in the bottom of Rodman's Hollow?" This is an excellent question that leads to the very geologic core of Block Island.

On one such trip to the hollow, I was with the third grade from the Block Island School. It was early April 2001, right after a rainstorm when the island received six inches of rain. Before starting our nature walk we all hypothesized that there would be a lot of standing water because of all of the slopes leading into Rodman's Hollow. And we were sure that there would be at least a puddle at the bottom of Rodman's, which is only 20 feet above sea level. (The commonly heard myth that the hollow is below sea level is untrue.)

The third-grade class at Rodman's Hollow, April, 2001.

Surprisingly, during our walk we saw no standing water. The bone-dry findings once again lead us to the question above, "Why isn't this a pond?"

Let's start with the basics. As with the rest of the island, Rodman's Hollow was glacially formed. It is the best example of a meltwater channel on Block Island. In fact, as the glacier that formed the island was melting, there was a raging stream that went through the hollow and continued for 70 miles, where it met up with the much-reduced ocean. (At this point in time, more than 20,000 years ago, a good bit of the present-day ocean was frozen and still part of the glacier.)

When the glacier finished melting, the stream dried up and no water remained in the hollow. Why? The simple answer is that the hollow's soil is extremely sandy with gravel, making for excellent drainage. This composition is due to the flow of the stream, where fine sediments that trap water were never able to accumulate in the hollow.

As with most classes that glean this new information, the third-graders searched around the hollow and found many places where sand and gravel poke through the vegetation. To illustrate this phenomenon, I reminded them of when you pour water on the beach, how quickly the water disappears (drains). It is the same principle with Rodman's Hollow, just on a much larger scale.

When you start to identify the plants in the bottom of Rodman's Hollow, they also support the answer to the question above. All plants tell the story of the soil they live in, and it quickly becomes clear that most of the species in this area are only found in sandy soils. Examples of these special plants include mouse-eared hawkweed, bushy rockrose, switch grass, and little bluestem.

Most of the ponds on Block Island that are rain-fed have a glacially deposited clay bottom that keeps the water from draining. Luckily, the bottom of the hollow isn't clay or it would be Rodman Pond instead of Rodman's Hollow (that saves us a lot of trouble because there already is a Rodman Pond).

THE GREAT BLOCK ISLAND NATURE AND HISTORY SCAVENGER HUNT

Complete all 11 items on the list by journeying to different locations on the island. (The easiest location to find each item is in parentheses.) Please leave all of the items located for this hunt where you found them.

HERE'S WHAT YOU MUST FIND:

1. An animal or bird footprint in the sand or mud. Draw it on a piece of paper. What kind of creature is it? (beach)
2. A bird feather. Trace it. (anywhere)
3. The year the Southeast Lighthouse was built. (SE Light cornerstone)
4. A turtle sunning on the rocks. Draw it. (any pond, especially the ones on Clay Head Preserve)
5. The name of one of the first settlers on Block Island. Write the name down. (Settlers' Rock)
6. An insect. (It must have six legs.) Draw a picture of it. (anywhere)
7. A spider. (It must have eight legs.) Draw it. (anywhere)
8. Three different leaves. Trace them. There's no need to pick the leaves, and beware of poison ivy.
9. A wildflower. Draw it. Please leave the flower for others to enjoy.
10. A gravestone over 100 years old. Write down the person's name and the dates. (Block Island Cemetery)
11. Something amazing! Draw a picture of it. (anywhere)

Spring's the time to see amphibians

Did you know that spring is the time of year to see amphibians on Block Island? These special creatures were the first land vertebrates to evolve from fish about 300 million years ago. Amphibians are terrestrial, but they still depend on a moist environment; their eggs are laid in water, where their larvae develop. While these animals may appear small and primitive, they are in fact members of a successful group that has outlasted the dinosaurs by 65 million years.

Block Island has only three species of amphibians: red-spotted newt, spring peeper, and green frog. These animals can be found in any moist area but are most often found in fishless ponds and swamps.

The red-spotted newt is a type of salamander. Newts are not as slippery as most salamanders, in fact their skin is rough. This species eats insects, leeches, worms, and frogs' eggs. Few predators eat newts because their skin gland secretions are toxic or at least irritating to mucous membranes.

The newt has three main phases: larvae, eft, and adult. Throughout the stages of this animal's life, the only constant characteristic is up to 21 red spots on its back. The aquatic larvae are olive to green, have gills, and measure 0.75 to 1.5 inches. They live in fishless ponds and after an undetermined amount of time, transform into terrestrial efts.

The efts measure 1.25 to 3.25 inches. They are bright orange to red and are found in upland habitat within a half-mile of their breeding ground. On Block Island and in other coastal locations the efts are mostly brown on their backs with orange on their bellies. After one to three years, the land-based efts return to the ponds and become adults. The adult red-spotted newt ranges from 2.25 to 4.75 inches. Both the male and female are olive-green; the male has a tail fin during the breeding season.

The spring peeper is the most numerous amphibian on Block Island, and the most vocal nighttime animal. This tree frog is often heard in chorus throughout Block Island in bushy areas above water. Their special toe discs allow them to climb up the shrubs to search for insects to eat and for locations termed calling stations.

The larval stage for a frog is a tadpole. The peeper tadpole is green and 0.25 inches long. The adult peeper is only 0.75 to 1.25 inches long with skin that is brown or gray. On its back is an imperfect "x." Its Latin name, *Hyla crucifer*, refers to the "x" or cross. The females are always larger than the males. It is shocking how small this animal is compared to the sound it makes. The peeper is active at dusk and during the night from March to November. In September and October it is often possible to see these frogs wandering though fields on a damp day.

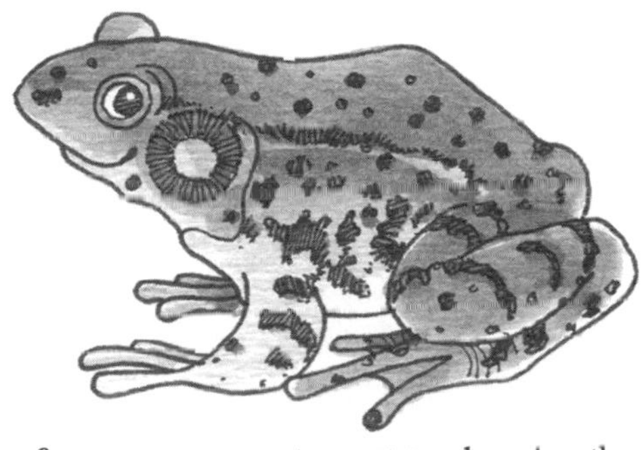

Green frogs are common to most ponds and wetlands on Block Island. Their call is like the strumming of a loose banjo string that is repeated three or four times with each note louder than the last. It is a true frog, with long legs, narrow waist, and smooth skin. Like Block Island's other amphibians this species eats mostly insects.

The tadpole for this species is dark green and about 1 inch long. The adult green frog is 3 inches long with dark spots on its lower back and sides. Its legs are brown with blackish bands. Males have a yellow throat and swollen thumbs. The green frog, if cornered, inflates itself, stands tall and utters a high-pitched "eek" before jumping into the water. This is the easiest Block Island amphibian to see because it is active both day and night from April to October and does not scare easily.

While amphibians on Block Island are very commonly heard and sometimes seen, they are declining in numbers at a rapid rate worldwide because of habitat destruction, acid rain, pesticides, and increasing ultraviolet light. It is amazing that a group of animals that has survived countless changes in the world for 300 million years is now in danger. So remember, the next time you hear or see a red-spotted newt, spring peeper, or green frog on Block Island, it is special and not to be taken for granted!

One busy robin

The signs that spring is here are abundant: the peepers calling, birds chirping, and the shad about to bloom. The American robin is also affected by the change in season. This is one robin's story.

Measuring 10 inches in length, with a red breast and dark gray back, the American robin is one of the most common birds on Block Island. Its song is a clear "cheery-up, cheery-ee." It is often seen hopping around lawns looking for worms and other food.

This story started one early May morning when, looking out my office window, I saw a female robin with a couple of pieces of straw in her mouth. Due to the fact that it was spring, I knew immediately that the straw was nesting material, and saw that the robin was starting to build a nest on a support beam outside my window.

In the shrubs nearby was a bright male robin watching the start of construction. Robin nests are often built jointly by the male and the female; however, in this case it was the female doing all the work. Determinedly, the robin would bring new material, place it on top of the nest she had started and then nestle into the pile.

While the female robin was away, a female house sparrow, a 6-inch small gray bird, would sneak in and steal some of the material for her own nest that was being built in one of the eaves of our building. Possibly because of the pilfering house sparrow, the next day the robin started to build another nest on the same beam, three feet to the left of her first one. The male still looked on from the shrubs nearby.

The base of the second nest was very much like the first, made of twigs and straw stacked on top of one another.

The house sparrow stayed busy removing parts of the new nest when the robins weren't around, and the second nest was abandoned before its completion. In fact, the first two abandoned, uncompleted nests were entirely removed by the industrious house sparrow.

Undaunted, the next day the robin then selected a third site on the same beam, four more feet to the left of the second nest. The male continued to look on from the bushes. About a quarter of the way through the building process, the female, for no apparent reason, abandoned this nest, too.

The next day, four days into the nest-building spree, a fourth try was located two feet to the right of the most-recently abandoned nest. It began in much the same way as the first three, but this one continued to grow.

While the base of the nest was constructed with hay, twigs, and mud, the top of the nest was made of feathers and fresh grasses. The inside of the nest was then lined with mud and soft material like fine grass and spider webs. The construction of the nest took about three days, with the female doing almost all of the work, even though the male was always in the area.

The completed nest was 10 inches in height, 8 inches in diameter, with grass, twigs and feathers everywhere. Basically, it looked as if the wind could blow it apart at any moment.

After five days the female had yet to lay any eggs, but she was around her nest throughout the day. Once the pale blue eggs are laid it's 14 days before any chicks emerge, and another 16 days before they fledge.

When the chicks fledge, the male takes over caring for them and the female builds another nest and lays a second clutch of eggs. Robins can lay up to three clutches in a single nesting season.

While it was a lot of work for this industrious female robin to actually complete a nest, it was neat to be able to watch the construction process from start to start to start to start to finish.

Only during the spring would one robin put so much effort into finishing one nest!

Spring migration on Block Island

After a long winter on Block Island listening to the calls of the same bird species day after day (mostly the white-throated sparrow's "poor old Sam Peabody" call or the Carolina wren's "teakettle" call), a birdwatcher looks forward to the first "foreign" bird song, signaling that spring migration is finally here.

Spring songbird migration is a very exciting time on Block Island, because you never know what warblers, thrushes, and vireos you will find. Unlike the fall, the songbirds are in their mating plumage and are easy to identify. One day you may see a beautiful but common magnolia warbler, and the next you may see the extremely rare Canada warbler.

Most of these songbirds are on their way back from Central and South America where they spent the winter, heading toward the northern United States and Canada, where they will nest for the summer.

Block Island is not on the direct path for many of these birds, but "fringe" birds still appear throughout the spring. However, when there is a southwest wind (what Block Island birders dream of at night), the songbirds are blown off the mainland and the island is overrun with colorful birds. On these days, it is possible to see more than nine species of flycatcher, five species of thrush, five species of vireo, 32 species of warbler and countless other species.

Once these birds are on Block Island, they seek out the island's coastal shrub habitat (bayberry, arrowwood, shadbush) for protection from migrating, sharp-shinned hawks, merlins, and peregrine falcons that are always looking for an easy meal. In addition to the need for protection from raptors, songbirds are also dehydrated when they arrive, so they require water. So, ponds covered by shrubs are the ideal place for songbirds.

Canada warbler.

The Clay Head Preserve has many of these secluded ponds and is by far the best place to see migrant songbirds on the island. By wandering the many trails, you can look for large flocks of birds. At first there will be almost silence, and then you will be bombarded by all sorts of wonderful songs. A flock! At this point, there are small birds everywhere that are yellow, red, blue, green, gray, black, orange, and brown; you cannot move your binoculars fast enough to see all the beautiful birds flying by you.

Magnolia warbler.

In a flock, certain species are always in the top of the bushes and other species are always on the ground; each species has its own place. Then, as quickly as the flock arrives, it will be gone and you will be left with nothing but silence and maybe a bird call in the distance. You can easily spend the whole day following these incredible flocks and see a different bird species each time.

Another great place to observe migrant songbirds is the Kurz property, east of Sachem Pond. Its many dead trees are full of insects that are an easy meal for the hungry birds. It is easy to find birds like the black-and-white warbler and the black-throated green warbler "working" over certain trees for food. Unlike the flocks at Clay Head, the birds here are much slower paced, giving you more time to study the birds and watch their behavior.

Although Clay Head preserve and the Kurz property both provide highlights of migration birdwatching, you can see amazing birds anywhere on Block Island's 6,188 acres. So, in the busy spring, take a little time each day to explore the places where these incredible songbirds hide and you will be rewarded with new bird sounds and amazing colors. Hope to see you out there!

Hooded warbler.

Small but powerful: the American kestrel story

The first American kestrel sightings on Block Island usually occur around the last week in March. This interesting little falcon, once known as a sparrow hawk, can often be seen around the island foraging in recently mowed fields and short-grass meadows.

The kestrel is nine to 12 inches long — about the size of a blue jay. What separates this bird from all other raptors is its rufous (reddish-brown) back. Both the sexes have a white face with a black mustache, the males being easily identified by their slate-blue wings.

This species has a fluid, swallow-like flight pattern until prey is spotted; then it hovers with wings beating rapidly (hence the nickname "windhover") and shoots down on its prey. After feeding, the kestrel will sit erect on a perch, usually a tree snag, bush, fencepost or wire.

The diet of this species consists primarily of large insects like grasshoppers, along with an occasional small mammal or bird. When the kestrel sees prey it swoops talons first, killing the animal instantly. The dead animal is then taken to a perch where it is ripped apart by the kestrel's hook-shaped bill and ingested. The kestrel will also take prey from the air when the opportunity presents itself. During the nesting season, the male of this species will cache food in grassy clumps for future use.

The kestrel prefers to locate its tree-cavity nest near open or partly open habitats. The male performs a courtship display around the nest site. He rapidly hovers in wide circles above the perch, then bends his quivering wing tips, calling out before returning to the perch. The female then joins him and they both bow at each other with the female calling continuously. In some populations there is courtship feeding, where the male feeds the female to woo her.

American kestrels

The cavity nest itself is in a tree or man-made nesting box minimally lined with material such as moss, vegetation and spider webs. Pairs usually have one brood consisting of four pinkish-white eggs with brown splotches. If there is an abundance of food the pair will have a second brood, usually using the same nest. The eggs are incubated by the male and female for 29 to 31 days. The nestlings are fed for 30 days by both parents. After fledging, the male continues to feed the youngsters until migration.

On Block Island, you can see this amazing falcon in almost any season except in the dead of winter. However, in the summer this species is rare because of the lack of suitable nesting spots on the island. Plans for a kestrel nest box from the Rhode Island Audubon Society are shown on Page 136. Should you want to help encourage this species on Block Island, build a nest box and place it on your property.

In the fall, the kestrel migrates as far south as Panama. During the winter, individuals will defend territories, with females being attracted to open habitat and males preferring denser vegetation, before returning north for the spring.

So the next time you are traveling near grassland habitat, look for the American kestrel perched on powerlines or soaring through the air. If you find one, watch its behavior: it will be an entrancing experience you will never forget!

Not all birds venture to Block Island

Spring has finally arrived, and the migrant birds have begun to return while resident ones, quiet all winter, have started to sing. This is an exciting time for birdwatchers, with American woodcocks singing at night and red-winged blackbirds doing their courtship display during the day. However, despite all this bird activity, there are some species common on the mainland that rarely, if ever, venture to Block Island.

The red-tailed hawk, the most commonly seen raptor on the mainland, is rarely seen here. This large hawk measures 19 to 25 inches and has a white breast, streaked belly, brown upper parts, and a rufous (brownish-red) tail. Typically this species soars, with its broad wings and rounded red tail making it quite conspicuous. But the animals don't like to cross open ocean. The only time one is spotted on-island is when it has been blown off course.

Turkey vultures are seen throughout the mainland scavenging for carrion. This black bird with a naked red head measures 26 to 32 inches with a 6-foot wingspan. When soaring, this species is easily identifiable by the two-toned blackish coloration of the wing underside. Like the red-tailed hawk, the turkey vulture avoids crossing open ocean unless it is blown over to the island by the winds. Usually this species can be seen about once a year on Block Island.

The great-horned owl is the largest owl in New England and has ear tufts or "horns." It measures 18 to 25 inches with brown plumage containing black barring. This owl also has a conspicuous white bib under its beak and a distinctive "hoo, hoo-oo, hoo, hoo" call. While there were reports of this species on Block Island and maybe even nesting in the 1980s, there have been no recent sightings. It is hard to speculate why this species disappeared from the island, but possible reasons include the loss of pine trees, more suitable habitat available on the mainland, and a better selection of rodent prey sources on the mainland.

Pileated woodpeckers can be found throughout New England forests but, to my knowledge, never on Block Island. This large woodpecker measures 16 to 20 inches with a bright red crest, black body and white cheek stripe that continues to the wing. In flight, white flashes from underneath the wing are seen with each wing beat. Block Island's lack of forest is the obvious reason for no recorded sightings of this species, but there may be other factors as well.

The tufted titmouse is one of the most common "feeder" birds seen on the mainland. This 6-inch bird is gray above, white below, with rusty flanks and a tufted crest. The titmouse has a very loud "peter, peter, peter" whistled call. Like the red-tailed hawk and the turkey vulture, this species doesn't like to cross the ocean. I know of only two records for this species on Block Island.

While Block Island is perfect for most of the avian species seen in New England, there are a few common ones on the mainland that are noticeably absent here. Thus, when one of the species above is spotted, it is an important record! And remember, just because a species is common doesn't mean it isn't of interest.

15 species you will see on Block Island

Common loon
American oystercatcher
American woodcock
Killdeer
Ring-necked pheasant
Northern harrier
Cooper's hawk
Downy woodpecker
Fish crow
Eastern bluebird
Yellow-rumped warbler
Red-winged blackbird
White-throated sparrow
Swamp sparrow
Song sparrow

Those amazing shad

Early May is a time of great anticipation on Block Island, waiting for the shadbush's display of natural splendor. When this species is in full bloom the island is covered in a sea of white, and it becomes quite apparent that this is one of the most common shrubs here. But more than that, it has a very interesting story.

This species received its name because the bloom usually coincides with the spawning runs of shad fish in coastal rivers. It is also known by many other names, including saskatoon, shadblow and Juneberry, with a number of related species found throughout North America. The most interesting alternative name for this bush is serviceberry, because in northern areas when it blooms it indicates that the ground has thawed enough to bury folks who have died during the winter.

The shadbush, *Amelanchier canadensis*, is a fruit-bearing, forest understory shrub or small tree, which normally grows from 10 to 20 feet in height. On Block Island it reaches gigantic proportions due to the relative lack of competition from larger trees, with some easily in excess of 30 feet. In fact, Harvard Forest researchers who recently visited the island indicated this place might be home to some of the largest shads in the world because of ideal growing conditions.

The trunks of the shad are quite striking, with individual stems from one or two up to a dozen or more sprouting from a central base, which in total can be up to nearly 3 feet in diameter. There is quite a bit of variation from plant to plant, with some trunks appearing to have rippling muscles under the dark gray bark, and others quite smooth. Lichens can be found growing on many, adding to their visual appeal. Wood from shad is hard and dense, and if they have to be taken down, are an excellent source of firewood when cured.

While young plants a couple of feet high or less seem to be able to resprout, cutting the larger shads off at the base will usually kill the roots, so one might want to be very thoughtful before destroying any. They also seem to benefit from the companionship of other shrubs, so clearing around them can sometimes have the undesired effect of exposing them to the full brunt of the weather. The leaves, which are small, oval and finely toothed along the edge, even provide a modest color display in the fall, though nothing in comparison to the awesome shower of blossoms in spring.

Shad abloom in Rodman's Hollow.

When the shadbush is blooming, in addition to being beautiful, the abundant flowers themselves are important to wildlife, and attracting a variety of pollen and nectar-seeking insects. Birds realize this and spend much of May foraging through the flowers looking for insects. This is especially important when the weather is cold and their insect prey is not active.

The fruit, which ripens in late June, hence the nickname "Juneberry," is rated by most botanical references as highly edible. People dating back to the Native Americans in many regions have enjoyed the fruit, which resembles a blueberry with a reddish hue. This fruit is easily distinguished from the blueberry by its larger seeds and noticeable almond-like flavor. On Block Island some people use them in pies and other recipes or just eat them off the bush.

The berries are also an important and extremely abundant source of food for many of our local breeding birds; especially fledglings that have recently left the nest and are in need of an easily accessible meal. Like the blossoms, the berries are profuse and usually ripen in the latter half of June, but this as with all natural things depends on the weather.

The birds, in turn, help disperse this showy plant when they pass or regurgitate the seeds, which may become more viable after this process. In addition to the food value of the fruit, shad provides structure for nesting birds as well as cover and roosting areas. Every type of bird, from the smallest songbirds like the common yellowthroat, to larger birds like the black-crowned night heron, nest in this important shrub.

In addition to the shads' value to wildlife and people and the incredible spring spectacle they provide for us, this shrub also helps soften the aesthetic impacts of development, especially as the non-native Japanese black pine continues to die off throughout the island. It is safe to say that without the majestic shadbush, Block Island would be without one of its best natural assets.

Meet the horsechestnut

In late May, if you go down Old Town or Payne roads you will notice the majestic horsechestnuts blooming. When you start to look carefully, you will find this species throughout the island, usually around old homesteads and roads. Thus this tree is a living link to the history of Block Island. These special trees are the oldest and largest on the island.

However, these trees are not native to Block Island. They were planted by settlers and came originally from Europe. The main reason they were planted was for shade. They can grow up to 60 feet in height with a large canopy.

The bark is scaly and grayish in color with a trunk that can reach a diameter of 3 feet. Each horsechestnut leaf is comprised of seven to nine wedge-shaped leaflets that are 2 to 8 inches in length. The buds at the end of each branch are more than one-half inch in length and very sticky.

Horsechestnut flowers.

The horsechestnuts are adorned with clusters of white flowers that range in length from 6 to 12 inches. The flowers also have very long hair-like protrusions coming from the center of the flower. These are called stamens, the pollen-bearing male reproductive parts.

In September and October, the fruits of this tree ripen. The thick and thorny husks that protect the fruit are about 2 inches in diameter. Broken open, the fruit looks similar to the American chestnuts of Christmas fame, but horsechestnuts are poisonous.

The horsechestnut tree at the corner of Old Town Road and Center Road.

Did you know that although Block Island does not have the American chestnut, it still sports one other member of this family? Oriental chestnuts can be found in the Nathan Mott Park along with a few other select places on the island. Its spiny fruit husk is what distinguishes it from the horsechestnut.

This time of year the horsechestnut is important to the birds of Block Island as a source of food because the flowers attract many insects that the birds eat. The denseness of the leaves also protects the birds from predators.

So remember, the next time you see a horsechestnut tree, appreciate it not only for its beauty but also for its place in history and the natural world!

****

Look for these birds in horsechestnut trees: black-capped chickadee, eastern towhee, gray catbird, song sparrow, American robin, blue jay, common yellowthroat, northern cardinal, Carolina wren, cedar waxwing, brown thrasher.

The Great Salt Marsh Scavenger Hunt

Can you hunt up all of the items listed below? The best places to search are Mosquito Beach (across from Scotch Beach) and Andy's Way. Have fun, and please remember to leave all of the actual items located for this hunt where you found them for others to enjoy. (Except, of course, the "something that doesn't belong in nature.")

Common slipper shell: This shell is one of the most common in the salt marsh. When alive, it is found attached to rocks and other shells. The slipper shell often stacks one on top of the other. How many shells can you find in a stack?

Quahog: A thick and strong-shelled, the quahog is oval-shaped with the point curved out to the side. Look for the beautiful purple on the inside of the shell.

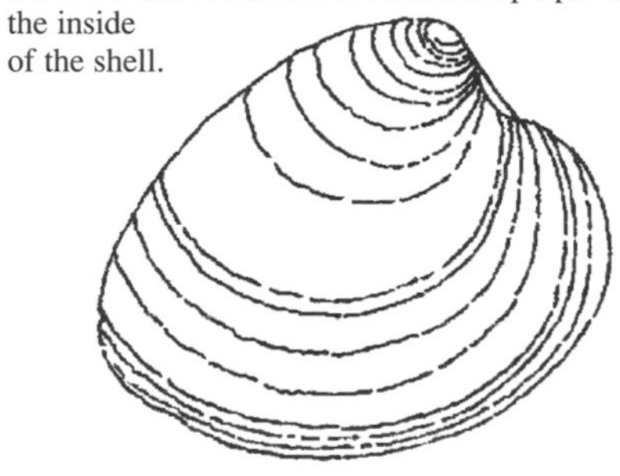

Blue mussel: It is named for its rich, blue color. It attaches itself to rocks and other mussels with its beard, which is formed by a sticky liquid poured out of the foot of the animal. It hardens in minutes and is surprisingly strong, even in heavy surf.

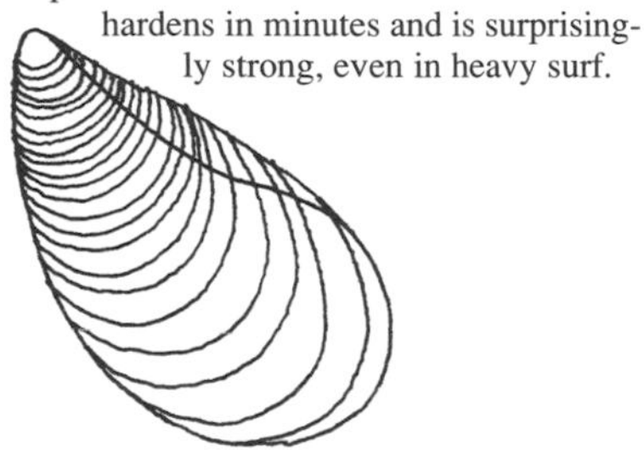

Jonah crab: Similar to the rock crab, this species is distinguished by its carapace (top part of shell), which is rounded on the front and pointed on the sides.

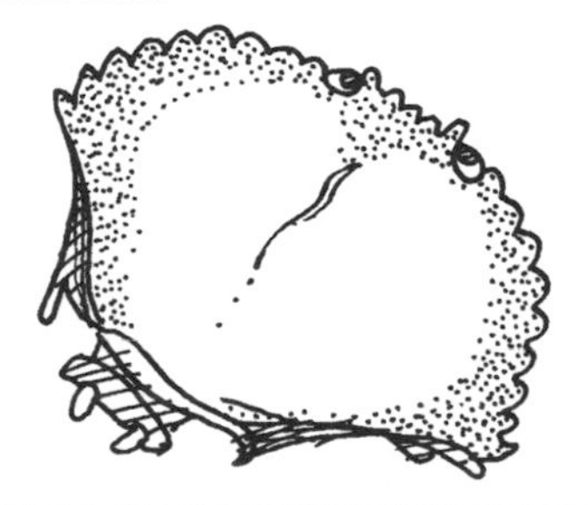

Surf clam: This is a very abundant shell on the beach. It is also one of the larger shells on the beach. It has an almost triangular shape. How large a surf clam shell can you find?

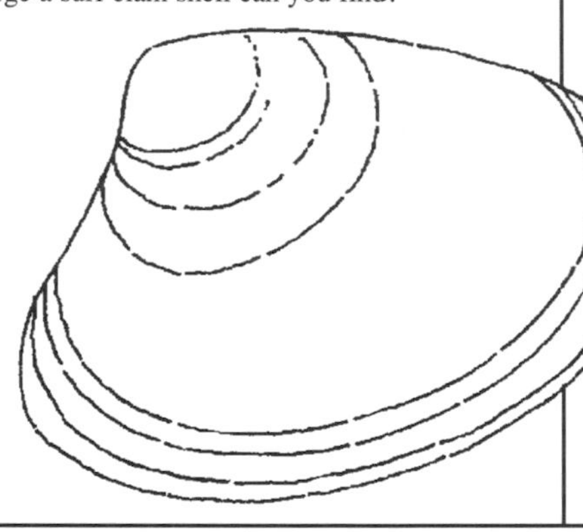

Bay scallop: This is a beautiful ribbed shell with wings at its base. This species' shell ranges from tiny to almost as large as a surf clam.

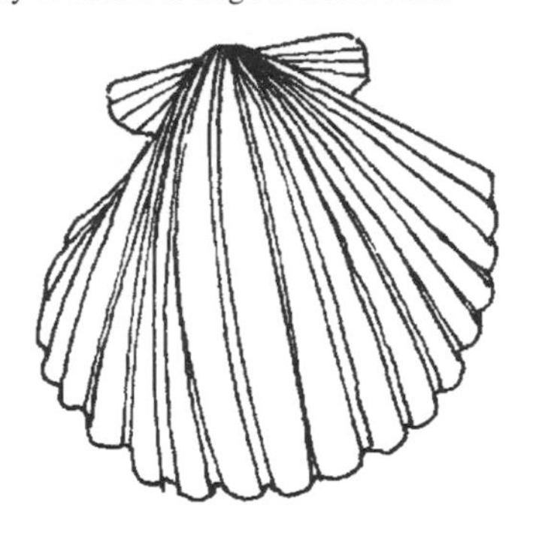

Periwinkle: It is olive to dark-gray in color and is a mobile home for an intertidal snail. These animals are often found stuck to rocks and feed by grazing on seaweed. Sometimes these shells are also used by hermit crabs, but when they are, they move much more quickly.

Bird feather: These come in all shapes, sizes and colors. While no longer important to the bird that lost the feather, other birds still use them to line their nests. How many different types of feathers can you find?

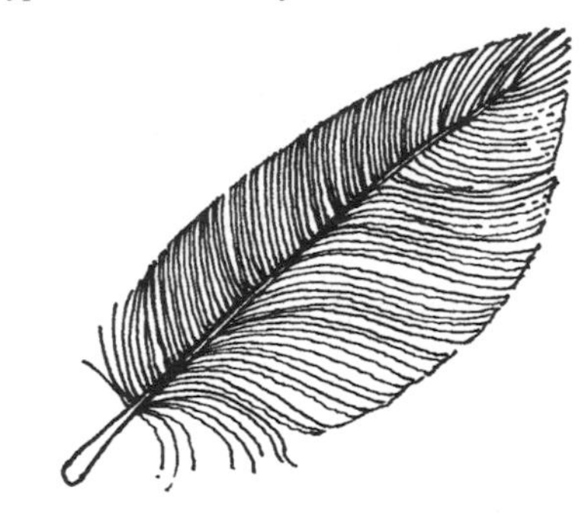

Razor clam: Shaped like a straight razor, this species is often found deep down in the sand. This is one of the harder shells to find around the salt marsh.

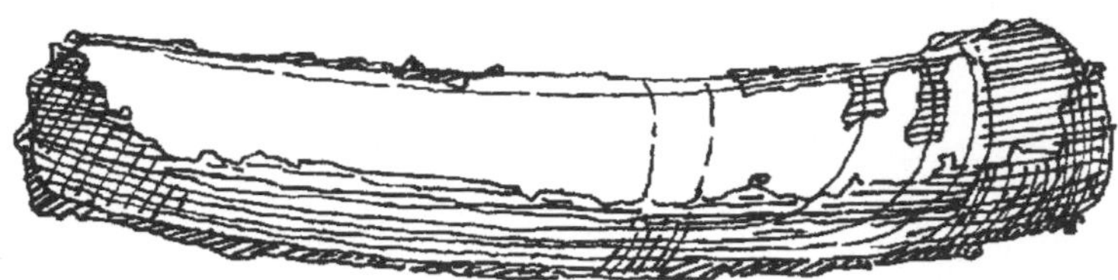

You're not done yet! Can you find:

- Whether it is low or high tide — record the time of your visit.
- A horseshoe crab shell — trace it.
- Something natural that floats on the water — draw a picture of it.
- Something that doesn't belong in nature — dispose of it (be careful of sharp glass).
- Something amazing — draw a sketch of it.
- Did you find them all? Which was the easiest? Which was the hardest?

The ever-important salt marsh

Have you ever been to a salt marsh? Land and sea meet in the marshes. Tidal creeks work their way inland, and clumps of grasses work their way into the saltwater. Salt marshes develop in quiet waters; thus there needs to be some sort of protection from the open sea. On Block Island, salt marshes can be found around Great Salt Pond. Two of the most visited salt marshes on the island are Andy's Way and Mosquito Beach.

Historically, it was believed that the noxious smells arising from the salt marshes were the cause of malaria and yellow fever, but as it turns out, a healthy marsh does smell at times without any bad effects on humans. The current fear about marshes is that they provide habitat for breeding mosquitoes.

Mosquitoes do breed in stagnant pools in the marsh, where the mummichog, a saltwater-marsh species of fish, cannot go to eat the mosquito larvae. Trenches have been dug in some marsh areas, like Mosquito Beach, so that fish can reach the mosquito larvae. However, the marsh extending from Skipper's Island to Beane Point has not been ditched and is the largest undisturbed marsh in the state.

Walking the beach at Andy's Way.

On Block Island, the salt marsh habitat is one of the most diverse (many different types of plants and animals live in it). In fact, once, in an after-school program with fourth-graders, we found 109 different living plants and animals between the Block Island Club and Skipper's Island.

When you walk out to a salt marsh, one of the first things you might notice is the large number of birds, especially at low tide. In the spring and fall, exposed tidal flats are important feeding stops for migratory shorebirds on their way north and south, like a McDonald's on Interstate 95 for humans. This time of year, birds such as the salt-marsh sharp-tailed sparrow and the yellowlegs nest in the marsh, while herons and egrets nesting at Beane Point spend their days feeding on fish in the marsh. Night herons are especially fond of fiddler crabs, which are only found in the salt marsh.

Upon close inspection of the marsh, you will realize that birds make up only a small part of the animal life that lives in this important area. This time of year, the fiddler crabs are marching, horseshoe crabs are mating, and green crabs are under many rocks. Ribbed mussels abound amongst the salt-marsh cordgrass, and common slipper shells, grass shrimp and periwinkles can be found in the small tidal pools. Many holes can also be seen in the sand. By carefully excavating the holes, soft-shelled clams and quahogs can be found. There are also many small animals such as worms that live in the sand and mud. While not of great interest to humans, the worms are food for many shorebirds.

On the shoreline of the pond, there are many different types of seaweed that group together in what is known as the wrack line. This area is an important place for insects to lay their eggs, and a key feeding area for shorebirds and swallows. Often, deer will venture to the wrack, lick the salt off the seaweed and even eat it.

If you get a chance to explore a salt marsh, check out how it changes with the tides. Different animals can be seen at different tides.

So visit the salt marsh and you will be amazed with what can be seen. Just remember that you are a visitor to this special area and it is important to give shorebirds a wide berth to feed (if shorebirds cannot feed, they will die). How many different living things can you find in the salt marsh?

One of Block Island's oldest species, the horseshoe crab

While exploring island beaches, you may be lucky enough to catch a glimpse of one of Block Island's oldest species, the horseshoe crab. These neat animals are considered to be living fossils, because their appearance has not changed in over 300 million years.

The horseshoe crab is an arthropod, which means that it has a segmented body, external skeleton, jointed legs, and compound eyes. This animal is not a true crab though; true crabs have 10 legs and horseshoe crabs have 12. Due to the structure of their mouth parts, they are more closely related to spiders and scorpions.

Horseshoe crabs have four eyes, two pairs on the front half of the shell, and five light-receptor organs beneath the shell. Adult females can weigh up to 10 pounds and reach 2 feet in length. Adult males are slightly smaller. The horseshoe crab has a spike-like tail called a telson that aids in maneuvering. When flipped upside down, the animal uses its telson like a lever to right itself. It is very important to note that this tail is not a stinger and cannot hurt people unless you touch the sharp tip.

Underneath the crab are six pairs of legs that can regenerate (grow back) if lost. The first pincer-like pair are feeding legs, the next four pairs are walking and feeding legs, and the last and longest pair are solely for walking. Legs are also used for clearing mud and silt when burrowing into the sand.

In between the legs are five overlaid flaps that comprise the gills. Each flap covers 100 paper-like leaves that absorb oxygen from water. They are called "book gills" because they lie on top of each other like pages of a book. They also act as paddles when the crab is swimming.

In the winter, horseshoe crabs migrate offshore and bury themselves in the mud. In the spring and summer they move inland to water ranging from coastland shallows to depths of 75 feet. Horseshoe crab mating occurs at peak evening high tides during the spring. These extreme tides are caused by full moons.

A female comes ashore towing a male after she has grasped the male's back with special claspers on her legs. The female then scoops a hole in the sand and lays about 1,000 green eggs, each about 1/10-inch in diameter.

The male is dragged by the female over the eggs to fertilize them. Some eggs are covered by sand. The ones that are not covered get eaten by gulls, eels and other fish. The female lays eggs in several locations to increase chances of survival. In one night the female can lay 80,000 to 100,000 eggs.

The eggs hatch in three to six weeks, and the hatchlings escape from the sand to the sea when the next spring high tide occurs. Horseshoe crabs molt (exit outside that shell, grow in size, and grow a new shell) several times during the first year and once a year thereafter until 10 years of age, when all molting will cease.

During the molting, the shell splits around the front rim. The crab, compressed within, walks out and expands 25 percent. The soft new shell hardens within 12 hours.

Migratory shorebirds are especially dependant on horseshoe crab eggs as they move north in the spring. Unfortunately, the horseshoe crab is declining at an alarming rate in many areas because it is being harvested for fertilizer, bait, and the pharmaceutical industry.

So next time you spot a horseshoe crab down in the water at Andy's Way, remember to treat it with respect because it is a window into the past.

Horseshoe crab invasion

When leading school programs at Andy's Way I am often asked, "Why are there so many horseshoe crab tracks here in the spring?"

In May and June, whenever there is a full moon and a nighttime high tide there are many horseshoe crabs to be seen. Extreme high tides are caused by the full moon. While Andy's Way is the best place to see this phenomenon, it can also be seen on the West Beach and sometimes at Mosquito Beach.

Females tow males ashore, lay eggs, and then drag the males over the eggs to fertilize them. It is very easy to see in the sand where dragging has occurred. In fact, one year with the Block Island School's second-grade we found 98 different tracks and a few straggling horseshoe crabs too.

The Block Island School's 2001 second-grade surrounds a horseshoe crab at Andy's Way.

The horseshoe crab populations in many areas are declining at an alarming rate because they are being over harvested. Throughout New England and the mid-Atlantic states, spring surveys are being conducted to monitor populations. In Rhode Island, Save the Bay and the Department of Environmental Management are conducting surveys throughout the state to determine numbers of horseshoe crabs. On Block Island, I have been doing counts since 2000 at Andy's Way and West Beach as part of this survey. Luckily for Block Island, there has not been a drastic change in the horseshoe crab population, yet.

During this time of year, if you happen to be at Andy's Way at low tide checking out the tracks, be sure to go to the northwestern part of this salt marsh and check out the fiddler crabs. These little creatures with purple carapaces (shells) live in holes in the sand. Males are easily distinguished from females by their one large claw. Around low tide, at this time of year, the males march up and down the beach waving their large claw. It is truly a spectacular experience.

The horseshoe crabs are easiest to observe during the spring breeding time. Remember to check the moon and tide charts for optimal viewing times. It truly is a primal experience that has been occurring since prehistoric times.

A close-up look at a female horseshoe crab dragging a male ashore.

Everyone can help preserve the dunes

Every spring since 1997, The Nature Conservancy has worked with the Block Island School, the Block Island Early Learning Center and the Town of New Shoreham with one goal in mind: to help preserve the dunes.

This has been achieved by carefully transplanting thousands of encroaching American beach grass plants from the Town Beach parking lot (soon to be destroyed by summer parking) to exposed dune faces. Before the restoration begins, each school group, just prior to planting, learns about the key role dune grass plays in the formation and stabilization of dunes.

The 2000 preschool class shows off the area the students just replanted.

Dunes are critical because they serve as a buffer, protecting the areas behind the dunes from flooding and erosion by wind and waves. Beach grass anchors the sand and holds it in place; without beach grass, stable dunes cannot exist.

The dunes are also important habitat, hosting a variety of highly specialized plants and animals that live in association with dunes. These include dusty miller, Block Island meadow voles, sea rocket and beach plum. In addition, this unique area provides an essential habitat for nesting birds like the gray catbird, song sparrow and common yellowthroat. It is also one of the favorite feeding spots for northern harriers searching for voles, and barn owls looking for Norway rats.

This species of beach grass, *Ammophila breviligulata*, is also known as maram grass or cape American beach grass. It is found throughout New England on sandy shorelines but is sensitive to disturbance. Thus, it cannot survive mild trampling or even a few passes with a vehicle over the same spot.

However, in the absence of disturbance, new plants often sprout from seeds stranded in the highest wrack or drift line from winter storms, or from underground runners. New growth naturally occurs on the bare slopes of the dunes and the upper beach facing the water. As soon as new plants take hold, they begin to trap sand. Over time, the number of plants in a bare sandy area will increase, holding more sand and growing upward as the sand accumulates, eventually forming a dune.

With disturbances to the storm-drift areas in the upper beach, it is difficult or impossible for grass to colonize areas seaward of existing grass patches. So when people play in, climb on, or walk near the dunes they are doing double damage. Existing plants are damaged, and sensitive seedlings and runners are not given a chance to colonize bare areas.

This is why the access paths to Crescent Beach have been formalized from Corn Neck Road, and rope fencing has been erected to delineate the paths to keep beach visitors out of this important habitat. People can still enjoy the beach without threatening the dunes by staying on the relatively flat part of the beach nearer the water. An added responsibility, as caretakers of the dunes, is to politely ask people to return to the beach when they are in the fenced-off sensitive areas.

The students' efforts over the last eight years continue to pay off by increasing the amount of this special habitat. Seeing bare sand turn to a lush dune system is certainly a job well done! However, without continued stewardship by the whole Block Island community this unique habitat type can still disappear.

Hopefully, everyone will learn what countless Block Island School students have: that dune preservation and restoration is hard, important work but also fun. For dunes' sake, do your part!

Dune restoration — before and after planting

The great Welcome Back Scavenger Hunt

If you're returning to Block Island, after being away for the winter, you may find all sorts of beach items sprinkled throughout your property, no matter where it is located on the island. While these items may seem out of place, there is a natural reason for this occurrence: the gulls and crows have dropped them while trying to extract the animal for food. See if you can find all nine items shown below, and learn a little about the food chain in the process.

Spider crab: Its carapace, or the top part of its shell, is brown to dull yellow, measures up to 4 inches, is spiny and covered with short hairs. Its legs can reach up to 1 foot in length. This species is a favorite of gulls because it is slow-moving and easy to catch.

Green crab: This carapace measures up to 3 inches wide and has five teeth on each side of the anterior (top) part of the shell. One of the most common crabs on the East Coast, it is originally from Europe.

Periwinkle: The most common snail on the island, measuring about 1 inch, and ranging from gray to dark brown in color with a white outer lip. Gulls and crows alike will grab these snails from the rocks at low tide and attempt to get the meat.

Quahog: The most common clamshell on the beach is a favorite target for gulls. In fact, you can find the shell shards on docks and pavement where gulls have dropped them to get to the meat. The quahog is white, often with a hint of purple on the inside of the shell.

Moon snail: This shell ranges from gray to tan in color and measures up to 4 inches. It is a predatory snail that eats other mollusks. It is the most common large snail on the beach and a favorite target of the gulls.

Crab claws: They come in all shapes and sizes. The most common are the rock crab (very angular), the green crab (greenish in color), blue crab (blue and red in color), and spider crab (elongated and greenish-brown in color). These are usually scavenged by gulls for the meat.

Lobster claws: Each lobster has two types of claws: a crusher, which is heavy and blunt, and a pointed, sharper claw used for tearing. Usually greenish in color and ranging widely in size, these claws are often found on the beach and are also scavenged by gulls.

Skate egg case: Also called mermaid's purse, this black leathery egg case is a common find on the beach. It measures up to 4 inches in size. An egg case floats for a year before it hatches into a skate, which is a flat fish. Unhatched eggs that wash up are a great source of food for all scavengers.

Channeled whelk: This large snail measures up to 7 inches. It is a rare find inland but quite common on the beach. This species is a predator that eats mostly shellfish. Because of its size, this species tends to be scavenged by gulls on the beach.

An Atlantic Torpedo, *Torpedo nobiliana*, washed up at Cormorant Cove in early April 2003. This species is a member of the electric ray family and is known to produce 220-volt charges. This individual measured 3 feet long, 2 feet wide, and weighed over 50 pounds. The largest known torpedo was 6 feet long and weighed 200 pounds.

The key characteristics of this species are its squared-off front, short snout, and coloration (brownish purple above and white below). This animal feeds on bottom-dwelling organisms, including flounder and small sharks, by enveloping them in its pectoral fins, stunning them with electricity, and then devouring them.

Lucky Block Rocks

Did you know there are good luck rocks to be found on Block Island beaches? On your next beach walk, (low tide is the best time to go), keep an eye out for smooth, dark gray stones that have a white stripe on them. If the stripe completely encircles the stone, then you've found a Lucky Block Rock. Don't lose it. Take only one home and keep it as a good luck memento of your stay on Block Island.

Did you know? There is no such thing as a "starfish." Out here on Block Island, when you walk the beaches at low tide, you will find common sea stars, blood sea stars, and purple sea stars… but no starfish.

I CAN'T SWIM ANYWAY!

The snakes of Block Island

With the onset of spring and warmer temperatures, the snakes of Block Island become active. There are only three species of snakes found on the island and none of them are poisonous. These neat creatures can be found on land and in ponds, and play an important role in the Block Island ecosystem.

All snakes evolved from lizards and are reptiles, which were the first truly terrestrial vertebrates. They are cold-blooded and have dry skin, have more efficient lungs than amphibians, and most reproduce by laying hard-shelled eggs.

Snakes have an elongated body with scales, without limbs, eyelids, or openings for ears. A snake continues to grow throughout its life, shedding its skin several times each year as it gets larger. Snakes flick their tongues often because this is the way they smell: a snake's tongue captures the scent outside the mouth and then places it in the mouth's Jacob's organ, where the scent is detected.

Common garter snake

On Block Island, and in the rest of New England, the most common snake is the garter snake, which got its name from its resemblance to the fancy devices that were once used for supporting men's socks. Depending on the individual, garter snakes can either be docile or try to bite in self-defense. When first captured, they release an unpleasant-smelling musk from glands at the base of the tail.

The garter snake is slender and can measure up to 22 inches in length. It has a narrow yellow stripe along the middle part of its back that runs the whole length of the snake, with two rows of blackish spots on either side of the stripe. The snake's belly is gray or a buffy white. It is important to note that the color and pattern of this species varies.

The most common foods for this species are frogs, fish, earthworms, leeches, mice, and small birds, which are all swallowed whole. Unlike most reptiles that lay leathery eggs, this snake bears live young in September. Garter snakes are most often found in fields, shrublands, under rocks and in gardens.

Northern water snake

The northern water snake, Block Island's largest snake, measures up to 33 inches. Its color pattern varies, but is most often a reddish-brown with black-edged bands that are wider on the back and narrower on the sides. Unlike the other snakes on Block Island, this species has a broad head and a gray belly with a stripe down the middle that ranges from yellow to pink.

The main staple of this snake's diet is fish. It eats the weak and diseased fish, keeping ponds from becoming overcrowded, thus allowing the remaining fish to grow bigger. The water snake reproduces by laying eggs in June that hatch in September. This species is found on the island in salt marshes, ponds and swamps.

Note well: this species often bites when handled and, like the garter snake, also releases a foul odor from its glands at the base of the tail.

Brown snake

Also called DeKay's snake after James Edward DeKay, an early naturalist of New York, the brown snake measures 11 inches and is thicker than the common garter snake. It is dull-brown in color, with a gray stripe across the back, flanked on either side by two rows of brownish-black spots, a black cap on the head, and a black mark behind the eye.

The brown snake's prey includes slugs, earthworms, and soft-bodied insects. Like the common garter, this species also bears live young in September. A fairly secretive snake, on Block Island it can be found in shrublands, marshes, and is very common in developed areas. In fact, the brown snake when found is often misidentified as a baby garter snake.

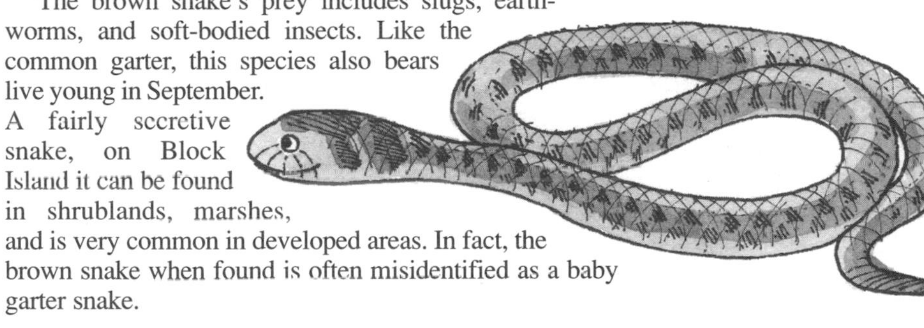

While not favored by many people, snakes are amazing animals and deserve to be left alone. Remember, they are part of what makes the Block Island environment unique!

A bird walk to remember

On Monday, June 9, 1997, the second-grade from the Block Island School and I went birdwatching at Nathan Mott Park. These students were extremely interested in birds and very good at looking and listening for them. In order to see birds you must have the equipment, and thanks to multiple donors, each student was able to have their own pair of binoculars. In addition to the optics, we were armed with multiple bird books including the Peterson's and National Geographic field guides.

At the onset of the expedition, the students learned that one of the best ways to find different birds is to know their songs, and that a great way to remember them is by putting words to the cheerful sounds. Due to the fact that this is nesting season, it is much easier to hear birds than to see them. The males are singing often to keep other males off their territory, and the females stay very close to the nests and are hard to locate. Thus, we spent most of the trip learning the different calls and then trying to track down and see the birds.

The bird songs that the second-grade heard and learned are all good to know because they are the most common ones that are heard during spring and summer. The advantage to knowing these calls is that you can sort out the songs you hear and then track down the ones that you don't know.

Luckily, we heard and saw many birds on our walk. One of the first birds we heard was the eastern towhee, which sings "drink your tea." When the students saw this bird, they noticed that it is easy to separate the males and females by the color of their backs: males have a black back and females have a brown back. What both sexes have in common is a white breast, red eye and rufous (a brownish-red color) on the flanks.

Many inquisitive gray catbirds were also singing during our walk. This species is a member of the mockingbird family and thus has quite a repertoire of songs, although not as talented a mimic as the northern mockingbird. They sound very similar to cats meowing (hence the name) and also make call that says "eric, eric, eric." These birds are gray all over, with a black cap, and rufous-colored feathers under the tail. The catbird is one of the most common passerine or "songbird" nesters on the island. The reason it is so common is because it nests in thick briars and bushes, which we have a lot of on Block Island.

The call of the common yellowthroat was another one we heard often. This species has just returned for the summer from its wintering grounds in Central America. Its distinctive song says "wichity, wichity, wichity, which." The class saw a few of these small yellow-throated birds and learned that only the males have black masks. The students loved the spunk of this bird and immediately started fondly referring to it as the "wichity bird."

As the group meandered inland, the distinctive sounds of fish crows could be recognized. The participants learned that there are actually two species of crows on Block Island (fish and American), and that they can only be separated by their size and call. The fish crow is smaller than the American crow and has a much more nasally sounding "caw" call. We were lucky to see six fish crows, which are definitely the rarer of the two crow species.

Toward the end of our trip, we heard a metallic-sounding chip note. I immediately pointed it out to the school group as the northern cardinal. As we searched to get a glimpse of this beautiful species, it serenaded us with its whole song, a sweet-sounding, "birdy, birdy, birdy." This is one of this species' two main songs, with the other being an equally sweet, "chew, chew, chew." The students then learned that cardinals are a relatively new sight on Block Island, only colonizing it as the coastal shrub habitat became dense and tall.

These songs described above are probably the most common on the island, and good ones to know as you travel through its wilds. Some of the other birds that were recorded on our trip were: song sparrow, American crow, mourning dove, herring gull, great black-backed gull, Carolina wren, American robin, eastern kingbird, chimney swift, common grackle, European starling, brown-headed cowbird, barn swallow and bank swallow.

I found that each member of the second-grade was an enthusiastic birdwatcher enjoying getting to know the avian inhabitants of Block Island. It will be fun to follow these budding birders as they grow into ornithologists over the next few years. These students definitely gleaned the most important birding lesson: the only way to learn your birds is to get outside, listen, observe and identify them.

Turtles on the Block

Spring is the best time of year to see freshwater turtles on Block Island. They can be seen sunning themselves on rocks around ponds, and also walking from pond to pond. On Block Island, there are four species of freshwater turtle. Each of these species plays an important role in the island ecosystem and should be left alone.

Painted turtle

This species measures 6 inches and is ovular in shape. The females are larger than males. On the carapace (the top part of the shell) there are three rows of blackish-brown scutes (panels) that are trimmed in yellow with no keels (ridges). On the edge of the shell, the scutes have fine red lines. The bottom part of the shell, or plastron, is yellow. The head, neck, and legs of this species are lined in yellow and red.

This is the most common species of turtle on Block Island. It sits in the sunshine in groups, on rocks around ponds. This time of year, with some luck, baby turtles (measuring 1 inch) can be seen heading toward the nearest pond from the spot where they hatched out of their leathery eggs.

Box turtle

The rarest turtle on Block Island, which may have been introduced, measures about 6 inches. The box turtle is dark brown with a variable intricate orange or yellow pattern on an oval, high-domed carapace. The plastron of this species is also yellow. Unlike the other turtles on Block Island, this species has a transverse hinge that allows the turtle to completely hide inside its shell. The box turtle is mainly terrestrial and soaks in mud or very shallow water. This species doesn't bask in the sun, but instead likes to hide under logs or rotting vegetation.

Snapping turtle

This is the largest turtle on Block Island, measuring up to 15 inches and weighing 35 pounds. The brown-black carapace of this species is oval and somewhat domed, with three rows of keels. This turtle's plastron is yellow and cross-shaped. With massive head, long neck, and a tail the same length as the carapace, this species is unmistakable. In June, this species is commonly seen, as females are looking for upland areas away from water to lay their eggs. The snapping turtle is an amazing swimmer that eats mostly aquatic vegetation. It should be noted that this animal can bite, and should be avoided when out of the water. It will not bite when it is in the water. This turtle often gets a bad rap, but plays an important part in the pond ecosystem here on Block Island.

Spotted turtle

This species is the smallest turtle on Block Island, measuring 4 inches. The turtle is yellow-spotted, with a smooth black oval carapace, which is somewhat flattened. Young turtles have one yellow spot on each scute and adults have several. The plastron is yellow with a black center and border. The head, neck and legs have yellow or orange spots. This uncommon turtle is often found in marshy meadows and moist shrubland areas. In the spring it can also be seen basking around ponds.

Turtles are fascinating reptiles that are neat to observe. Please make sure to leave them alone to carry out their important role in the Block Island environment!

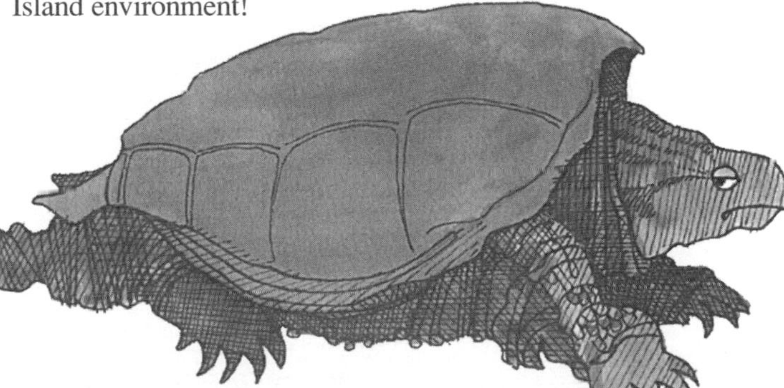

Why biodiversity counts

Do you know what biodiversity is and why it is important? Biodiversity is a term describing variety of life on earth and the essential interdependence of all living things. Without understanding this, it is virtually impossible to conserve the natural world around us, and in a sense ourselves.

Since the spring of 1999, students have been learning the importance of biodiversity. Block Island School fifth- and sixth-graders, their science teacher Shannon Cotter, and I have taken part in Biodiversity Counts, an interesting science program sponsored by the American Museum of Natural History (AMNH). The Biodiversity Counts program is a pilot program in which only 100 schools nationwide were initially selected to participate.

Fifth-graders working in the field with Scott Comings in 1999.

To document biodiversity, the many forms of life in one area must be inventoried and observed. In order for the documentation to be accurate, it must be done over time. The Biodiversity Counts program is a site-specific study in which the students monitor an established area for animals, specifically arthropods (insects, spiders, worms, etc.), and plant life.

Over the years, biodiversity documentation has occurred at the Fresh Swamp Preserve, Fresh Pond Preserve, Surf Beach, and the Faulkner property across from the school. During the last few years, we have been inventorying a beach site and an inland site, to demonstrate to the students the similarities and differences in biodiversity.

The observations span throughout the year with the majority of them occurring in the spring semester. By doing this, the students are able to see the drastic changes in the seasons. They are observing the environment around them as it goes from being dormant to thriving with life.

Several times each week, the young scientists venture to one of their sites and record the animals and plants they see. As would any scientist doing field research, the students map their sites, keep detailed records and diagrams of what they discover each day, and record the weather, time of day, and any other relevant information.

In the spring when students do not go out into the field, they utilize other components of the Biodiversity Counts program, such as reading current scientific articles written by AMNH scientists. The students also study various field guides to identify the many plants and animals found on their various sites, learning to use the Latin names for these organisms.

An integral part of this program, as with all scientific research, is organizing the data that have been collected, and creating posters that display the results and conclusions. These posters, which include common and Latin names, sketches, photographs, tools used, and conclusions, are unveiled each year at the school's display night.

After documenting hundreds of different plant and animals species over the last seven years, there are a few that stand out. These include a freshwater arthropod called a fairy shrimp, which is found only in vernal ponds (ponds that dry up during the summer); a Carolina wolf spider, which is the largest spider in New England; a predacious diving beetle; a lilypad forktail (type of damselfly); and a species of purseweb spider named *Atypus niger* (no common name). All of these were first-time records for Block Island; with the two spiders and diving beetle being first records for the state.

This program clearly has had an impact on the students, who often continue to search for plants and animals, especially spiders, even after school. Additional proof of this impact can be seen as graduates of the Biodiversity Counts program continue their studies in high school, where they are more prepared for life sciences and, if they choose, to become naturalists.

No matter what year, the students have been and continue to be visibly excited about the field study component of the Biodiversity Counts program, repeatedly asking when they would be able to go exploring again. The students, past and present, have learned a great deal about the plants and animals that live on Block Island. But the most important thing they have learned is that they are doing scientific work that has and will continue to benefit the island.

Summer

The summer season on Block Island is one of extreme activity, whether plant, wild animal, or human. It is a time of beautiful (usually) weather, rampant plant growth, bird nesting, beetle activity, interesting butterflies, and amazing seashore life. This special season on Block Island is a time that is cherished by many, from visitors to year-round residents.

Cool coastal breezes are commonplace in the summer, and for the most part humidity is fairly low. It is always surprising, the dramatic difference between the cooler temperatures and lower humidity on Block Island compared to mainland Rhode Island. Another wonderful thing about being on the island is that on hot days, the ocean is an easily accessible way to cool off.

Summer is the time when plants explode, growing significant amounts. One of the best examples of this is blackberry, which can grow over 12 feet in a season. Some of the more interesting flowering plants this time of year are bushy rockrose, butterfly-weed, and common milkweed. In addition to flowers, it is also a great time to gather fruit like shadberry, blackberry, and high-bush blueberry.

After setting territories in the spring, birds are actively nesting in the beginning part of the summer, and feeding fledgings toward the end of it. There are over 50 bird species that nest on Block Island. Some of the more interesting ones are American oystercatcher, black-crowned night heron, yellow-crowned night heron, barn owl, northern harrier, and grasshopper sparrow. It is important to note that all of these species are state-endangered.

Summer is also the season when the federally endangered American burying beetle is most actively searching grassland areas for carrion (decomposing animals). This beetle is Block Island's rarest animal and the island is one of five places it is found in the world. Other rare beetles include the clay banks tiger beetle and the rhinoceros beetle; both not found anywhere else in the state.

There are many butterflies to see during the summer months. These include monarch, viceroy, red admiral, tiger swallowtail, and American copper. These beautiful insects feed on nectar and are a welcome sight in any garden. For me it is always fun to see how many different butterfly species I can find in one summer.

Observing seashore life is a highlight of any summer. Whether watching piping plovers attempting to nest or fiddler crabs marching during the full moon, it is safe to say, there is a lot to enjoy. This is, of course, the season when the beach is full of vacationers, but it is also an active time for the biota in this habitat. Some of Block Island's most fragile species exist only on the beach.

For the Block Island community, summer is an extremely busy season with little time to relax. However, it is also a time to catch up with old friends returning to the island and sometimes to even feel anonymous, which does not happen in any other season. It is always wonderful to see summer come, but it's also great when it ends.

Summer is a season like no other on Block Island. No matter how many island summers you have seen there is always a lot more to take in, which makes it all the more exciting.

A special place for plants and animals

Just as there are many people who live here who think Block Island is a special place, there are plants and animals that share this same sentiment. In fact, there are over 40 state and federally threatened or endangered species that inhabit Block Island. For the state, this special place has become the last refuge for many flora and fauna that were once found throughout Rhode Island.

The rarest plant on Block Island is the state-endangered bushy rockrose or *Helianthemum dumosum*. This coastal plain species is endemic to southeastern New England and Long Island, N.Y. Other than one record in South Kingstown in 1977, Block Island is the only place in the state where this herbaceous perennial is found. Bushy rockrose plants can be found on dry grasslands throughout southwestern Block Island. These grasslands, known by scientists as morainal grasslands, are a globally imperiled habitat type.

The bushy rockrose's branching stems are almost horizontal, forming compact bushy mounds that reach 2 inches in height. Flowers with pale yellow petals occur singly near the tips of the main branches from late May to June. The biggest threat to this flower is loss of morainal grassland habitat due to natural succession and human disturbance.

The showy state-endangered northern blazing star, *Liatris borealis,* is also found on morainal grasslands and areas with sandy soil. While found throughout New England, Block Island has the only populations of this wildflower in the state of Rhode Island. The biggest island population is at Turnip Farm, which has over 15,000 plants.

This beautiful plant stands 14 to 30 inches tall with purple spiked flower heads numbering as many as 20 per stalk, which bloom in the fall. Many people have a domestic species of this plant in their garden called gay feather, *Liatris spicata*. The major threats to this plant are habitat succession to shrubs and grazing by deer. This is why in areas with many clustered plants we have erected fencing to keep the deer from grazing on this rare plant.

Block Island's rarest animal is the elusive American burying beetle, *Nicrophorus americanus*. Block Island is the only place east of the Mississippi where this once-common beetle is still found. The American burying beetle is so rare that it is a federally endangered species with only a few populations in the entire world. This nocturnal animal is most common in the southwestern part of the island.

Block Island's American burying beetle.

The American burying beetle is large, measuring over 1 inch long, and is black in color with one orange spot on the thorax (middle segment of the insect), and four orange spots on the abdomen (last segment of the insect). At night, this beetle flies around trying to locate carrion (dead animals) by using its antennae and smell. When an appropriately sized carcass (between 80 and 150 grams) is found, the beetle loosens the earth and drags it underground. This is an amazing task because the beetle will pull hundreds of times its weight.

A cavern is then built and the fur or feathers of the animal are plucked. After mating, the female lays her eggs on the carrion, and the young are raised eating the rotting meat. The major threats to this special animal are loss of grassland habitat, light pollution, and competition for carrion.

Another elusive nocturnal animal on Block Island is the state-endangered barn owl, *Tyto alba*. Although this animal is found throughout the world, the island is the only place in Rhode Island where this once-common owl still nests. On the island, the barn owl likes to nest in the bluffs, in holes about 5 inches in diameter just below the bluff crest. Depending on the year, there are between three and five nests on the island.

The barn owl is very distinctive with a heart-shaped face, light-colored breast, rusty-brown back, and measures 16 inches. It is the largest owl on Block Island except in the winter when the larger migrant snowy owl arrives. The call of this species is a truly unmistakable raspy, hissing screech. This predator eats mostly rodents, and in the daytime roosts in stands of trees. The major threats to this species are loss of hunting areas and decline in the rodent population.

Another state-endangered raptor found on Block Island is the northern harrier, *Circus cyaneus*, once known as the marsh hawk. The island is the only place in the state where this animal, which is declining in the region, nests on the ground. Depending on the year, there are between 10 and 15 nests found on the island.

The northern harrier can often be seen gliding throughout the island looking for rodents and birds to eat. Males are gray-backed and females brown; both have a white patch on the rump. This bird measures 22 inches, with a 4-foot wing span. The major threats to this species are disturbance of nesting areas and loss of habitat.

Often a source of food for the barn owl and northern harrier, the Block Island meadow vole is considered a subspecies of the mainland meadow vole because it has a longer snout and a shorter tail. With some further scientific research we may find that this animal is a separate species endemic to Block Island.

The meadow vole, *Microtus pennsylvanicus,* is slightly larger than a mouse, with a brown back and a gray stomach. This animal eats grass, grass seeds and berries, and is most often found in clumps of switch grass and in American beach grass in the dunes. The major threats to this species are loss of grassland habitat and disturbance to the dune habitat.

The six species described above are just a few of the many found throughout Block Island. Remember, this is a very special place and the plants and animals that live here know it, too!

Test your knowledge of animals that love Block Island

1) What state-endangered bird nests in the bluffs?
A) great blue heron C) barn owl
B) bald eagle D) yellow warbler

2) What do monarch catterpillars eat?
A) grass C) daisies
B) milkweed D) pizza

3) Which insect's only home in New England is Block Island?
A) mosquito C) luna moth
B) rhino beetle D) American burying beetle

4) In Rhode Island, which hawk only nests on Block Island?
A) sharp-shinned C) Cooper's
B) northern harrier D) none of the above

5) What Block Island rodent may be a separate species?
A) meadow vole C) muskrat
B) white-tailed deer D) white-footed mouse

6) How many different species of amphibian does BI have?
A) ten C) three
B) five D) one

7) Which federally threatened species nests on BI's beaches?
A) piping plover C) American oystercatcher
B) herring gull D) none of the above

8) How many species of state-endangered night herons does BI have?
A) two C) none
B) one D) four

9) What BI state-endangered bird sounds like an insect?
A) song sparrow C) savannah sparrow
B) grasshoper sparrow D) none of the above

10) How many species of bats can be found on Block Island?
A) four C) one
B) none D) three

Answers: 1-C; 2-B; 3-D; 4-B; 5-A; 6-C; 7-A; 8-A; 9-B; 10-D

Natural habitat quiz

Block Island is host to many great natural habitats. Each one of them has special plants and animals that can only live in a specific area. Test your knowledge below and see how much you know about Block Island's habitats. (If you need help, turn the page.)

1) How many types of habitats does Block Island have?
A) Four B) Ten C) Seven D) Six

2) What is Block Island's most endangered habitat type?
A) Wetland C) Morainal grassland
B) Shrubland D) Salt marsh

3) What habitat type is most at risk due to human disturbance?
A) Shrubland C) Grassland
B) Wetland D) Beach / Dune

4) What is the most common habitat type on Block Island?
A) Wetland C) Stand of trees
B) Shrubland D) Salt marsh

5) What is the least common habitat type on Block Island?
A) Grassland C) Beach / Dune
B) Salt marsh D) Wetland

6) In what type of habitat is an American oystercatcher most often found?
A) Salt marsh
B) Grassland
C) Shrubland
D) Wetland

7) In which type of habitat is the wildflower northern blazing star most often found?
A) Morainal grassland
B) Beach / Dune
C) Wetland
D) None of the above

Answers: 1-C; 2-C; 3-D; 4-B; 5-B; 6-A; 7-A

Block Island habitats

Did you know that Block Island has many different types of habitats? Each habitat contains a certain set of plants and animals. On the island, there are seven main habitat types: beach system, salt marsh, wetland, grassland, morainal grassland, shrubland and tree stand. It is amazing to think that all of these habitats exist on Block Island's 6,000 acres.

Beach system

The beach system is the most sensitive to human disturbance. It is comprised of three parts: beaches, dunes and bluffs. The beach part is home to the federally threatened piping plover and the wrack line (where seaweed bunches up). The latter is important to shorebirds, gulls, and many early successional plants. The front part of the dunes is covered with American beach grass, and the back is mostly bayberry, beach rose, and beach plum. This area is host to a variety of animals like the Block Island meadow vole, white-footed mouse, and northern harrier.

The bluffs are extremely important as a location for birds like the belted kingfisher, barn owl (only nests in Rhode Island) and bank swallow (over 8,000 nest on Block Island). The clay banks tiger beetle is also found in this area, and Block Island is its only recorded location in the state. When you are visiting this habitat, remember to stay near the water because that causes the least disturbance!

Beaches and dunes: the sensitive habitat.

Salt marsh

The salt marsh habitat is the least common habitat on Block Island. These special areas are formed in protected areas where freshwater and saltwater meet. They are one of the largest habitats and also one of the most diverse. In fact, with one group of students, we found more than 150 species of plants and animals between the Block Island Club and Andy's Way. In addition to its diversity of species, the salt marsh is very important as a rest and refueling spot for migratory shorebirds.

The endangered northern blazing star found in morainal grasslands.

Some of the animals you might see are black-crowned night heron, American oystercatcher, fiddler crabs, four species of clams, two species of mussels and common slipper shells to name a few. In the salt marsh, many specialized plants (able to survive in saltwater) can be found like glasswort, salt-meadow grass and seaside goldenrod. There is truly no place like a salt marsh, but when exploring, never trample vegetation or disturb the birds.

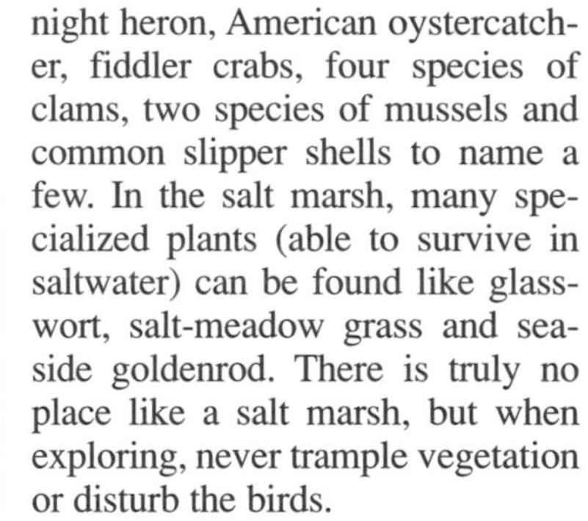

Wetland

The wetland system is one of the most important on Block Island and is very sensitive to disturbance. It is comprised of three main parts: vernal ponds, freshwater marshes, and ponds. Vernal ponds are ponds that dry up for part of the year. Due to this cycle, they contain no fish, which means they are inhabited by lots of insects, amphibians, and reptiles (because these animals and insects are not eaten by fish). In Massachusetts, vernal ponds are thought to be so important they are protected by law from any disturbance. Freshwater marshes are mostly composed of plants like cattail, Phragmites and buttonbush. They are a haven for animals like the muskrat, red-winged blackbird, marsh wren, and yellow warbler. Ponds have mostly open water and are used by many different types of animals including ducks, geese, and swallows. There are many species of aquatic plants in the ponds, with

The Clay Head Swamp, a wetland.

specialized shrubs like winterberry and chokeberry found at the water's edge. The wetland system is needed by all of Block Island's animals (including us) to survive.

Payne Farm, a grassland habitat.

Grassland

The grassland habitat contains some of Block Island's most unique species. These habitats are managed grasslands, which means they are mowed every few years to prevent them from becoming shrubland. Plants that can be found in a grassland include milkweeds, asters, goldenrods, blackberry, and switch grass. The grasslands are home to the federally endangered American burying beetle, which is Block Island's most globally rare species. Other animals that are found in this special area are the state endangered grasshopper sparrow, northern harrier, and savannah sparrow. In the spring and fall, this habitat is also used as a feeding area for migrating hawks and falcons. The grasslands on Block Island are a refuge for many of the plants and animals that were once common throughout Rhode Island.

The rose-breasted grosbeak, a migrating songbird often found in shrubs.

Morainal grassland

The glacially-formed morainal grassland habitat consists of hilltops made predominantly of sand and rock. It is a type of grassland that does not have to be mowed because the soil is so sandy that only certain plants can inhabit the harsh habitat. While many of Block Island's rodents thrive in this area, the most interesting species are plants. The hilltop is mostly covered with grasses called little bluestem and switch grass. However, there are also two state-endangered plants called northern blazing star and bushy rockrose. This special habitat is globally imperiled and disappearing at an alarming rate in New England.

Shrubland

Shrubland is the most common habitat on the island. Shrubs often get a bad rap when they are called "junk" by people who do not know their importance. The shubland is populated with bayberry, arrowwood, shadbush, black cherry, chokeberry, and elderberry. It provides cover for most of Block Island's animals, and its berries are an extremely important source of food for first-year songbirds in the fall. Without this food source, many of these small birds would starve to death. In a planning exercise that was done by The Nature Conservancy for the Massachusetts islands, it was found that the shrubland is a preferred habitat. In fact, they are converting their forest back to shrubs because of its importance.

Tree stand

The tree stand habitat is the closest Block Island comes to possessing forest habitat. The groups of trees are made up of both exotic (Japanese black pine, oriental chestnut, sycamore maple) and natural (red cedar, red maple, sycamore) species. They are important to cavity-nesting birds like the northern flicker and black-capped chickadee. There is also evidence to suggest the migratory songbirds in the spring and fall key in on these habitats because of their high density of insects. The amount of bird life in this area is truly amazing.

While everyone has his or her favorite habitat, each one plays an important role in the formation of the island ecosystem. This is why stewards of the island should always respect and manage each habitat. In the world of science, this practice is called mosaic management. By doing this, we will hopefully be able to keep all of the island's flora and fauna; for in this case, the sum is truly greater than its parts.

Dead Japanese black pines.

Bird sounds of the summer

Many people are very excited to learn all the different bird songs they hear on Block Island. However, when they find out how many there are during some seasons, they are completely overwhelmed.

The beauty of summer is that it is when there are the fewest species of birds on the island. Thus, it is when there are the fewest number of songs to learn and a great time to start.

People always ask me what is the best way to learn bird songs? The answer is to spend time outside and attempt to track down the bird songs you don't know.

When you find a bird, watch it sing and you will never forget the sound. It is also helpful to draw the song in a notebook (whether it goes up or down in pitch), and to put words to the song. As you progress with your song studies, it will become easier. When fall approaches, you will already know the resident bird songs and it will make learning the migrant birds much easier.

To get you started in your studies, let's go over five of the most common songbirds heard on Block Island. Knowing just these will help immensely when out birdwatching, or can greatly impress friends and family.

Eastern towhee

Thc loud "drink your tea" of the eastern towhee is the most easy to hear and recognize. This bird is found in shrubs, and often forages on the ground scratching with both feet. The towhee is 8.5 inches long, with the males black above, rufous on the sides and white below. Females look the same except they are brown above.

Black-capped chickadee

The black-capped chickadee has two calls that can be heard throughout the island. This bird has a scolding call, "chickadee dee dee" and a clear whistle "fee-bee." This bird measures 4.25 inches in size, has a black throat and cap, gray back and wings, and white breast. The chickadee is one of the most fearless birds, approaching quite close to people. It may even land on you if you stand still near a feeder.

Carolina wren

The deafening sound of the Carolina wren is unmistakable. Its "teakettle, teakettle, teakettle, tea" can be heard in any patch of shrubs. It makes a loud noise for such a small bird, measuring 5.5 inches. This bird is rusty above, with white throat, and tan below. When moving around, the bird's tail is always straight up. Like almost all wrens, it is very feisty and has a lot of personality.

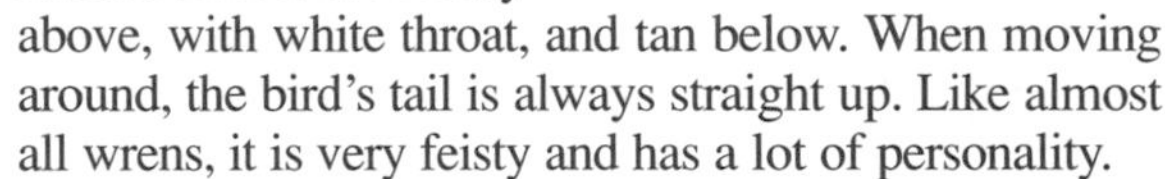

Gray catbird

The gray catbird is the most common songbird on Block Island. Its catlike "meow" is a familiar sound coming from the shrubs, as is its "eric, eric, eric," call. This species is closely related to the mockingbird, and is a good mimic that commonly makes a "sloppy" robin song. This 8.5 inch bird has a black cap, gray body and rufous feathers under its tail. A very curious bird, it can often be seen in the yard.

American robin

The American robin is the most common lawn bird, and also has an excellent song to learn. Its sweet-sounding "cheerily cheer-up cheerio" can be heard in any yard on Block Island. This 10-inch bird has a black head, rufous breast and brown back, and is often seen foraging lawns for worms and other insects.

Knowing these five songs will give you a starting point to learn all the wonderful bird sounds of Block Island. I will be out listening and learning, the question is will you?

Call versus Song

Bird calls and songs are differentiated, somewhat arbitrarily by the length and complexity of the vocalization. Calls serve a variety of specific functions, are usually inherent rather than learned and are often understood across species. Songs which are unique to each species are used by males to attract females and to defend their territories. They are well developed and must be partially or entirely learned.

The black-crowned night herons of Beane Point

In late June of each year, the dense poison ivy understory is crashed through in an effort to get a count of the wading birds nesting in trees on Beane Point. This census is led by Chris Raithel of the Rhode Island Department of Environmental Management with help from other ornithologists and assistants.

The Beane Point property is part of the U.S. Fish & Wildlife Service's Block Island National Wildlife Refuge. It contains conifers (mostly Japanese black pine) surrounded by coastal shrub (bayberry, arrowwood, chokeberry), and abuts the beach, encompassing nearly the whole peninsula.

This part of the refuge is where Block Island's largest colony of the state-endangered black-crowned night heron is found.

This medium-sized heron measures 23 to 28 inches, is chunky, with a black head and back, gray wings and white breast. There is no difference in appearance between the male and female. The immature of this species is brown all over with white streaks. At night the black-crowned night heron's loud, flat "quok" can be heard anywhere around the Great Salt Pond.

Young black-crowned night heron nestlings.

Most of the black-crowned night herons nest in pine trees located in the more secluded areas of the Beane Point property. This species' nest is composed of sticks, twigs, and reeds that are loosely woven together to make a platform. The nest's interior is scantily lined with finer material, such as moss and needles. These nests are found in the "crooks" of trees, usually as high up in the tree as possible. This species is considered a colonial nester so nests are normally in groups.

It is also important to note that night herons are extremely sensitive to disturbance and will only nest in quiet areas. This is one of the main reasons that Beane Point is closed to the public during the nesting season. In fact, in the 1960s, this species used to nest at the end of West Beach Road until too much traffic from the dump forced them to flee to Beane Point.

Once the nest is constructed, this night heron lays between three and five eggs that are light blue-green in color and about 2 inches in size. Both the male and the female then incubate the eggs for 24 to 26 days. After the eggs hatch, it is another 42 to 49 days before the nestlings fledge.

When searching for black-crowned night heron nests there are many clues as to where they are located. First would be the "quok" of the adult as it is flushed off its nest; another clue would be the "white-wash" (droppings) at the base of the nest and on the tree, and finally the eggshells below the nest.

Systematically, the Beane Point property is walked looking for any one or all of these signs. The area where the night herons nest is very dense and thus it is very important to go slowly and to look in the thickest of spots. When a nest is located, it is important to check for other nests because many times the nests are right next to each other.

This survey usually takes about four hot hours, trekking through the poison ivy. On average, 25 to 40 active nests are found. The majority of these nests are grouped on the northwestern end of Beane Point. Usually great and snowy egret nests are also found and recorded.

The number of black-crowned night heron nests is slowly declining from years past because suitable nesting habitat is disappearing. Its main type of nesting tree, the Japanese black pine, is dying from turpentine beetle damage and other diseases, resulting in fewer large trees on Beane Point for this species to nest in. Due to this phenomenon, black-crowned night heros have recently been spotted nesting in small numbers around Sands Pond and in the Boy Scout Camp.

If this article has piqued your interest and you want to see a black-crowned night heron on Block Island, I recommend going to Andy's Way and scanning the marshy area to the north, or venturing to the Coast Guard Beach at dusk. In one of these two places, you will surely see one of these amazing animals in its classic crouched hunting pose, looking to spear some fish.

THE GREAT FOURTH OF JULY NATURE SCAVENGER HUNT

Check off all 12 items on the list by journeying to different locations on the island (the easiest place to find each item is in parentheses). Please leave all of the items located for this scavenger hunt where they are found.

Find the following:

1) **American goldfinch** – a small yellow bird with black wings. (Any yard or feeder.)
2) **American oystercatcher** – 18-inch shorebird with orange bill. (Any beach at low tide.)
3) **American beach grass** – grass covering the dune — see it from afar. (Any dune area.)
4) **American robin** – common lawn bird. (Anywhere… every where.)
5) **American grasshopper** – the large field grasshopper. (Found in an unmowed field.)
6) **American copper** – a common, small, brown butterfly. (Any path or greenway.)
7) **Red-winged blackbird** – robin-sized black bird with red and yellow on wings. (Any swampy area.)
8) **White crab shell** – crab shells that are on the beach and are quickly bleached by the sun. (Any beach.)
9) **Blue jay** – blue bird bigger than a robin. (Any yard or feeder.)
10) **Sea star** – also known as a starfish. (Found on any beach at low tide.)
11) **Northern blazing star** – a wildflower with alternate leaves. (Fenced-in area at Turnip Farm, which is located off Old Mill Road.)
12) **The North Star** – star at the end of the handle of the little dipper. (An unlighted place on a clear, dark night.)

A mistaken identity

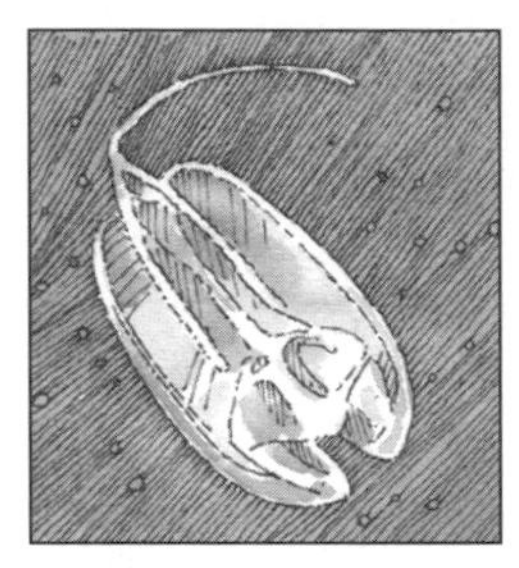

Every August, a number of people ask me questions about the little blobs of jelly they see bobbing along while swimming in the ocean. Visitors often think they are bluefish or striped bass eggs or some kind of jellyfish.

Well, they are none of these, rather, they are a species of animal plankton called a salp, which filter plant plankton from the water. According to Peterson's, *A Field Guide to the Atlantic Seashore*, salps are primarily an offshore organism, but can be found inshore in great abundance when current and prevailing winds dictate, which is often the case in mid- to late-summer on Block Island.

Unlike jellyfish, salps do not have stinging cells, and pose no threat to people. They are part of the ocean's rich, organic "soup," which in turn provides food for large animals, like whales and basking sharks.

Did you know…

There is no such thing as a seagull!

Out here on Block Island you will see herring gulls, great black-backed gulls, ring-billed gulls and even Franklin's gulls. But no "seagulls."

Patriotic animals

Every year around the Fourth of July, I think about all the "patriotic animals" that can be found on Block Island. There are insects such as American grasshopper, American copper and American painted lady, and birds such as American crow, American robin, and American redstart. Let me tell you a little about my three favorite patriotic animals.

One of the hardest patriotic animals to see is the elusive state-endangered American bittern. This bird is always solitary and usually hides among the marsh vegetation. It is 28 inches tall with a wingspan of 42 inches. Like all members of the wading bird family, when it is flying its feet point out behind the tail. This bittern is brown above and whitish below with dark maroon stripes on its throat. Its bill is yellow, large and pointed which is used to spear fish and other aquatic animals.

The American bittern moves extremely slowly and often stands with its neck and bill pointing straight up which makes it almost impossible to find in the marsh vegetation. The most intriguing thing about this patriotic animal is its unmistakable song, a booming, gulping "bloonk-adoonk" repeated over and over again. This song sounds just like water being pumped through a pipe. Currently it is unknown whether this species still nests on Block Island. During the spring and fall the best places to see this secretive animal are Andy's Way, Middle Pond, and Ambrose Swamp.

Although not as rare as the American bittern, the American oystercatcher is an uncommon nester in Rhode Island. Due to how few nests there are in the state, the oystercatcher is state endangered. On Block Island, there are five nesting pairs. These birds are hard to miss if you go to the salt marsh (Andy's Way, Cormorant Cove) at low tide. The 18-inch shorebird has a large red/orange bill, black head, and brown back. When flying, white patches can be seen on the wings. And it makes a very distinctive call that sounds like a car alarm. This bird nests on the cobbles of the beach and is very protective of the nest, often driving off much larger predators.

American oystercatchers.

The oystercatcher got its name from what it eats: oysters and other bivalves, like mussels. The oystercatcher has a long bill that is strong and doesn't bend easily. The bird sneaks up on an open bivalve and plunges its bill between the shells, severing the adductors (muscles that keep a bivalve sealed shut) before the bivalve can close. Young oystercatchers learn this unique way of feeding by watching their parents.

The American goldfinch is by far the most common of my three favorite patriotic animals. This songbird measures 5 inches. The males are bright yellow with black wings and cap, while the females are a duller olive with black/brown wings. This bird is found anywhere there are thistles, birdfeeders, fields and roadsides. The song of the goldfinch is a sweet-sounding series of trills and twitters. The easiest way to find this bird is to observe it as it flies: it undulates (folds its wings back and starts to drop and then flaps again) and sings out the call note that sounds like "potato chip."

The nest this bird weaves into the fork of a tree branch is so tightly woven that it holds water. The inside of the nest is lined with caterpillar or spider webs. The male collects the nesting material and then gives it to the female to construct the nest.

These are the stories of just three patriotic animals, but there are many more to be told. So on the Fourth of July, take a walk in the outdoors and keep an eye out for patriotic animals. They will be showing their true colors!

A male American goldfinch.

The moths of Block Island

In the summer, it is amazing how many different types of moths will come to a porch light when it is left on at night. With the help of lepidopterist (butterfly and moth expert), Mark Mello, from the Lloyd Center for Environmental Studies, The Nature Conservancy has been working to inventory the moths of Block Island since 1996.

How many moths do you think can be found on Block Island? So far, 350 different species of moths have been identified, but more incredibly, Dr. Mello believes that up to 650 species may inhabit this small island. This extremely high number of species makes it one of the most diverse forms of life on Block Island.

Moths are separated from butterflies in two ways, but there are always exceptions to the rule. Moths are active at night (nocturnal), and butterflies during the day (diurnal). Moths have feather-like antennae, whereas butterflies' are narrower and clubbed at the end.

The best way to catch and identify moths is by using a black light reflected on a white sheet. This is set up at dusk and then the light is checked frequently; moths are collected and identified. Another method of capture is using a light trap: a black light mounted on a aluminum funnel that is placed in a 5-gallon bucket and left on overnight. Moths come to the light, hit it, and drop through the funnel and into the bucket, caught until the trap is checked.

The final method is to mix a can of beer with some sugar and at dusk paint this solution on a tree trunk; then wait to collect the moths that are attracted. With all traps, the moths that can be identified are released; ones that need further identification are collected (to collect moths, a state permit is needed).

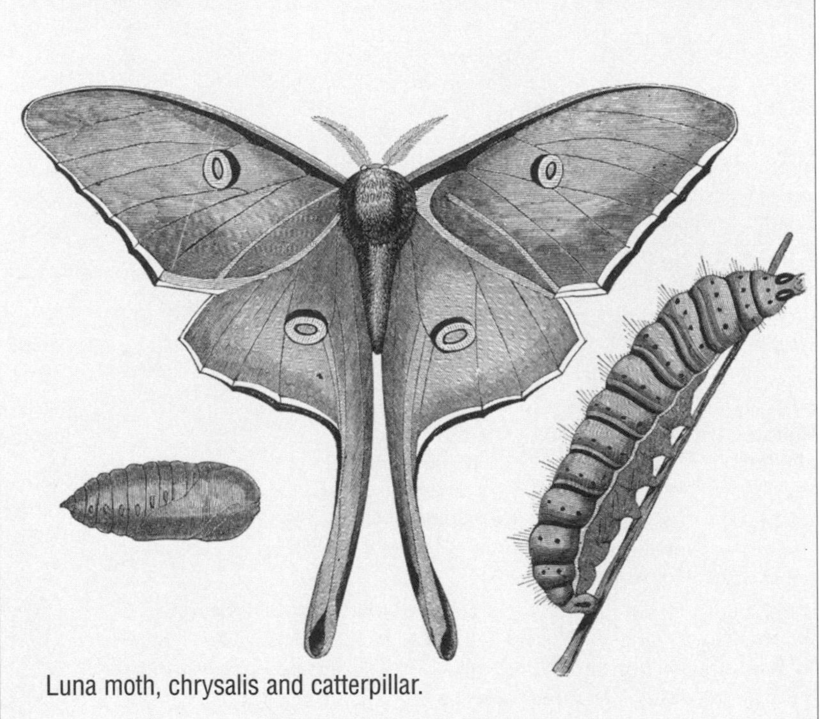

Luna moth, chrysalis and catterpillar.

Whether observing moths coming to your porch light or actively pursuing moths, there are many books that can be of great help. For the beginner, *Peterson First Guide to Butterflies and Moths*; for the intermediate, the *Peterson Field Guide to Moths*; for the expert, *The Moth Book*. These books contain all you ever wanted to know about moths and more, but let me tell you about the four most interesting moths that can be seen this time of year.

The Io moth, which is named for a mythical Greek maiden, measures 2 to 3 inches and has a conspicuous black eyespot on each of its hind wings (back two wings). In the male, the forewings (front two wings) are bright canary yellow, whereas in the female they are brown. This is a beautiful moth that is often attracted to lights.

The giant leopard moth is truly unmistakable. This 3-inch moth is white with black spots and a blue abdomen. The female is always much larger than the male and its abdomen often more brownish in color. This species lives in gardens and shrubs, and is a common visitor to outdoor lights.

The cecropia moth, with a wingspan of 6 inches, is the largest moth in North America. Its body is red with a white collar and white bands on the abdomen. The wings are dark brown with white hairline scales and red and black mixed in. Each wing also has a distinctive crescent-shaped spot. Cecropia moths do not live long (about two weeks) because the adult cannot eat. In fact, it doesn't even have a mouth or proboscis. Its only purpose is to mate and lay eggs.

The luna moth has spectacular colors and a remarkably long swallow-like tail. Its wingspan can reach up to 5 inches. This moth is light-green with springtime emergers having a pink/purple outline, and summer emergers having a green one. It is truly the most majestic moth on Block Island.

If you have your lights on at night you will surely see these amazing creatures. But remember, if they are at your lights they are not reproducing or looking for food. So it is always important to have low-voltage outdoor lights, and as few as possible, so the moths can go about their nightly business.

Planting native on Block Island

The Random House College Dictionary gives these definitions:

Native: originating naturally in a particular country or region, as plants or animals.

Exotic: of foreign character, not native.

****

One of the biggest threats in America today is from foreign invaders in the form of aggressive plant, insect, and animal species not native to the United States. It may seem hard to believe, but these "exotic" species often wreak havoc on the habitats they invade, causing the destruction of food and breeding habitat for native fauna (animals), the loss of much native flora (plants), the destruction of important food and ornamental crops, and the ruination of some of the country's most beautiful landscapes.

On Block Island we are not immune to the onslaught of exotic species. Rick Enser, Rhode Island Natural Heritage biologist, says "65 percent of Block Island plants were not originally found on the island. At least three mammals have been introduced to the island, and nobody knows how many insects.

Exotic species

While we cannot put the genie back in the bottle, we can help by not planting certain aggressive exotic species, and, by monitoring or removing the invasive exotics already present on our property. The following are plants to avoid when planning a garden.

Asiatic bittersweet is a woody vine with yellow fruits that split open to reveal bright orange seeds. Birds love the plant, so it is spread quite rapidly, strangling everything in its path. This plant is very obvious in the fall when all the berries can be seen. Please do not use bittersweet to make wreaths because wherever the seeds drop, plants will surely follow.

Multiflora rose is a sweet-smelling bramble with 9- to 12-foot-long arching stems rising directly from the ground. This species is the first to turn green in the spring, and also is one of the first to flower. Despite its beneficial qualities for birds, it overgrows and crowds out native plants. It is especially destructive to the blackberry patches we all enjoy.

Purple loosestrife is an attractive plant with purple spiked flowers and square stems. It's an aggressive weed, despite its elegant appearance, which can overrun native wetlands, destroying cover and food sources for many wetland species. A mature plant can produce up to 2.5 million seeds a year. Luckily, on Block Island, there are only a few populations of this plant and they are not expanding.

Other exotic species to avoid include all barberry species, tree-of-heaven, all buckthorns, black swallow-wort, autumn and Russian olive, Japanese honeysuckle, and Japanese knotweed. At this point you're probably saying, what should I plant?

Native species

There are many native plants that are beautiful and attract all sorts of birds and other animals. These native plants, if planted in their appropriate habitat, will require less watering and maintenance, and will have a higher resistance to insects and diseases, allowing you to avoid the use of pesticides and fertilizers. The following are a few great plants to use in your garden.

Arrowwood is a shrub with many trunks and white flowers in the spring and blue fruit in the fall. This plant attracts birds in the fall when its fruit is the main part of many migratory birds' diets.

Pokeweed is another great plant to attract birds in the fall. This plant has large purple berries (poisonous) and purple stalks. Thought by many people to be a weed, it actually is a favorite of the birds due to its large, juicy fruit.

There are also many beautiful wildflowers that are colorful in the garden and also important to local insects. Finally, **little bluestem** is a native grass that is blue-green in the early spring but then turns to tan for the summer. This grass is very important to the Block Island meadow vole.

The plants above are just suggestions. Ask your local landscapers for native plants that match your specific garden tract. As all gardeners know, there is no perfect plant for all situations, but native plants help make your garden a more productive part of the Block Island ecosystem.

Native plant options

Common Name	Latin Name
Flowers:	
butterfly-weed	*Asclepias tuberosa*
New England aster	*Aster novae-angliae*
common yarrow	*Achillea millefolium*
virgin's bower	*Clematis virginiana*
rose-mallow	*Hibiscus moscheutos*
Joe-pye weed	*Eupatorium dubium*
Shrubs & Trees:	
elderberry	*Sambucus canadensis*
shadbush	*Amelanchier canadensis*
winterberry	*Ilex verticillata*
beach plum	*Prunus maritima*
cockspur hawthorn	*Crataegus crus-galli*
highbush blueberry	*Vaccinium corymbosum*
red cedar	*Juniperus virginiana*
red maple	*Acer rubrum*
sweet pepperbush	*Clethra alnifolia*

Mammals of Block Island

Compared to mainland Rhode Island, Block Island has very few mammals. This lack of mammalian diversity adds to the interest of the island's ecosystem. Some of the mammals that are now seen on the island are native, while others have been introduced. The following is an account of each.

Block Island meadow vole

This animal is a subspecies exclusive to Block Island. It has a longer tail and shorter snout than the mainland vole. It loves switch grass and other tall grasses on Block Island. The island vole is slightly longer and fatter than a mouse, measuring 7 inches, including a 2-inch tail. In the winter it has a brown back with a gray stomach, and in the summer it is all buffy- brown. The vole nests in grass clumps and under boards, between six and 17 times a year, each bearing one to nine young. Active both night and day, this species eats grass seeds, insects and berries, and is a source of food for barn owls and northern harriers (marsh hawks).

White-footed mouse

This mouse is Block Island's other native mammal. It measures 7 inches in length, including a 3-inch tail, and has a reddish-brown, black back with white stomach and feet. This animal has countless litters of five young from April to November, in nests made in shrubs, trees, or grass clumps. Mostly nocturnal, except in extremely cold weather, this species eats seeds and berries. It is also a favorite meal for many of the raptors that live on and migrate through Block Island.

House mouse

Not native to anywhere in the United States, this mouse came to the island aboard ships, and soon spread throughout the island. It measures 7 inches long with a 3-inch bi-colored tail (brown with black tip). This species' body color ranges from grayish buff to a reddish-brown with a little white on the stomach. The house mouse is easily separated from the white-footed mouse because it has brown feet. It is found in developed areas including structures, but can also be found in open fields. Its nests are made in the shallow underground, in foundations, under woodpiles or other objects. The house mouse is a prolific breeder, having as many as 13 litters a year of six young per litter. Active both night and day, this animal eats a variety of seeds, stems, insects, berries, and household food. This mouse is an important food source for both hawks and owls.

Muskrat

Originally brought to the island to keep the ponds clear of vegetation, this neat animal has rich brown fur and a silver belly. It is much larger than the Norway rat, measuring 23 inches, including a 10-inch tail. The muskrat builds a stick, mud, cattail lodge in either a pond or bank, and has two to three litters of six to seven young per year. This species is an excellent swimmer and mainly eats aquatic vegetation. It is active both during the day and at night, and is lodge-bound only on the coldest of days. Muskrats, which are significantly larger than any other rodent, can often be seen moving slowly on the roadside. They are a positive part of the Block Island system. Please try to avoid hitting them with your car.

Norway rat

This rodent came to the island as another unwelcome passenger aboard ships. Also known as the brown rat, it has a brownish-gray back with a whitish-gray belly measuring 15 inches long, including a 7-inch tail. It digs a network of tunnels that are 2 to 3 inches in diameter in the ground, and has up to six litters a year of about eight young each. This mostly nocturnal species eats insects, seeds, stored grain, and garbage. The Norway rat is the major food source for the barn owl. In fact, the more rats there are, the more barn owl young and multiple nesting attempts from one pair there will be.

Silver-haired bat

By far the most common of the three species of bats on the island, it is a positive thing to have about the island because it eats mosquitoes and other insects. Measuring 6 inches, this species is nearly black except for silver-tipped hairs on the nape of the neck. In June or July, one or two young are born in either a tree hollow or an abandoned bird's nest, and remain there for about three weeks before they are able to fly. This is a migratory species that spends about five months a year on Block Island, flying to the southeast United States in the winter. The other two species of bats that can be found on Block Island are: little brown bat and eastern pipistrelle.

White-tailed deer

Brought over to the island in the 1960s, the white-tailed deer is an animal that can easily be seen around the island and unfortunately in your garden. Although the bane of many people's existence due to Lyme disease and garden damage, this large mammal is still fun to watch. It measures 3 feet in height to the shoulder, and 6 feet in length, with a foot-long tail. In the winter this species is grayish-brown, and in the summer it becomes a reddish-brown. In the late spring, females have one to two young a year, depending on the amount of food resources available. When a deer is scared, notice how it raises and wags its white tail. This is to warn other deer in the area of danger. As everyone who has a garden knows, deer eat herbaceous material throughout the year.

As you journey around the island, may you see all of the mammals that have a positive effect, and only see the others in the distance.

Other mammals on the Block

Feral cats – These wild cats come in all shapes and sizes. Originally abandoned, they have become adept hunters and have had many litters, which unfortunately increases Block Island's cat population. While these animals help keep the rodent population down, they also kill a tremendous amount of wild birds throughout the island.

Domestic rabbits – There are a few rabbits that can be found in town and, every once in a while, out in the wilds of Block Island. Again, abandoned especially after Easter, few rabbits are equipped to survive the harsh winter on the island. At this point the rabbit population is very small but it needs to be monitored to ensure that a population explosion does not occur.

Rock-flippin' family fun!

Did you ever lift up a rock just to see what crawled out from under it? Here's your chance to learn more about all those wiggly creatures that live there.

Find a rock that looks like it has been on the ground for a long time… then flip it over. Carefully observe all the animals you see.

Can you find all the creatures pictured on this page? Can you find more?

Please return the rock to its original position when you're done. Remember, the rock is the roof of their home.

Ground beetle: This elongated, hard-shelled insect is black in color. Make sure to check out its mandibles, or jaws. They are really neat!

Daring jumping spider: This friendly spider has green fangs (harmless), and three distinctive orange dots on the back of its abdomen.

Meadow cricket: It hops out as soon as the rock is flipped over. It has a black body with brown wing coverings.

Sow bug: It is also called a potato bug. It is the most common creature you will find under a rock.

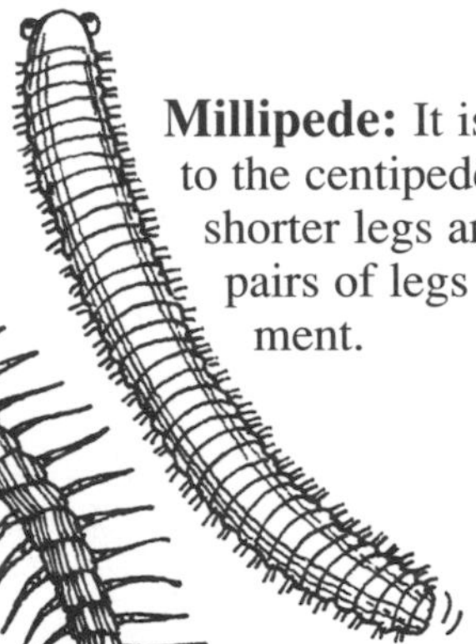

Millipede: It is similar to the centipede, but with shorter legs and two pairs of legs per segment.

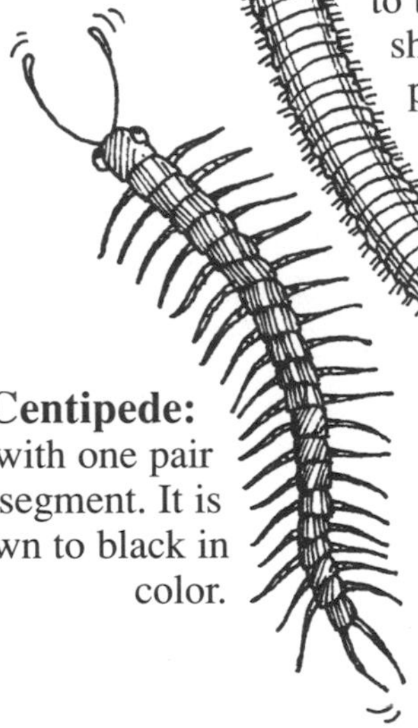

Field Ant: This mid-sized ant is black in color. See if you can find any ant tunnels, or individual ants carrying white egg sacs.

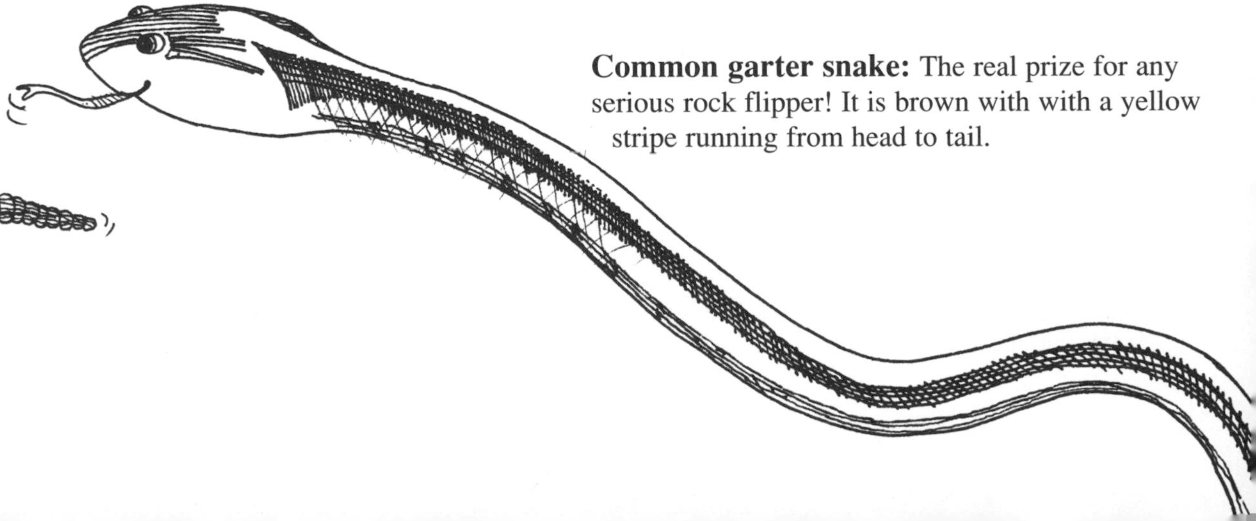

Centipede: A creature with one pair of legs per segment. It is often brown to black in color.

Common garter snake: The real prize for any serious rock flipper! It is brown with with a yellow stripe running from head to tail.

Earthworm: A red to black segmented worm of varying lengths. What's the longest earthworm you can find?

Backyard species

On Block Island there are many different animals to be seen around the yard. Whether you are sitting on the porch or working in the garden, animals abound if you know where to look for them. In any yard, at any given time, it is possible to see even rare and endangered species. For many of them, Block Island is an important refuge, a last stronghold — in the state, and for some, the region. However, there are also many common species that can be seen much easier and are neat in their own right.

Earthworm

This species is also known as a night crawler, and measures in length up to 8 inches. Its body is cylindrical and soft with many segments. The earthworm is purplish to orange in color, and is often seen in the yard surfacing after heavy rains. This animal is extremely important for having good soil in the garden because it aerates the soil with its movemenment.

Sow bug

Also known as a pill bug, and in the science community as an isopod, this species is a crustacean, like lobsters and crabs. It measures up to 0.5 inches in length, and is oval in shape when seen from above. The sow bug is covered with grayish-brown plates that protect the animal. It has seven pairs of short legs, and feeds on decaying plant matter. When disturbed, the sow bug rolls into a ball. This is by far one of the most common species in the yard.

Common green darner

This is the largest dragonfly on Block Island and can often be seen flying through the yard. It measures 3 inches in length with a green body. If the abdomen is blue, it's male; if it's reddish-brown, it's a female. This animal hunts insects and often flies the same flight path over and over again. Some green darners live year-round on Block Island; others migrate through in large numbers in the spring and fall.

Cabbage white butterfly

This butterfly is quite common on Block Island and can easily be seen around the yard. It measures about 1.5 inches, and is white on top with charcoal tips on the forewing. Males have an additional two charcoal dots on the forewing, whereas females only have one. This species is mustard-yellow in color underneath, with gray and black spots. This species is native to Eurasia and was accidentally introduced to North America in 1860.

Common garter snake

The garter snake can measure up to 22 inches in length and is slender. It has a narrow yellow stripe along the middle part of its back that runs the whole length of the snake, with two rows of blackish spots on either side of the stripe. The belly of this snake is gray or a buffy-white. It is important to note that the color and pattern of this species is variable. The garter snake eats mice and unwanted garden insects.

Gray catbird

The gray catbird is the most common songbird on Block Island. This 8.5-inch bird has a black cap, gray body and rufous feathers under its tail. Its catlike "meow" is a common sound coming from the shrubs, as well as its "eric, eric, eric" call. This species is closely related to the mockingbird, and is a good mimic that commonly makes a "sloppy" robin song. A very curious bird, it can often be seen hopping around the yard, especially after the lawn is mowed.

Song sparrow

This species is one of the most common songbirds on Block Island, nesting in every terrestrial habitat. It is brown above and white below, and measures about 6 inches in length. A large brown dot in the middle of its breast separates it from other sparrows. The song sparrow's song – two sweet-sounding notes, a twirl, and two more sweet notes – can often be heard in the backyard. Depending on the time of year and availability, this bird eats seeds, fruit and insects.

There are many neat species of animals to be seen around your Block Island backyard, each with its own amazing story. So, when you are on your deck or out in the garden, don't forget to observe Block Island's special creatures.

It's all happening at the beach

What do you think of when you hear the word "beach" on Block Island? Most people would say sand, ocean, shells, sun, party, and summer. Few would think of it as an important habitat that is home to some of the island's most threatened plants and animals. Of all the different types of habitats that make up the Block Island ecosystem, the barrier beach habitat is the most at-risk due to extreme use in the summer.

When first learning about the barrier beach on Block Island, it is important to realize that there are four basic zones that comprise this habitat: near-shore marine, beach, primary dune, and back dune.

The near-shore marine zone, which is the area where most people swim and play, is full of many species of fish, sea turtles, and sea birds. If you are lucky, you may have seen some of these amazing creatures. Some of the animals that occur in this area are striped bass, bluefish, common loon, herring gull, and in the winter, seals. Occasionally, sea turtles can be observed close to shore here. The biggest threat to this part of the system are oil spills, balloons and plastics that look like food to the larger animals, and disturbance from boats, jet skis, and people that get too close. Leatherback turtles are especially vulnerable to dying from ingesting plastic balloons and bags. While there is little we can do to prevent oil spills, we can pick up balloons and plastics when we see them, and be respectful of the animals when we are in the near-shore marine area.

Inland from the near-shore marine zone is the beach zone, which despite its appearance as a strip of lifeless sand, supports a variety of plants and animals that can live nowhere else. The federally threatened piping plover, American oystercatcher and other shorebirds, plants, and insects depend on the area between the low-water mark and the sand dune for their survival. This zone contains the greatest number of species in the beach region, with some even living on top of one another! Plants that live on the beach have special adaptations that resist salt and dryness, and have seeds that float. The wrack line, which is composed of seaweed, plant material, and marine-animal remains, is another important component of this zone. In addition to trapping seeds, it is where many insects breed and in turn are eaten by a variety of animals. Disturbance by people and vehicles is the main threat to this sensitive area. Visitors on foot can help this habitat by staying close to the ocean and not stepping on vegetation. If vehicle use is absolutely necessary, make sure to follow all regulations and restrictions.

The primary dune zone is stabilized by American beach grass, which over time catches and holds the sand, transforming a plain into a 20- to 30-foot high dune. This zone is important because it protects inland areas from wind and waves. It is also home to the Block Island meadow vole, white-footed mouse, and ring-necked pheasant. Throughout the grass are other beach plants like seaside goldenrod, dusty miller, rugosa rose, and beach pea. The major threat to this area, like the beach, is disturbance from people. The more individuals climb in the dunes, the less vegetation there is to hold the sand, and the greater the chance the dunes will erode during windstorms and other weather events. It is extremely important for visitors passing through this area, on their way to the beach, to use marked trails. The dunes are not a playground, restroom, or a photo stand.

Finally, the back dune zone harbors stands of switch grass and salt-tolerant shrubs like bayberry and beach plum. This group of plants forms a dense undergrowth that is ideal for many Block Island animals, including migratory songbirds, eastern towhee, and song sparrows. Again, the major threat to this area is disturbance. Just as with the dunes, it is important to stay on marked paths, especially because poison ivy and deer ticks are common here.

There are a few other important things to remember when visiting this sensitive barrier beach habitat. Beach litter, while it seems harmless, can injure or kill animals. Did you know that it takes an aluminum can 200 years to degrade, and a plastic bottle 450 years? Pets should be on a leash or at home, for they can harm or disturb wildlife when not restrained, and can also annoy other people. Finally, if you get a beach fire permit, be sure that your fire circle is away from the beach grass and that it is completely out when you leave.

Anyone who has been for a walk on Crescent Beach recently should be amazed at how good the beach habitat looks; let's try to keep it this way. Enjoy the beach, as we all do. Just remember many unique plants and animals depend on it to survive!

Seaweed

The smell of seaweed on the beach, no matter where I am, makes me think of Block Island. There are many different types of seaweed that can be seen on the island's beaches and in its waters. The best place to observe seaweed is in the ocean's intertidal zone, where it forms an underwater miniature forest. These areas are refuges for many of the animals found in this area.

When seaweed is washed up on the beach, piles form the important wrack line, where insects lay their eggs, seeds for dune plants are found, and shorebirds forage. It is always fun to walk the wrack after a major storm and see what new types of seaweed have washed up. While seaweed comes in all colors, sizes and shapes, there are five main types that are easily found on Block Island beaches. This is their story.

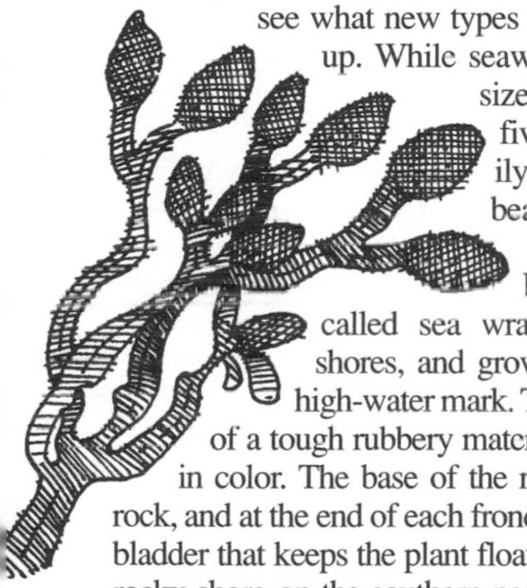

Brown rockweed, also called sea wrack, is found off rocky shores, and grows mostly just below the high-water mark. This seaweed is composed of a tough rubbery material that is green to brown in color. The base of the rockweed is attached to a rock, and at the end of each frond (branch) is a dimpled air bladder that keeps the plant floating during high tide. The rocky shore on the southern part of Crescent Beach is covered with this species, and which can be seen floating at high tide and out of the water at low tide.

Green sea lettuce, which is a type of green algae, is bright-green and very thin. Like the brown rockweed, this species is a rocky shore species. It is extremely delicate, attaching to rocks with a thin connection; and when you hold it up to a light it is possible to see through it. The bright color of this species makes it quite easy to spot in the wrack line. One of the best places to see this species is off Clay Head.

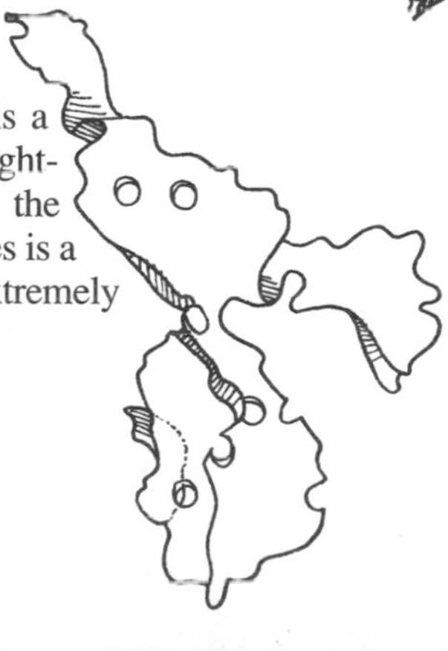

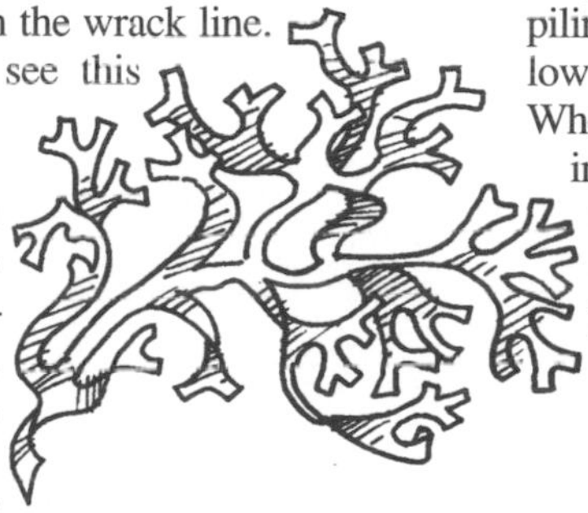

Irish moss is a type of red moss that is dark purple to green in color and has a profile similar to cauliflower. When on the beach, this species loses its color quickly due to the sun. This seaweed grows in dense clumps around the low-tide line. In the past, there was an Irish moss industry on Block Island, with it being harvested to use in puddings. The low-tide area on the southern part of Crescent Beach is a good place to locate this species.

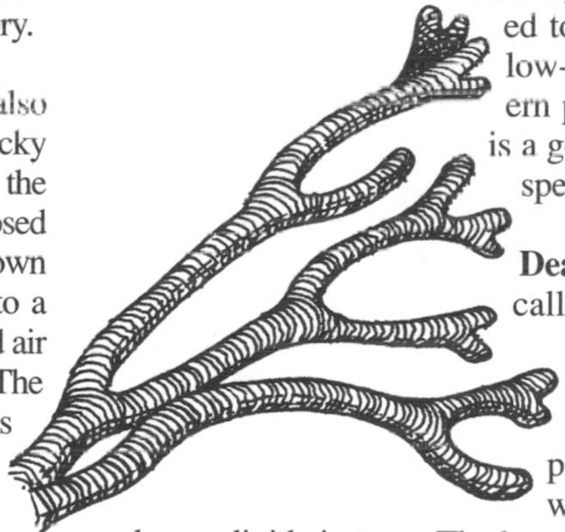

Dead man's fingers, also called green fleece and Codium, lives in rocky intertidal areas. It is a dark green velvety plant that floats erect with branches that always divide in twos. The branches, with some imagination,look like "fingers" floating in the ocean, hence the name. Most often it can be found attached to large shells like surf clams and oysters, or to small stones. This species is very common on Block Island and can be spotted off any rocky shore.

Brown kelp is a brown algae that is the most common type of kelp on Block Island. Its fronds are long and tough, and rich-brown in color. It attaches to rocks and pilings with finger-like anchors, and is rarely exposed by low tides except for the full moon low tides in the spring. When a spot covered by kelp is found while snorkeling, it is always interesting to see what is taking refuge in this dense area. A good place to see this species is in the deeper water past the Irish moss and brown rockweed.

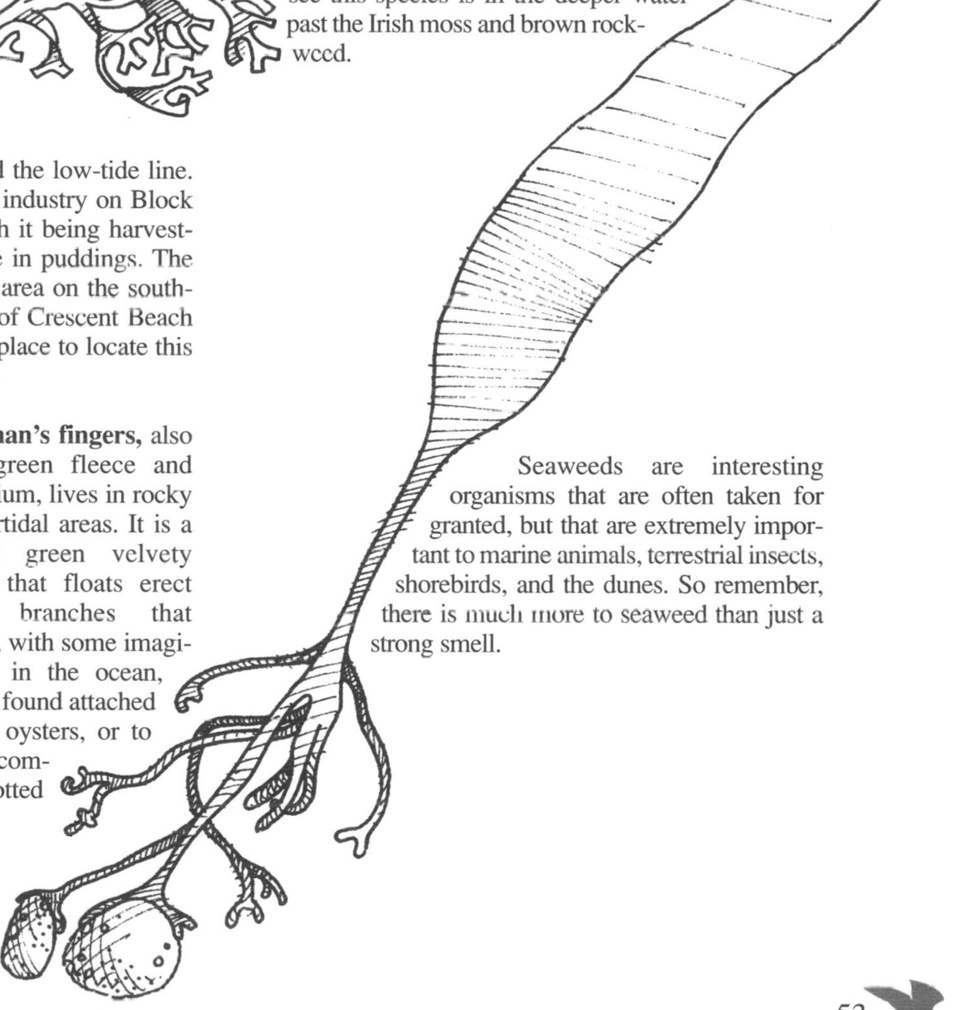

Seaweeds are interesting organisms that are often taken for granted, but that are extremely important to marine animals, terrestrial insects, shorebirds, and the dunes. So remember, there is much more to seaweed than just a strong smell.

The beach-monitoring study

Beach litter on Crescent Beach is always of major concern. Since 1997, as part of the education and outreach activities for The Nature Conservancy, I have been coordinating the National Marine Debris Monitoring Program for the Ocean Conservancy. This long-term study, which is funded by the Environmental Protection Agency, has over 200 "standardized" beach sites throughout the United States that are monitored by volunteers during the same time period every 28 days.

On Block Island, the 500-meter (approximately 1,500 feet) research area lies between Scotch and Mansion beaches. For the purposes of the study, the sites must be ocean-facing and mostly sandy beach.

On a monitoring day, a group of volunteers, often students from the Block Island School, go out and walk this stretch of beach in a zigzag path between the base of the bluffs or dunes and the ocean. Every piece of litter encountered on this stretch of beach is picked up, recorded on a data sheet, and removed. It usually takes about two hours to complete the monitoring of this section of beach.

The beach monitoring on Block Island began in August 1997, and so far this stretch of beach has been monitored 97 times. Many volunteers have helped us with this study, with the students from the Block Island School having done yeoman duty, accounting for the bulk of the work. This study would not happen without the help of volunteers and students. Many hands make light work!

The amount of beach litter removed from the 500-meter stretch of beach over the three years is staggering! The greatest amount of litter collected over the last 97 monitoring excursions is as follows: 4,030 pieces of plastic, 1,594 balloons, 1,312 pieces of rope greater than one meter, 1,308 pieces of Styrofoam, 1,266 pieces of rope less than 1 meter, 841 plastic beverage bottles, 809 beverage cans, and 626 floats and buoys. The total number of pieces of litter removed from between Scotch and Mansion since 1997 is 20,439.

Sixth-grade students from the Block Island School participating in the beach-monitoring study.

This study is designed to distinguish litter that washes up from litter that is left by beachgoers. Items such as plastic pieces, rope, balloons, floats, and the like probably washed up, while items like beverage cans, cigarette butts, plastic food containers, and such were probably left behind by beachgoers. The purpose of this study is to figure out the amount of garbage washing up on the beaches, and to measure the effectiveness of the marine dumping laws.

Some of the items that wash up are of special concern because of their impact on sea turtles; these include plastics and balloons (the top two in frequency). When they are floating in the water they look like jellyfish, a common food source for sea turtles, which then eat and choke on the look-alike foreign objects. Another concern is long pieces of rope (third in frequency) because marine animals (whales, dolphins, seals, and sea turtles) can get tangled in this type of debris and drown.

When you consider that 20,439 pieces of litter were removed on just 500 meters of beach, it makes you wonder about the rest of the island's beaches. If we had been collecting garbage on all the island's beaches, and they had the same density of garbage as the study area, we would have pulled off over 650,000 pieces of garbage since 1997. Actually, it probably would have been more because Crescent Beach, the site of the study, usually has less litter than the west and south beaches.

After hearing a number as large as that, I bet you are asking, "What can I do about this problem?" Three simple things that people can do are:

First, carry out everything you bring to the beach.

Second, remove beach litter that you find already there.

Third, if you're on a boat, don't throw litter in the water. If you bring it on board, please carry it off.

If everyone did these three things, we would find a lot less garbage on the beach.

The Great Wrack Line Scavenger Hunt

Wrack is seaweed and the remains of other marine plants and animals stranded by the tide on the beach. It provides food and shelter for flies and bugs, which are eaten by fish, birds, and other special mammals. Walk along a wrack line and see how many of these species you can find. When finished, please place all items back where they were found for others to enjoy.

Deadman's fingers— This very common seaweed is soft with thick, green spongy branches. It is also called green fleece.

Crab carapace— This is the top shell part of a crab. There are many types of crabs to be found including green, blue, Japanese mitten, and rock.

Bird feather— It's soft and floats on the breeze. It's designed to help birds fly and to stay warm.

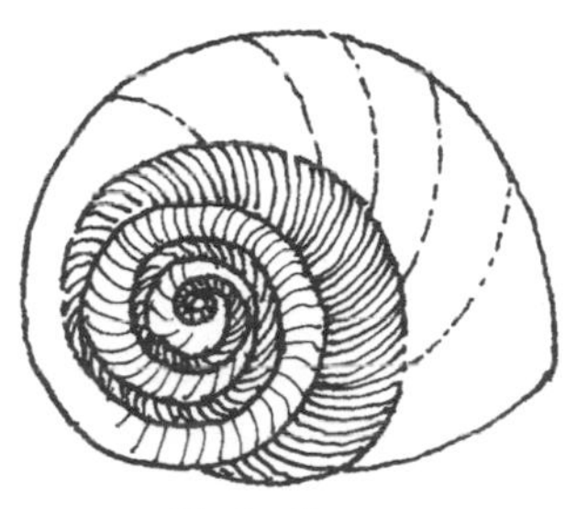

Moon snail shell— It's white, and can be up to 4 inches in size. This shell is home to a large beach snail.

Irish moss— This seaweed varies in color from green to purple to transparent. In the past it was used to make a very tasty pudding.

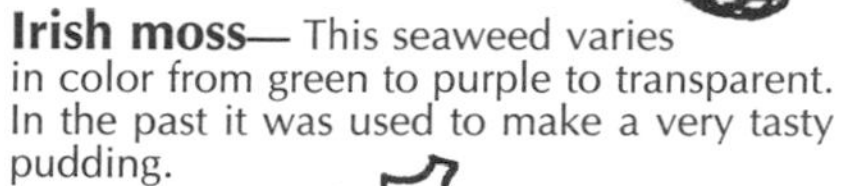

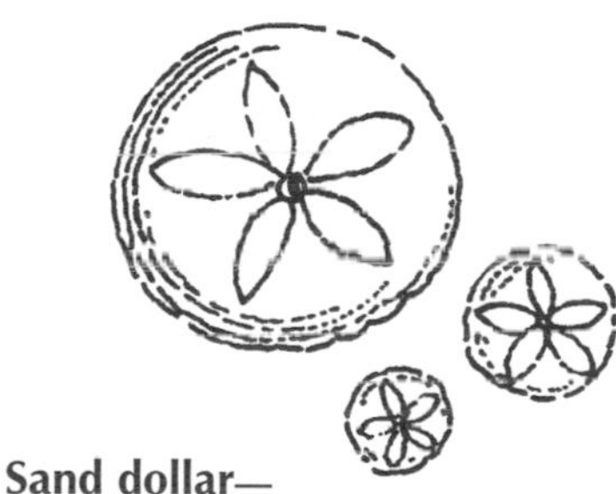

Sand dollar— Flat with five section patterns on top, it is gray to white in color. While big ones are hard to find, there are many that are smaller when you look carefully.

Blue mussel— It's smooth and small in size. It's a bivalve, which means the two shells are connected by a hinge.

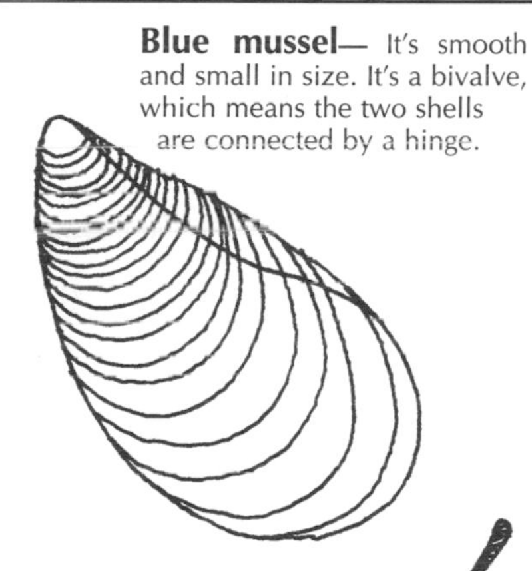

Crab or lobster claw— These are green to red to white in color depending on the amount of time in the sun.

Brown rockweed— This seaweed is flat at the bottom and has air bladders at the top that help the plant float above the rocks it attaches to.

False angel wing— White and fragile and up to 2 inches in length, it is a bivalve mollusk, which means it has two shells connected by a hinge.

Skate egg case— It's black and leathery, and floats in the ocean for a year before it hatches.

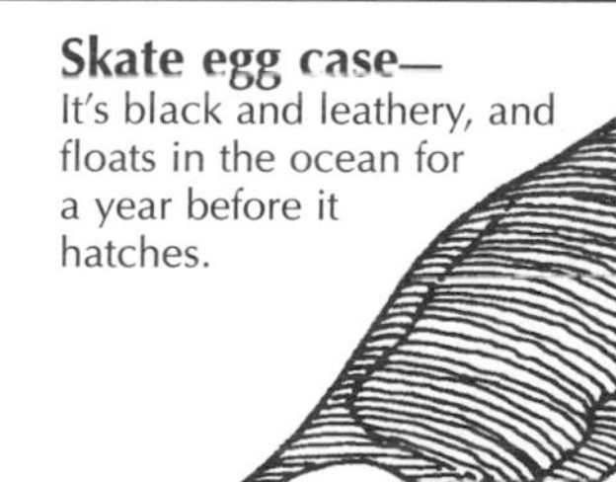

Periwinkle— They are small and brown, and provide homes for an intertidal snail.

Did you find them all?
Which was the easiest?
Which was the hardest?
Which was the smelliest?

Gulls

While many people consider the gulls on Block Island "flying rats," they are actually quite interesting. These scavengers eat all sorts of things, and their important role in the ecosystem is essentially as one of nature's garbage removers. On Block Island, the gull rookery south of Sandy Point is the largest in Rhode Island.

The herring and great black-backed gulls are the two main species of gulls on Block Island. In their adult form they are easily distinguished, with the herring gull having gray wings with black tips and the great black-backed gull having black wings outlined in white. When immature, it is very difficult to distinguish between the two species because they look very similar.

The island used to support more gulls before the dump became a transfer station. Over the last 10 years there has been a lot of competition and a decline in numbers. In May, the gulls begin to nest and the competition between the species is greatly increased. Currently, the great black-backed gulls are outcompeting the herring gulls.

This has been well-documented by a yearly count of nests (426 great black-backed, 187 herring gulls in 2004). This count is more of a painful chore, walking through poison ivy and getting pooped on and dive-bombed for a few hours. One time I actually got hit in the head by a gull's wing and it drew blood. I have now found it is helpful to wear a hat and carry a stick to keep the birds away. The two main areas where gulls nest on Block Island are south of Sandy Point and on the way out to Beane Point from West Beach Road. Anyone visiting one of these areas should make sure to stay at least 20 feet away from the nearest nest.

These gulls do not have elaborate nests, but can easily be spotted by the adults standing nearby and a lot of fecal material in the area. There are usually between one and four eggs in each gull's nest. As the chicks hatch and become older, the adults leave the nest to find food. When they return, chicks peck the red dot on the gull's bill, which is a cue for the adult to regurgitate its food and feed the chicks.

Gulls eat all sorts of food including clams, mussels, and crabs, not to mention garbage and food that may have been left by people visiting the beach. Due to their size and mobility, they sometimes hit things like wires and break their wings. It is not an uncommon sight to see a gull with a broken wing walking around various parts of the island. There are no facilities on Block Island to rehabilitate these birds, thus it is better to let nature take its course. Many of these birds survive quite a long time feeding on discarded food and dead animals.

In addition to the herring and great black-backed gulls, it is also quite possible to see ring-billed and laughing gulls. These two are smaller in size and the ring-billed, like the name says, has a black ring around its bill. The laughing gull is distinguished by a dark head and black wingtip. Rare gull sightings include glaucous gull, black-legged kittiwake, lesser black-backed gull, and Bonaparte's gull to name a few.

Gulls are a part of the fabric that is Block Island. At one point they were so rare that some of the land in the Block Island Wildlife Refuge was originally conserved for them. They have returned in large numbers and are now a common occurrence on the island. No matter where I am, when I hear the call of a herring or great black-backed gull I think of Block Island. For this reason I appreciate these species, and I hope you will too.

Those crazy crows

Did you know that there are two species of crows on Block Island? There is the American crow, one of the most common birds seen around the island, and the fish crow, which is less common. Both crow species are some of the smartest birds in the world, adaptable and extremely opportunistic. While they can be bad for crops, specifically corn, they also have a tremendous benefit for humans, eating large quantities of destructive insects and pests, and also removing potentially harmful decomposing animals.

The American crow is found throughout North America and is a permanent resident on Block Island. This animal is midnight black in color and measures 21 inches in length with a fan-shaped tail. Its flight is a steady wing flapping and its call sounds like "caw-caw."

This species can be found in any habitat on Block Island searching for food. The American crow is an omnivorous feeder, which means it eats both animals and plants. Its favorite foods include snails, salamanders, small birds, wild fruit, grain, mice, eggs, insects, and carrion. On Block Island this crow also forages in a manner similar to gulls, taking clams and mussels and dropping them from the sky to open the shells. Then the birds land on the ground to ingest the meat. An adult of this species eats its weight in food every day, consuming eight to 10 full meals.

American Crows reach breeding maturity between 2 and 4 years old. During the breeding season they become very quiet and solitary. When a male finds a female, a complex mating ritual takes place either on the ground or in the trees. Once they have mated, the male and female perch together, touch bills, and preen each other's feathers. This species is also a cooperative breeder living in family groups of up to eight individuals. The individuals that are not sexually mature assist with all aspects of nesting and caring for fledged offspring.

American crow nests are found just below the tops of large trees, which on Block Island means that they are in either Japanese black pines, large shads, or black cherry. Both the male and female build the nest, which is 12 inches in diameter and made of twigs, grasses, and tree bark. Three to seven blue, gray, or green eggs with brown blotches are laid by the female. Both of the parents incubate the nest for 18 days and the chicks fledge after about five weeks.

Some neat American crow facts include: in winter they roost together in large groups to stay warm; they fly up to 50 miles a day searching for food; and often when foraging they have multiple high-perched sentinels serving as lookouts for danger. These crows also have complex vocal cords, which allow captive crows to pronounce words.

The fish crow is very similar to the American crow in appearance. It is also dark black, but slightly smaller measuring 17 inches and with a very nasal "kwak" or "ah-ah" call. It also has a faster wing beat than the American crow. Size and wing beat speed can be very deceptive in the field, so the best way to distinguish this species is by its call.

The fish crow is slowly expanding its range north from the southeastern United States. On Block Island, this species is less common and most often found around the beaches, at the Abrams Family Animal Farm (next to the Manisses), and around Clay Head. Fish crows are also omnivores, eating much of the same types of food. However, one of this crow's favorite foods is dead fish, hence its name. It is also a common predator of heron and egret eggs.

Fish crows have a complex mating ritual that includes a courtship fight and touching wings and heads. It is not a communal breeder and it is believed that pairs are monogamous. Nests built in the highest notches of an evergreen or large deciduous tree are constructed of sticks and twigs and are lined with bark and pine needles. The female then lays four or five greenish eggs with brown blotches. Both the male and female incubate the eggs for 18 days, and chicks fledge after 21 days.

The fish crow is the most sociable and gregarious of all North American crow species. In fact, first year fish crows like to play with each other. This species is also rapidly expanding its range in a "leapfrog" pattern: new colonizers move from an established area, skip a spot, and inhabit a new area. It is believed that this happens because fish crows are keying in on heron and egret colonies.

Unlike in mainland New England, the West Nile virus has not affected crow populations on the island. As of 2004, there are no recorded cases of this virus on Block Island. Should you find a freshly dead crow (less than a day old), call The Nature Conservancy to arrange for testing of the animal (do not touch the animal).

Despite the many negative feelings about crows, often derived from misinformation, they are extremely interesting animals and deserve our respect.

Underwater Scavenger Hunt

Grab your snorkel, mask and swim trunks, and head to your favorite stretch of ocean to see if you can find the following things. Please refrain from touching or disturbing any of the animals or plants.

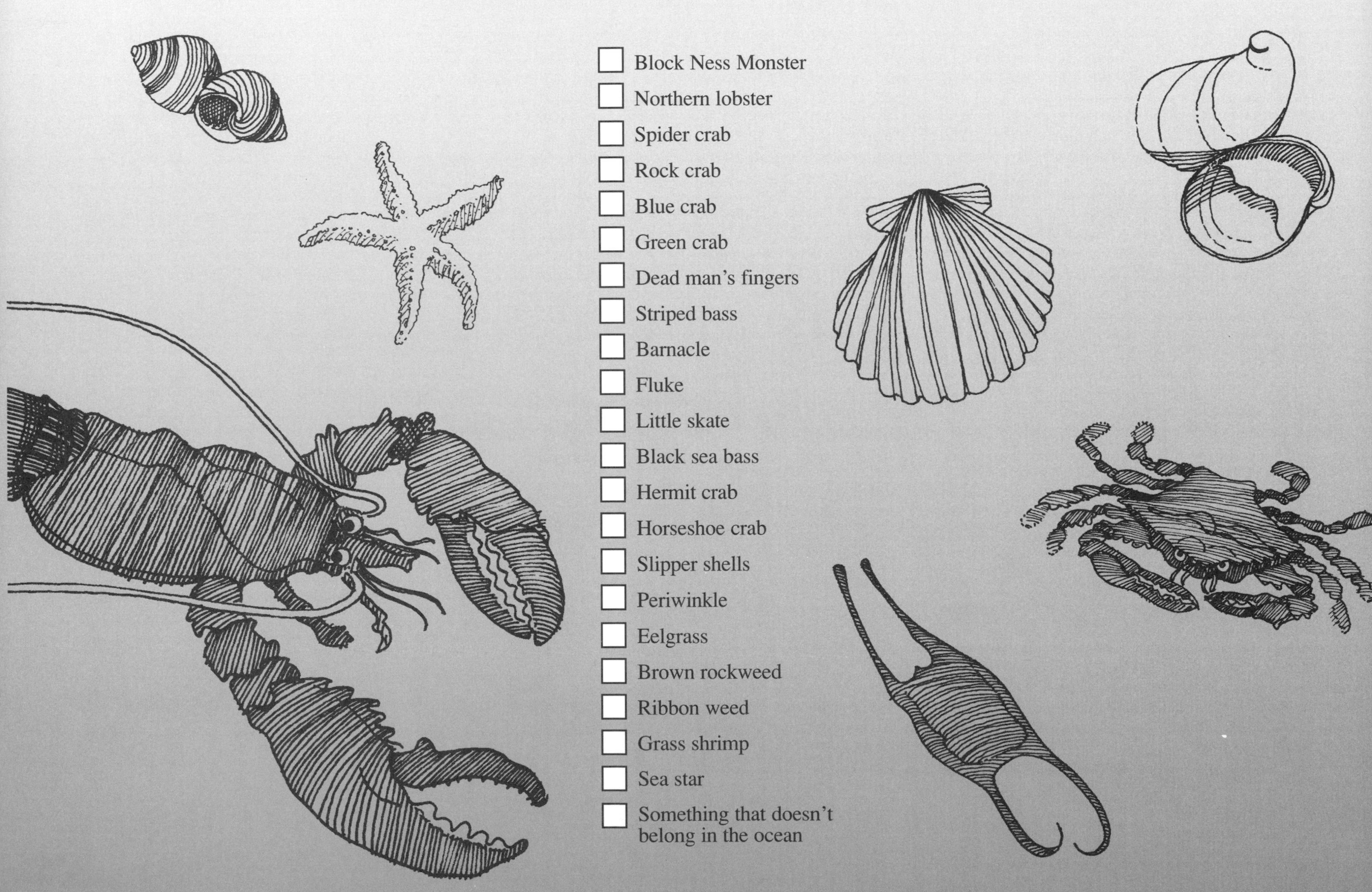

- ☐ Block Ness Monster
- ☐ Northern lobster
- ☐ Spider crab
- ☐ Rock crab
- ☐ Blue crab
- ☐ Green crab
- ☐ Dead man's fingers
- ☐ Striped bass
- ☐ Barnacle
- ☐ Fluke
- ☐ Little skate
- ☐ Black sea bass
- ☐ Hermit crab
- ☐ Horseshoe crab
- ☐ Slipper shells
- ☐ Periwinkle
- ☐ Eelgrass
- ☐ Brown rockweed
- ☐ Ribbon weed
- ☐ Grass shrimp
- ☐ Sea star
- ☐ Something that doesn't belong in the ocean

The Great Block Island Hands 'n' Knees Beach Hunt

Block Island's beaches are beautiful, and taking long beach walks, looking for treasures in the tideline, is something everyone does at least once during their summer vacation.

But for a real adventure on the beach, get down on your hands and knees and take a really close look at a small portion of the tideline. In an area no larger than 6-feet square, how many treasures can you find? How many are natural things? How many are trash?

In addition to the items pictured here, what else can you find? Here's a short checklist to help you get started:

— Sea glass	— Bottle cork
— Surf clam	— Fish head
— Bird bones	— Fishing lure
— Fish netting	— Skipping stone
— Magic rock*	— Coins
— Really round rock	— Plastic bottle cap
— Blue mussel shell	— Balloon
— Sea star (Starfish)	— Driftwood
— Pirate's chest	— (What else?)

* A magic rock, lucky rock or wishing rock is a dark rock that has a white stripe all around it. They're easy to find on Block Island.

Crab carapace

Feather

Quahog shell

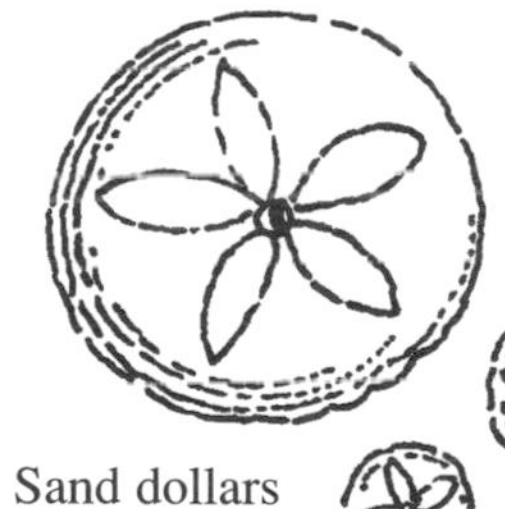

Sand dollars

Brown rockweed

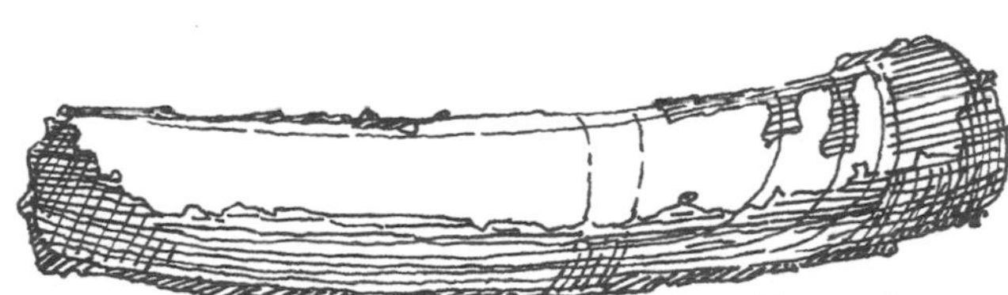

Razor clam

Bay scallop shell

Skate egg case

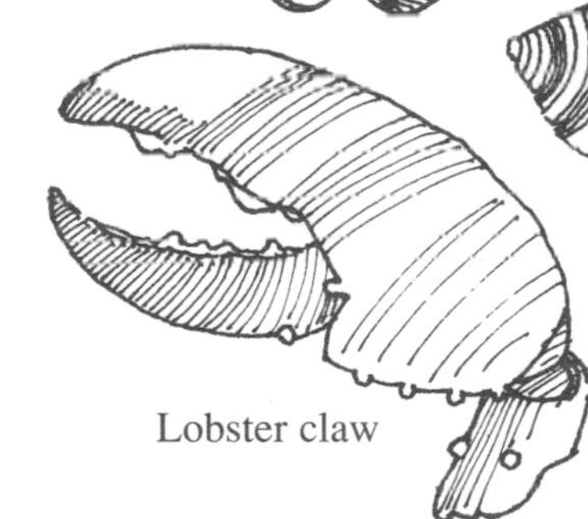

Lobster claw

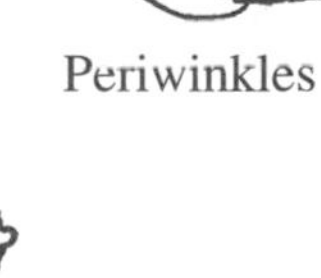

Periwinkles

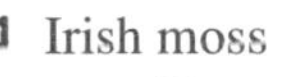

Irish moss

Sea turtles

Summer is a great time to see sea turtles on Block Island. These magnificent creatures are reptiles, thus they are cold-blooded, breathe air, and have leathery eggs and scaly skin. As with observing whales and dolphins, you have to be in the right place at the right time to see these animals. There are four species of sea turtle that can end up in Block Island waters in the summer and early fall.

Green sea turtle.

The green sea turtle is the most common sea turtle around Block Island. This species gets its name from the green-colored fatty tissue under its shell. It is easily distinguished from other sea turtles because it has a single pair of prefrontal scales (scales in front of its eyes), rather than two pairs as the other sea turtles have. The shell of this turtle is a splotchy dark brown on top and a yellowish-white below, and is often covered in green algae growth. Adults reach 4 feet in length and weigh 400 pounds. This species is herbivorous, eating sea grass and algae with jaws that are especially serrated to aid in the tearing of this vegetation. Its diet is what makes its fat layer green. This is the only species of sea turtle that is herbivorous as an adult. The green sea turtle can live up to 80 years, but there has been a significant increase in mortality in the population in recent years. Threats to this species include entanglement in fishing gear and death from incidental bycatch in commercial fisheries.

The loggerhead sea turtle is the second most common sea turtle around Block Island. The loggerhead gets its name due to its extremely large head and powerful jaws. Its shell is heart-shaped and reddish-brown above and a dirty-yellow below. The scales, or scutes of the shell, are rough and do not overlap. Adults can reach 3.5 feet and weigh 350 pounds. This species is carnivorous, eating mostly animals that live on the bottom of the ocean like horseshoe crabs, clams, and mussels. Its powerful jaws easily crush the shells of its prey. This species lives up to 50 years, although its population is listed as a federally threatened species in the United States. Ingesting plastic that looks like prey is a major cause of mortality for this species, along with getting caught in fishing gear and being harvested for meat.

The leatherback turtle is the largest sea turtle around Block Island. The leatherback gets its name from its shell, which is composed of a layer of tough rubbery skin that looks like leather. This species' shell has five ridges and is black with light-colored spots above and whitish below. Its extreme size, reaching up to 8 feet in length and 1,300 pounds, also separates it from all other sea turtles. This species has a delicate jaw that would be damaged by eating anything other than soft-bodied animals. In fact, it eats jellyfish almost exclusively. The leatherback is believed to live over 50 years, and is currently listed as federally endangered. Major causes of mortality include ingestion of plastics, entanglement in fishing gear, and being struck by boats.

The hawksbill turtle is the rarest sea turtle around Block Island. The hawksbill gets its name from its narrow head and sharp hawk-like beak. This species' shell is elliptical in shape with overlapping scutes that are amber in color. It is a smaller sea turtle, reaching 3 feet in length and weighing 150 pounds. This species' jaw is not serrated, and its diet consists of sponges, shrimp, squid, and anemones. It is not known how long hawksbill turtles live, but it is believed to have a shorter lifespan than other sea turtles. The animal is federally endangered because of the excessive harvesting of its prized shell, which is still used to make hair ornaments, jewelry, and other decorative items in some countries.

One thing we can do to help sea turtles is to pick up plastic and balloons whenever we are on the beach. These are amazing animals that are very hard to see around Block Island, thus, every time I see one it is a very special experience. Whenever you are on or near the water, keep an eye out because you never know when you might glimpse a sea turtle.

Saltwater fish: not just for grilling

Normally on Block Island, when the subject of saltwater fish comes up, people like to talk about their favorite grilling recipe or where the best place is to catch these amazing creatures. While this is interesting information, most people know very little about the life history of the common saltwater fish in Block Island waters. Here is their story.

Striped bass:

This important game fish is green-gray on top, shading to silver below, with six to eight blackish-brown stripes on both sides of the body that run from the gills to the base of the tail. Some older fish have a rosy-colored patch under the pectoral fins (bottom fins in the front of the fish). This species has separate dorsal fins (fins on the back) that are spiny and carry a mild neurotoxin. Striped bass can range in size up to 6 feet, and weigh in at over 60 pounds. Bass are generalists, eating many types and sizes of fish, lobsters, crab, eels and shellfish.

The striped bass is anadromous, which means that it migrates from the ocean to freshwater for the purpose of reproduction. Most stripers spawn in rivers from New York to North Carolina. The female, when in river habitat, lays hundreds of thousands of eggs, which are then fertilized by the male. Once they have hatched, young fish remain in the river for several years before migrating to the ocean. This species can be found along the East Coast of North America from Nova Scotia to Florida.

Bluefish:

The bluefish is another important game fish. It is greenish-bluesh above, with silvery sides, and a black splotch at the base of the pectoral fin. This species has a large mouth with many sharp teeth. A bluefish can range in size to about 3.5 feet, and weigh up to 25 pounds.

Also a generalist, this species feeds mostly on fish and crustaceans.

Oceanic in nature, the bluefish can be found either inshore or offshore. It spawns from late spring to early August off the East Coast. During the winter months, bluefish go south toward the Carolinas but their exact wintertime location is still debated.

Fluke:

Also called summer flounder, it is a flatfish that spends most of its life on the ocean floor. It has both eyes on the left side of its body when viewed from above. The eye side of the fish is scattered with 10 to 14 black spots, which help it blend in with the ocean floor. The fluke actually has the ability to change coloration, and patterns to help it hide. The other side of the fish is white. It can range in size up to 35 inches, and can weigh over 20 pounds. An excellent predator, it eats small fish, squid, sea worms, and other crustaceans. Spawning for this species happens during the fall migration and on the wintering grounds. This species is found in brackish and coastal waters from Nova Scotia to Florida.

Tautog:

Also known as blackfish, it is popular for both commercial and recreational fisheries. Usually this animal is a dull blackish to dark green color with irregular mottled sides, and lighter in coloration on the chin, throat and lips. The tautog is slow in growth and lives up to 30 years, reaching up to 20 pounds and 3 feet in length. It is strongly territorial and feeds mostly on shellfish (especially mussels) and crustaceans.

While spawning, mature female tautog may lay over 600,000 eggs during spring. Spawning reaches a peak in June, and may last throughout the summer. This animal is found along the Atlantic coast between Nova Scotia and Georgia, with the largest populations occurring between Cape Cod and Chesapeake Bay.

Black sea bass:

The sea bass is blue to black to dark brown in color and blotched throughout, resembling a fishnet pattern. Often found around rock jetties and on rocky bottoms, this species can range in length up to 2 feet and weigh up to 8 pounds. Also a generalist, this bass feeds on different species of crab, juvenile lobster, small fish, and squid.

Unlike the striped bass, this species is strictly confined to salt water. While much is unknown about the life history of the sea bass, it spawns from the middle of May to the end of June. While it moves along the East Coast, depending on temperature, its range is from Maine to Florida and the eastern Gulf of Mexico.

These fish live in a world that is rarely seen but in which many interesting things occur. So when swimming or snorkeling in the ocean, keep an eye out for these amazing animals.

Block Island ponds

A bird's eye view of Block Island displays just how common ponds are on the island. Local lore insists that there are 365 ponds, one for every day of the year. While this number may generously include a few puddles after it rains, it is still amazing how many ponds, approximately 330, can be found on this small island.

Throughout Block Island, many different types of ponds can be found. Some are rainfed while others are spring fed; some have clay bottoms while others have sand; and some are surrounded by vegetation while others are completely open. These subtle differences in the ponds affect the types of species that inhabit them.

From 1997 to 2001, The Nature Conservancy hired Mark Chandler from the Edgerton Research Laboratory of the New England Aquarium to inventory the ponds of Block Island. This information was then used to document the importance of Block Island wetlands in the region.

One of Block Island's many ponds.

For the first three years of the study, Chandler and his team of three (which usually included me) inventoried 58 ponds, which were a representative sample of the ponds of Block Island. The inventory work for each pond included: a survey of both aquatic and terrestrial vegetation, amphibians, reptiles, fish (density and species), insects (density and species), water clarity, pH, dissolved oxygen in the water, and nitrogen amounts. All of the data, when combined, painted an excellent picture as to the health of a pond and potential factors affecting its condition. Every pond was then re-inventoried during the fourth year of the study to see how it had changed over time.

Ponds were found to fall into one of three categories: fishless ponds, which had the highest density and diversity of insects and amphibians; ponds with introduced fish like bluegill sunfish and largemouth bass, which had fairly low overall diversity; and ponds with only native fish like brown bullhead, golden shiner, and pumpkinseed sunfish, which had slightly less diversity than fishless ponds.

The Block Island ponds with introduced fish were found to be very similar to ponds with the same characteristics across New England. Ponds with only native fish were found to be extremely rare in the region because of rampant fish introduction by anglers. Finally, fishless ponds were also found to be extremely rare in the region and the most interesting of the three types.

In the final year of the study, Chandler focused exclusively on fishless ponds, monitoring them throughout the spring, summer, and fall. He found that they were the most diverse in the spring and the least diverse in the fall. This makes sense because many of these ponds are vernal and tend to dry up for part of the summer. He also found that these ponds, because of their small size, were negatively affected in a dramatic way by even a minor disturbance.

For most of the ponds surveyed, the overall health was good to great. However, some ponds had too many nutrients because there was not enough of a vegetative buffer to filter them out. Chandler has three simple rules to keep your pond healthy: "have at least a 50-foot vegetative buffer around the pond, do not use lawn fertilizer in areas where it could run off into a pond, and do not introduce any new fish to a pond."

In addition to being beautiful, ponds are an important habitat for many species of plants and animals. This pond inventory project found that there are many healthy functioning ponds with high diversity throughout the island. While these ponds are common on Block Island, many of them are unique to New England and should be treated with respect.

Birds need rain, too

Not to overstate the obvious, but... birds need the rain, too. During extremely dry summers, which can be easily determined with a quick tour of the island, lawns are brown, ponds have a large beach or are dried up, and many plants look wilted. It is clear that many habitats are affected by the lack of rain, or more specifically no long-soaking rain for some time. With songbird migration beginning in the early autumn, it is important to explain how the dry summer impacts the birds that are and will be migrating through Block Island in the fall.

During the fall, songbirds moving from the north to the south stop on Block Island for a period of time that ranges from one day to a few weeks. While they are here, they are drinking and eating to continue their trip south. When the birds reach this key stopover site, they need to drink water, preferably from areas that are covered with shrubs so hawks cannot find them.

After rehydrating, the birds start to forage to restore fat deposits lost during migration. Dr. Jeffrey Parrish from Brown University was the first to prove, from a study conducted on Block Island, that these migrants in the fall switch from eating insects to eating mostly fruit because there is so much of it during this time of year. The shrubs and their fruit are extremely important to the birds migrating through Block Island. Dr. Parrish also found that recently arrived migrants are dehydrated more than anything.

In a dry summer, the continued lack of rain causes many of the larger ponds and wetlands to recede from the shrubby edge, and some of the smaller ones to dry up completely. Thus during drought periods, songbirds have to be out in the open in order to get a drink of water, exposed to hawks and other predators. This means that there is a reduced chance of survival for songbirds. It is nearly impossible to predict just how big an impact this will have.

The yellow-breasted chat, a fruit-eating bird that may be affected by the lack of rain.

A warm, dry summer also affects the fruiting shrubs. Important ones like black cherry (food of choice in August) have fewer berries than usual. The arrowwood, normally food of choice in mid-September, ripens in late August or sometimes even drops its fruit and withers. Thus, there is also a negative change in the fruit cycle during dry summers. Food that is normally present in large quantities for birds may not be available, which means that the songbirds probably spend more time and energy searching for food. This translates into a longer stopover period (good for birdwatchers) and a higher chance of mortality due to perils of migration (predation, starvation, running into an obstruction). Again, it is hard to say the degree of impact this has, but we must remember that birds have survived many a dry summer in the past.

The effect of the lack of rain during any given summer on migrating birds in the fall has yet to be determined. It may cause a higher mortality rate for these songbirds while they visit the island. Hopefully, they can shift their diet to insects if they cannot find enough fruit, and can find the few ponds that still have a lot of shrubs nearby. Remember, if it is a dry summer, pray for rain!

Keeping Track of Rainfall

If rainfall amounts are of interest to you, the following steps will help you keep track:

1) Purchase a rain gauge at a garden center or nature store.
2) Place rain gauge on level ground away from obstructions that could alter the results.
3) Set up a rainfall log book.
4) Wait for it to rain.
5) After each rain event - check the gauge, record the measurement in the log book along with the date, and then empty the gauge.
6) Repeat steps four through six for desired period of time.

By tracking the rainfall you can gather interesting information that can also be very useful when deciding when the garden needs to be watered!

Freshwater fish

Block Island's many ponds are beautiful to behold from afar, but there are also many neat creatures below the surface, specifically fish. Some of the ponds have only native fish, while others have fish that were introduced by anglers. Block Island's ponds featuring only native fish are extremely rare in New England, and thus it is important to not transport fish between ponds. There are many species of fish that can be found in freshwater, but seven stand out as the most common. This is their story.

The golden shiner is a native fish that gets its name from its color. This shiner has a back that is golden in color, with sides that are light olive with silvery reflections, and a belly that is silvery-yellow. It is one of the smaller fishes in the pond growing up to 6 inches. This species forages on microscopic creatures called zooplankton, water fleas, insects and algae. During the day this species stays close to aquatic vegetation, and ventures out to open water at night. The golden shiner is only found in ponds with good water quality, thus it is a good indicator species of a pond's health. This species is consumed by birds, bigger fish and turtles, and is often used by anglers as bait.

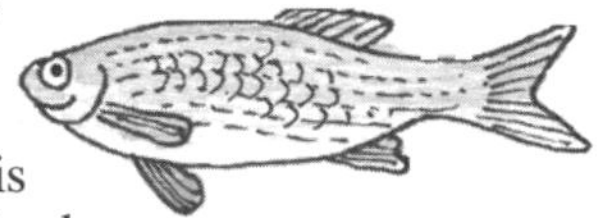

The brown bullhead is a type of catfish that is native to Block Island. This bullhead is olive-brown above – shading to grayish-white on the belly – with sides that have black mottling. This species is easily distinguished by the black barbells, which are light in color at the base and extend from the chin. This species can reach 15 inches in length and weigh over 2 pounds. A bottom dweller, the bullhead forages at night when its sensitive barbells help it find food in the darkness. Its diet includes aquatic insects, worms, small fish, snails, freshwater clams, and algae. This species is able to survive in polluted waters that kill most other fish. It is also able to survive out of water for a few hours if kept moist. Many scientists believe this species can move between ponds in wet weather. The bullhead is an important food source for both large fish and wading birds.

The chain pickerel is native to Block Island and gets its name from the chainlike markings it has on its sides. This pickerel has an elongated snout, is olive to brown above, white on the belly, and has a dark bar under the eye. This animal can reach 31 inches in length and weigh up to 9 pounds. It is found in ponds with a lot of aquatic vegetation, which it hides in and then ambushes prey as it passes by. Mainstays of its diet include small fish, frogs, newts, and insects. Like the golden shiner, this species is only found in ponds with good water quality. This pickerel is mostly preyed upon before it reaches maturity by birds and bigger fish, and is a favorite for anglers year-round.

The yellow perch is a fish that is native to Block Island, with a green to golden yellow color above and a white belly. Its most distinguishing characteristic is six to eight vertical bands found on its back and flanks. This species reaches 15 inches in length and weighs as much as 2 pounds. During most of the day this perch lives in deep water and congregates in schools. However, it is crepuscular, which means it feeds at dawn and dusk in shallower water. Its diet includes smaller fish, insects, and snails. It likes ponds that have less aquatic vegetation and decent water quality. The yellow perch is eaten by bigger fish and wading birds, and is debatably the easiest fish to catch and thus enjoyed by all anglers.

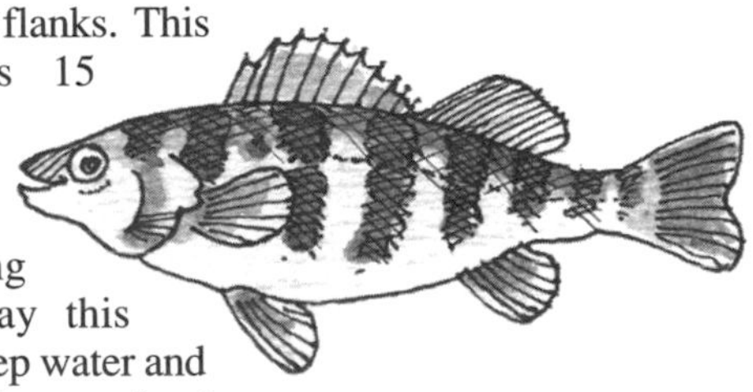

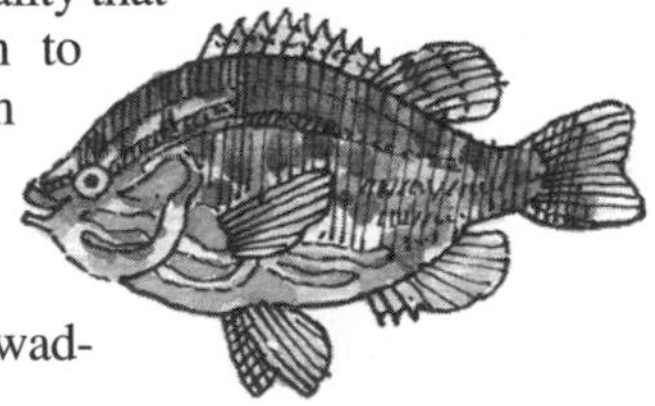

The pumpkinseed sunfish is native to Block Island and gets its name from the orange dots that are found throughout its body. This species is the most vibrant fish on the island with yellow, green, and blue above, yellow on the belly, and a flat, oval-shaped body. This sunfish can reach a length of 7 inches and weigh less than a pound. It is found in ponds with good water quality that have submerged vegetation to hide in. This species feeds on the water surface and on the bottom, eating mostly insects, snails, and freshwater mussels. Larger fish and wading birds are the major predators of this species.

The bluegill sunfish was introduced to Block Island ponds probably by anglers. Shaped like the pumpkinseed sunfish, this species is easily distinguished from it by a dark spot found at the base of the dorsal fin (fin on the back of the fish). The bluegill is olive-green above, bleeding to an orange-brown color on the sides, and reddish to yellow color on the belly. Typically, this species can reach 12 inches in length and weigh up to 2 pounds. The bluegill likes ponds with good water quality and filled with aquatic vegetation. Due to its small mouth, it can only feed on zooplankton and insects, with a preference of feeding in covered areas to avoid predators. This sunfish is an important food source for larger fish and wading birds.

The largemouth bass was introduced to Block Island ponds by anglers because it is an amazing game fish. It is oblong in shape with an upper jaw, which when closed, extends past the eye. This species is dark green above, fading to silvery green on the sides, and white on the belly.

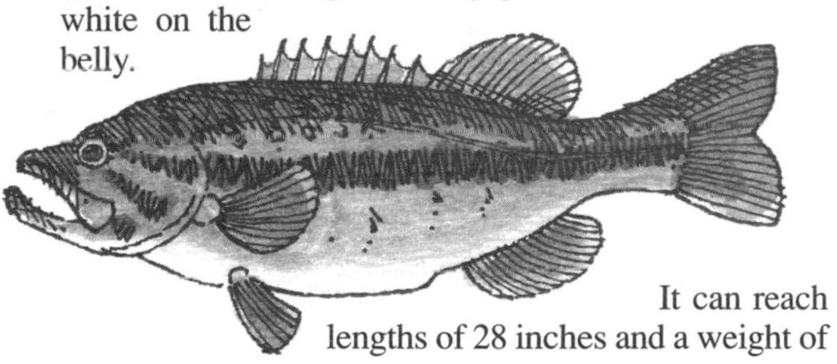

It can reach lengths of 28 inches and a weight of 12 pounds. This bass is a solitary fish that likes weedy ponds and feeds by ambushing prey. The largemouth is crepuscular and eats almost anything it can catch ,including fish, insects, worms, frogs, snails, and snakes. This is the top fish predator in the pond and is a favorite of anglers.

Fish play an important role in Block Island's ponds. Whether you enjoy angling or are happier just observing fish in ponds, you must agree, they are very interesting creatures.

How many of these fish have you caught?

- [ ] Golden shiner
- [ ] Brown bullhead
- [ ] Chain pickerel
- [ ] Yellow perch
- [ ] Pumpkinseed sunfish
- [ ] Bluegill sunfish
- [ ] Largemouth bass
- [ ] Other?
- [ ] Other?
- [ ] Other?

The great all-around-the-pond scavenger hunt

Go to your favorite pond on Block Island and see if you can find the things on the checklist below. How many other things can you find?

Remember to leave everything where you found it for other people to enjoy.

Barn swallow

Common green darner

- [ ] Dragonfly
- [ ] Great blue heron
- [ ] Barn swallow
- [ ] Muskrat
- [ ] Painted turtle
- [ ] Water strider
- [ ] Lily pad
- [ ] Northern water snake
- [ ] Common green darner
- [ ] Cattails

Northern water snake

Meet the northern harrier

While I was driving back from the Transfer Station one weekend, an amazing female northern harrier swooped in front of my car. She was soaring around the dunes looking for her favorite food source – the Block Island meadow vole.

Did you know that Block Island is the best place in Rhode Island to see the graceful northern harrier? In fact, it is the only place in the state where this species nests. While commonly seen on the island, the harrier is considered endangered in the state and declining in New England.

Formerly known as the marsh hawk, the northern harrier is easily distinguished from other raptors by its white patch above the tail. Males are about 18 inches in length and gray-backed, while females are 24 inches in length and brown-backed. Both the male and female have white breasts. Their wingspans range between 38 and 48 inches in width. Young birds can easily be spotted in the autumn and winter with their russet breasts.

The harrier can often be seen gliding low over the ground looking for prey. In addition to the preferred vole, other food sources include songbirds, snakes, frogs, grasshoppers and other insects, and carrion. When prey is spotted, this hawk pounces talons first and kills the unsuspecting animal. It then takes the food to a secluded area where the hawk uses its curved bill to rip apart the meat into bite-size chunks.

If you are really lucky, in the spring you will witness the harrier sky dance. This is when a courting male performs a series of dives from a near-stall high up in the sky. During the dive this individual does a variety of maneuvers, including barrel rolls and u-shaped loops, and pulls up at the last second before hitting the ground. While this is all happening the male repeatedly calls in a nasal whistle "pee, pee, pee." Chances are good that if you see this behavior there is a nest in the area.

On Block Island the northern harrier nests on the ground at the edge of thick vegetation. It is estimated that there are between 10 and 15 nests on the island. The nest is a flimsy composition of sticks and grass, and is lined with fine materials like spider webs and moss. Females usually lay five bluish-white eggs that hatch in 32 days. It then takes an additional 35 days for the nestlings to fledge. The female does most of the work around the nest while the male hunts and flies by the nest dropping food. This is called a prey pass.

In the spring of 2004, in partnership between The Nature Conservancy and the University of Rhode Island, a three-year northern harrier study began. Master's degree candidate Mike Byrne is the principal investigator of a project that's primary focus is the breeding ecology of this bird. Hopefully, his research will serve to answer a number of unknowns, as well as build up a baseline of information on the status of breeding northern harriers on Block Island.

In his first season Byrne found six nests and followed their productivity. This was a good sample size of nests, but clearly not all of the harrier nests that are on Block Island. After the chicks fledged, Byrne followed the young and noted their behavior. As with all scientific studies, especially one as complicated as harrier nesting, this first year was used to gather preliminary data to refine the study for the next few years.

The most important components of the upcoming year of the study are to accurately survey the number of harriers actually breeding on the island, see if their nests are successful, and to identify crucial nesting areas. As part of this process harriers will be caught and color bands placed on their legs. By doing this, each individual hawk can be identified using binoculars and catalogued at its nesting site.

In the final year of the study, the goal will be to identify dispersal areas for juvenile harriers. This will be done by placing satellite collars on a few individuals to track them and see where they end up. The collars are non-invasive and will fall off in about three months. The prospect of this is extremely exciting and may prove that Block Island is a harrier source population for New England (individuals leave here to repopulate other areas).

At this point you may be asking what you can do to help. Well if you happen to be out walking and see nesting behavior (sky dance or prey pass), please call The Nature Conservancy (466-2129) and report it. Doing this adds many pairs of eyes to the study and will help ensure we are able to find all the nests on the island.

We are extremely lucky to have the majestic northern harrier soaring around the island in such large numbers. It is truly something special to enjoy!

Those amazing newts

What is a newt? A newt is a type of salamander. On Block Island, there is only one species of salamander, the red-spotted newt. Newts are not as slippery as most salamanders; in fact, their skin is rough. These animals are mostly aquatic, with a land stage, and can be found throughout the island.

The red-spotted newt is found from Canada's Maritime Provinces west to the Great Lakes and south to central Georgia and Alabama. It has three main phases: larva, eft, and adult. (For more information see Page 19.)

Due to this animal's size and habitat on Block Island, you must be very lucky to see one of these newts in moist wetlands. One late-summer day, Chris Blane brought a red-spotted newt in the eft stage into the office, and I proceeded to bring it up to the Block Island School for a quick show and tell. Special thanks go to Blane for thinking of the students when he saw the newt.

The students enjoyed seeing this elusive animal, and for many it was the first time. They were amazed at how sticky the animal's feet were, which enabled it to climb up the jar. They were also intrigued that the animal's skin was so thin that all the internal organs could be seen in the light. The red-spotted newt got to meet most of the Block Island School students and then was released close to where it was found.

Upon being released, the newt stopped, appeared to take its bearings, and then ran off toward a rotted log near a small pond. The newt then climbed into the log and disappeared. Whenever you are near small fishless ponds, keep your eyes peeled and you just might get lucky and see a red-spotted newt.

Nathan Mott Park Scavenger Hunt

Can you find all of these items in Nathan Mott Park?
Please leave any items located during this hunt where you found them for others to enjoy.
And don't touch the poison ivy!

Poison ivy: Don't touch this one. "Leaves of three, let it be." This plant is common in the park and one of the major reasons it is good to stay on the trail.

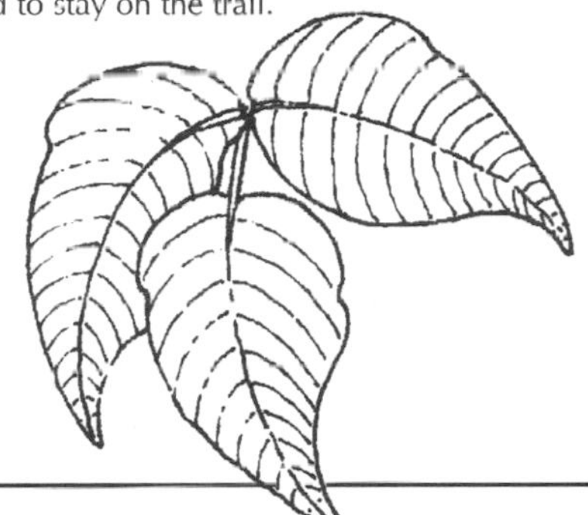

Pine cone: How many different types can you find? Many of the pine trees in the Enchanted Forest were planted by BI students in the 1930s. The seeds in the cones are an important source of food for seed-eating birds.

Spider web: How many different types of spider webs can you find? During the day spiders hide in the leaves at the end of their web. At night they move to the center and wait for insects to hit the web and get stuck.

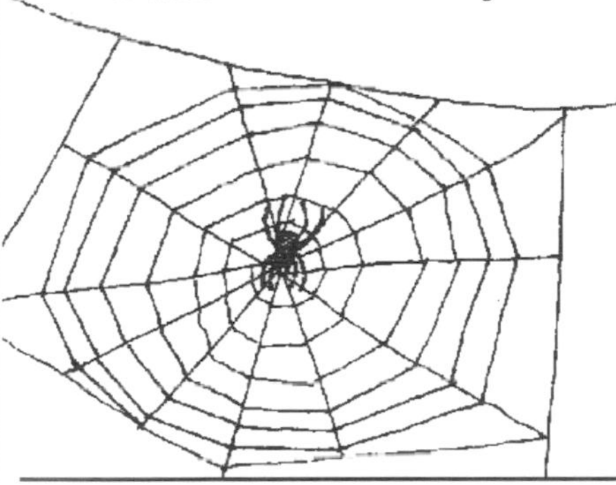

Blackberries: There are a lot of places in the park where this ripening fruit can be found. Blackberries are an important source of food for both mammals and birds. When you see a gray catbird, look for purple stains around the beak.

Catbird feathers: As you walk through the park you may see piles of gray feathers in the middle of the trail. This is where a catbird has been eaten by a hawk. When the hawk grabs the bird with its talons the bird releases its tail and downy feathers.

Did you find them all? Which was the easiest? Which was the hardest?

Exploring the habitats of Nathan Mott Park

People spend so much time on the beach in the summer that they often forget the natural wonders of Block Island's interior. Nathan Mott Park is a great place for your first foray away from the surf and sand. A majority of the island's natural habitat types can be found within its 40 acres.

Once the farm of Nathan Mott, the property originally included the western half of the Block Island State Airport and was inherited by Mott's daughter, Lucretia Mott Ball. Following her death in 1941, the property was bequeathed to the Nathan Mott Park Corporation, thereby beginning the land conservation movement on Block Island. In 1996, the trustees transferred ownership to the Block Island Conservancy, with a management easement to The Nature Conservancy.

The meadow is one of six habitats in Nathan Mott Park.

As you enter the park from the Center Road entrance across from the airport, you will notice that there are dense shrubs all around, primarily bayberry, arrowwood, black cherry, chokeberry, shadbush, and elderberry. These fruiting shrubs are an important source of food for both resident and migrating birds in the fall. Stop and listen; see how many different types of bird calls you can hear. Some of the more common songs heard in this part of the park are the gray catbird's "meow"; the eastern towhee's "drink your tea"; and the Carolina wren's "teakettle, teakettle, teakettle, tea."

This is where the land conservation movement on Block Island began.

Continuing on you will reach a meadow area that is mowed once every four years. Notice all of the wildflowers starting to bud and bloom. Look for white-tail deer beds in the meadow, and see if you can find the small trails made by Block Island meadow voles (a grayish/brown rodent slightly bigger than a mouse) and white-footed mice. People often ask what the viney plant is that's found throughout the meadow with the hanging seedpods. This invasive plant called black swallowwort is slowly out-competing many of the meadow plants.

Climbing the hill, you reach a ridge where thc soil becomes very gravelly with coarse sand. This area is part of a morainal grassland. As a result of intense development pressure from people building houses on these gravelly hilltops, this type of habitat is globally imperiled. Certain specialized plants are found only in such harsh areas with dry soil conditions. Look for a yellow-flowered plant with hairy leaves called mouse-eared hawkweed; also be sure to check out all of the neat mosses and lichens. They are able to grow here because they have no competition from plants that need better soil and moisture to survive. While examining this interesting area, be sure to stay on the path because this habitat can be disturbed very easily.

Just past the sandy-soiled area on you left is a small vernal pond (dries up in the summer, but remains wet the rest of the year). While quiet now, this area is hopping with life in the spring and fall. During these seasons, all three of Block Island's amphibians are in this pond: spring peepers (small treefrog), green frogs and red-spotted newts (salamander). Due to the fact that there are no fish in this pond, it is full of insect life whenever there is water in it. In the spring and fall, the pond is extremely important for migratory birds that

Recently constructed stairs eliminate erosion problems.

are dehydrated when they arrive, and use this shrub-covered pond to drink while safely away from dangerous hawks. Keep an ear out for the "sweet, sweet, sweet, I'm so sweet" call of the yellow warbler.

Down the trail on your right is a hawthorn tree. Although not native to the area, it is still used by migrating yellow-bellied sapsuckers. Look closely at the trunk for lines of small holes. When the bird migrates through in the spring and fall, it drills these holes and waits for the sap to drip out. The sap attracts insects, so the bird gets its protein and sugars at the same time with little effort. Be sure to also notice the thorns and small but interesting leaves of the hawthorn.

Shrubs are still enchanting to many songbirds.

As the trail gets narrower you will notice the vegetation changes from shrubs to a thorny bush with broad waxy leaves. This plant is called sweet greenbriar and the habitat type is appropriately called thorn scrub. Although some people refer to this type of habitat as "junk," it is actually extremely important to nesting birds. The small songbirds are able to navigate the greenbriar and make a nest that no predator can reach. Essentially it is like the bird nesting in a dense tangle of barbed wire.

Past the thorn scrub you will see a few remaining large trees; this area was once known as the Enchanted Forest. The forest was originally planted by local naturalist Earl Dodge and Block Island School students in the 1940s. A majority of trees in this area, composed of Japanese black pine, spruce, sycamore maple, and oriental chestnut, were removed in the spring of 2004 because they were an obstruction to airport traffic. This project was mandated by the Federal Aviation Administration. Many of the trees in this area were standing deadwood due to disease and age. The area will now be managed as a meadow, which will benefit declining grassland species and leave open dramatic scenic vistas.

After climbing the hill and catching your breath, go to the left and be sure to take in the amazing view – one benefit from the loss of trees. As you continue straight you will venture back into shrubland and eventually reach a permanent pond. This beautiful spot has a nesting pair of wood ducks and is one of the few places in the state where the lilypad forktail (a small damselfly) is found.

Also note the different shrub you see; this is winterberry, a deciduous plant that is in the holly family. In November the fruit of this plant turns reddish-orange and is a great contrast to the dull gray of the rest of the vegetation that has already lost its leaves. Both rodents and birds eat the fruit throughout the early part of the winter.

At this point, you have seen all the different habitats that Nathan Mott Park has to offer. You can either continue on and loop back through Turnip Farm (for the more adventurous), or retrace your steps (chances are you will definitely see something you missed on the way out).

Do you know how many different habitats you saw? The total is six: shrub, meadow, morainal grassland, vernal pond, thorn scrub, and pond. Seeing all these different habitats in a relatively small area is a great demonstration of how densely packed the natural world is on Block Island. So while staying on Block Island be sure to take a hike into the interior of the island and explore its diverse natural world.

View from recently cleared area, looking east.

A journey down into the hollow

View toward Black Rock from Rodman's Hollow.

The summer is an excellent time to explore Rodman's Hollow. This area, a glacial outwash plain, was formed when the glaciers that made Block Island receded. It is also the first conservation acquisition, purchased in 1972 by the Block Island Conservancy, which was formed for this purpose. Over the next three decades land has been added to the preserve, and it now encompasses over 175 acres. It is one of the few places on Block Island where the view from the road to the water is conserved in perpetuity for all to enjoy.

This hike starts by walking down Black Rock Road, which is now more of a trail. Be sure to keep an eye out for bikes and horses that also use this road. Take the first left to begin a wonderful loop trail through the hollow. Most of the habitat in the hollow proper is coastal shrub, which is composed of shadbush, black cherry, and bayberry. In early May Rodman's Hollow is a sea of white due to the blooming shadbush.

Take a right at the fork in the trail, which leads to an amazing hilltop view. From here it is possible to see Lewis Farm, Black Rock and much more. Note that most of the habitat to the west and south is grassland. This area is managed by mowing biannually, to ensure the survival of the federally endangered American burying beetle and the state-endangered grasshopper sparrow.

Continuing on, bearing left at the next fork, which is where the descent into the hollow begins. During this walk you will notice a few grassland areas with lots of different mosses and lichens. These special habitats are called morainal grasslands. Looking skyward, this is also one of the better places to see the soaring northern harrier as it is looking for its next meal.

The trail descends rapidly; watch your footing because much of the sand and rocks are unstable. Once the bottom is reached you are standing on the lowest spot on Block Island, which is only 20 feet above sea level. The shrubs in this area are huge because they are protected from the wind, and bird activity is high because of this protection.

Further down the trail on the left is a large morainal grassland that has a bushy rockrose population. This rare wildflower grows along the ground and has a yellow flower that blooms this time of year. This is one of Block Island's two populations, which are the only ones that still exist in Rhode Island.

As the hike continues be sure to stay left because there is a spur that goes to Fresh Pond. At this point you will start the ascent back to Black Rock Road. In this area there are many nesting songbirds including: northern cardinal, song sparrow, common yellowthroat, eastern towhee, and gray catbird. By being quiet and standing still, this time of year it is possible to watch these birds gathering food in their bills to feed recently hatched young.

The hike on the loop is soon completed and you return to Black Rock Road. Turn left to visit the beach and right to get to Cooneymus Road. In the summer, I find this hike to be perfect in the early morning or late afternoon. Avoid the hollow during the middle of the day because the breeze does not reach its interior, making it extremely hot.

A summertime hike in Rodman's Hollow is a wonderful journey that embodies all that is beautiful about Block Island.

The sign at Rodman's Hollow

Dragonflies and damselflies

If you have been walking on the Greenway trails in the spring, summer, or fall, you surely have seen the dragonflies and damselflies patrolling the paths looking for insects to eat. Dragonflies and damselflies are referred to by scientists as odonates because they are both in the insect order Odonata, which means "toothed" and refers to the serrated jaws of the adult.

An easy way to tell dragonflies and damselflies apart is by their wings. A dragonfly's stationary wings are held flat like an airplane, and the damselfly's wings are folded together over its back. Damselflies are also usually much smaller and more delicate than dragonflies.

Students from the Block Island Early Learning Center after a successful odonate collection trip in Nathan Mott Park.

For a number of years, inventory work has been conducted on odonates in Rhode Island, producing a list of 113 species. This is incredible diversity for such a small state. However, about 75 percent of the inventory work has occurred in one area, the Wood-Pawcatuck River Watershed.

In 1998, Virginia Brown of the Rhode Island Natural History Survey, started the Rhode Island Odonata Atlas Project, a systematic effort to record odonates in every corner of the state. It was undertaken with volunteers assigned to do much of the collection work throughout the state. Brown, an acknowledged expert on these fascinating creatures, then identified and catalogued the specimens.

At this point, you may be asking yourself, why odonates? Well, they are good indicators of water quality and the health of a water system. Plus, it is important to know what species occur in each type of habitat. Odonates live in the water as camouflaged larvae, and terrestrially as adults (although adults must lay their eggs in the water). In addition to their important role in wetland and terrestrial ecosystems, odonates eat flies and mosquitoes and, in turn, are eaten by fish, turtles, frogs, birds, and other insects.

From 1999 through 2001, I was the primary collector of the odonates on Block Island during their active period, which is generally May to October. The way to collect dragonflies and damselflies (once you have a permit from the state) is to go to places they frequent with an insect net, and then swing the net when they pass by. You will quickly learn that these creatures, which fly up to 35 miles an hour, are extremely hard to capture. It takes many hours of practice to get even one in the net.

Once captured, the odonate is placed into a glassine envelope (this is the type of envelope that stamps are placed in). The envelope is then placed into a jar of acetone for 1 minute, the insect is positioned, and replaced in the acetone jar for 24 hours. This insect, now a specimen, is placed in a climate-controlled cabinet – documenting in perpetuity that this species occurs here. It is important to note that we only take a representative sample of each species, which does not hurt the population.

I spent many hours collecting throughout the island's abundant ponds and fields to get an accurate sample of the odonates of Block Island. Due to the fact that I was often standing stationary in the ponds, sometimes I collected more leeches on my legs than odonates in my net! While I was collecting, I also had a lot of help from volunteers, the kids from Camp Mohegan in the summer and the students from the Block Island Early Learning Center and Block Island School in the spring and fall. Thus it was truly a group effort.

The Rhode Island Odonata Atlas recorded a total of 135 species; of these 32 occurred on Block Island. The most important record from Block Island was a lyre-tipped spreadwing (a type of damselfly), only the second record for the state. There were also 11 new species records for Block Island, including the lilypad forktail, a damselfly first reported in Rhode Island in 1998.

Pond species such as the common green darner, ruby meadowhawk, and the Halloween pennant were more abundant on Block Island than the mainland. However, stream and river species were found only on the mainland because Block Island does not have these types of habitats. The project as a whole recorded 21 new species for Rhode Island in addition to countless new county records.

When you are outside in spring and summer, keep an eye out for dragonflies and damselflies – they are truly amazing fliers and great fun to watch. Hopefully, you will be as captivated by them as I am.

The original "webmasters"

Surveying a lawn on a wet summer morning, it is impossible to miss the plethora of dew-laden spider webs that are illuminated by the morning sunlight. Until recently, little was known about the diversity of Block Island's resident spider population. Spiders are distinguished from all other arthropods by their two body segments and four pairs of legs.

Spiders can be found in every type of habitat from wetlands to forests, but had never been inventoried officially, on Block Island. From 1998 to 2000, in the spring, summer and fall, I helped conduct a spider inventory project on Block Island in partnership with Geoff Balme, a doctoral graduate from the University of Rhode Island. It was a very simple partnership where I collected the spiders and Balme identified them.

It is important to note that this study found no spiders on Block Island that are dangerous to humans but most spiders will give a mild bite if disturbed and some people do get minor allergic reactions to them. Spiders do play an important role in the island's ecosystem by keeping insect populations down which also benefit humans.

There are many ways to find and catch spiders. One method, called sweep netting, involves walking down a path or roadside and swinging an insect net in the vegetation. Every few minutes the net is checked for spiders. Another method uses pitfall traps, which are deployed by digging an empty coffee can or jar into the ground so that the lip is flush with the ground. These traps are then checked once a day in the morning to see what has fallen in.

Sifting leaf litter through an insect net is also a way to find spiders. Searching and picking is another method – essentially looking for spider webs and then collecting the spider. This can also be done at night by using a headlamp and watching for the spiders' eyes, which reflect the light. The final method involves rolling over logs and rocks to look for spiders that hide under these objects for protection. By using these different methods you hope to get as accurate a sample as possible from each area.

I searched for spiders in all sorts of habitats including pond, meadow, shrub, beach, pine stand, and under and around various homes (crawlspaces and outbuildings are excellent places to find spiders). My search for spiders has been helped by many of The Nature Conservancy interns, Camp Mohegan, Block Island Early Learning Center and the Block Island School (all grades). With all of the help from these volunteers we were able to cover more area and capture more spiders. In addition to helping with the inventory work, the participants were able to learn a lot about spiders. Hopefully now, when they see a spider, they will observe it instead of stepping on it. Although we have captured spiders from many different areas, there is always more spider inventory work to be done. But for now we have a good baseline and should focus on other uninventoried species.

Once a spider is captured, it is ready to be preserved and identified. It is important to note that in order to collect a spider you must have a permit from the state. A spider is preserved by being placed in a 70-percent solution of anhydrous ethyl alcohol in a glass vial. The date, time, location, and collector are then recorded on the vial.

At this stage of the inventory program, the specimens were turned over to Geoff Balme, and then the tedious part began: the identification. Spider identification is extremely difficult because it involves mostly microscope work, examining very specific and sometimes trivial aspects of the spider. Another identification challenge for spiders in New England is that they have not been studied recently, and many of the species' keys are 80 to 100 years old. This means having to translate scientific terms that are no longer in the mainstream.

The results of the inventory work tallied 21 families, 55 genera, and 85 species of spiders found on Block Island. Some of the more common spiders were the black and yellow argiope (a spider 1 inch in size and black and yellow in color); yellow flower spider (small, all yellow in color, which hold their legs like crabs); daring jumping spider (small, black in color with green fangs and three orange spots on the abdomen), and common grass spider (mostly brown with a white stripe down the middle of the body, makes a funnel web in the grass). The most interesting spider catalogued, the first record for the state, is called *Zygoballas sexpunctata* (there is no common name for it). Until this survey, this small, nondescript brown spider was previously known to occur only as far north as New Jersey.

As with most inventories, the smaller the animal, the less likely it has been recorded, and the better the chance that it is rare.

Remember, spiders come in all shapes, sizes and colors, and are truly an important part of the unique Block Island ecosystem.

The usual suspects

There are more than 300 bird species that have been recorded here on Block Island. Records have been kept since the late 1800s.

But if you're a beginning birder, a summer visitor, or simply someone who has at one time wondered, "What the heck is that?" the 30 birds on the next three pages are what we refer to as "the usual suspects."

Red-breasted merganser

Mallard

Great blue heron

Great black-backed gull

Herring gull

Double-crested cormorant

Belted kingfisher

Northern harrier

Ring-necked pheasant

Mourning dove

Carolina wren

American robin

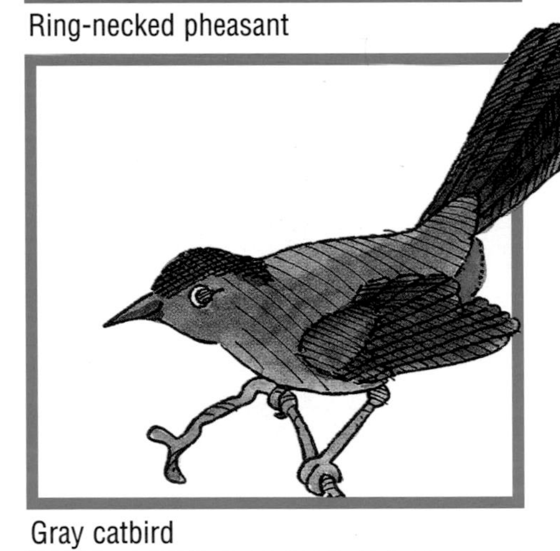

Gray catbird

Northern mockingbird

American goldfinch

Song sparrow

Common grackle

Red-winged blackbird

Eastern kingbird
Barn swallow
Tree swallow
Black-capped chickadee
Blue jay
American crow
Northern cardinal
Eastern towhee
European starling
Brown-headed cowbird
Yellow warbler
Common yellowthroat

The birds of spring

Spring is a wonderful time to observe birds on Block Island. They are in their alternate plumage, which is colorful and ornate for mating. The birds show off many bright oranges, reds, yellows and blues rarely seen in nature. Whether a hardcore or occasional birdwatcher, this is an amazing time to watch these very special creatures.

White-eyed vireo

Ovenbird

Indigo bunting

Chestnut-sided warbler

Hooded warbler

Bay-breasted warbler

Least flycatcher

Veery

Blackburnian warbler

Summer tanager

Black-and-white warbler

Mourning warbler

Wilson's warbler

Blackpoll warbler

American goldfinch

Blue-winged warbler

Chipping sparrow

Common yellowthroat

Wood thrush

Magnolia warbler

Block Island is a great place to observe all of these avian species, because they are in vegetation close to the ground. On the mainland, they would be in the forest canopy, more than 30 feet in the air. By watching birds on the island, "warbler-neck," which is caused by looking for birds high up in trees, can be avoided.

So remember to keep an eye out for flashes of color, and see how many of these birds you can find.

Some of the beautiful wildflowers that bloom on Block Island.

How many can you find?

Ox-eye daisy

Slender blue flag

Queen Anne's lace

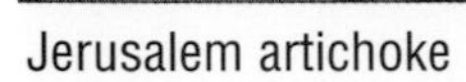

Jerusalem artichoke

New York aster

Bull thistle

Butter-and-eggs

Rosa rugosa

White water lily

Lance-leaved goldenrod

Maryland golden aster

Black-eyed Susan

Rough-leaved goldenrod

Red clover

Northern blazing star

The birds of autumn

In the fall, there are many bird species in their basic plumage, which is drab and nondescript, that stopover on Block Island during fall migration. The drab plumage helps these creatures, vulnerable to predators, to blend in with their surroundings. The fall is a time that tests even the most experienced birdwatcher, with extremely subtle differences between some avian species.

Sharp-shinned hawk

Yellow-rumped warbler

Canada warbler

Yellow-breasted chat

Blackpoll warbler

Cedar waxwing

Tennessee warbler

Red-eyed vireo

Red-breasted nuthatch

Blue-headed vireo

Hooded warbler

Rose-breasted grosbeak

White-crowned sparrow

Northern waterthrush

Kentucky warbler

Whip-poor-will

Yellow warbler

Nashville warbler

Savannah sparrow

Brown thrasher

On Block Island, in the autumn, the best places to see these birds are in areas with fruiting shrubs and wetlands, especially after a strong northwest wind. Interestingly, most of the individuals observed during this time are hatching-year birds (birds born this year) because adults tend to stay more inland during migration. It is the young ones that make a "navigational error" and end up on the island.

In the fall it is always spectacular to see birds everywhere, even if they are sometimes confusing to identify.

September is a wonderful time to see colorful butterflies and moths

September is a great time to look at butterflies and moths! They are easily seen in a variety of habitats and vary in size, shape and color. In my mind they are almost as much fun to watch as birds, which is saying a lot.

Butterflies and moths make up the *Lepidoptera* insect order. *Lepido* is Latin for scale and *pteros* for wing. All species in this order have wings that are covered by rows of tiny overlapping scales. You should only handle animals in this order if you have been trained in how to do it. Mishandling can knock the scales off and then they cannot fly.

To attract these animals to your property it is helpful to have native wildflowers that bloom during the day and night. Also at night, make sure to turn off all exterior lights when not in use because they will attract moths and keep them from fulfilling their nightly duties.

So when venturing around the Block in September, be sure to keep an eye out for these special creatures, for they are truly amazing.

Monarch butterfly— The most recognized butterfly on Block Island, this species measures four inches and is orange with black veins and margins. Males of this species have one black dot in the middle of each hindwing. Monarchs lay their eggs on common milkweed, which hatch into caterpillars that eat the milkweed leaves and synthesize its toxin. The caterpillar then encases itself in a chrysalis (a cocoon-like structure) and eventually emerges from it as a butterfly. Thanks to the milkweed toxin, the adult tastes bad to birds which are potential predators. It should also be noted that this species migrates to Mexico in the fall and returns in the spring. This butterfly is easily found around milkweed and a host of other wildflowers.

Viceroy butterfly – A mimic of the monarch trying to take advantage of the fact that birds avoid the bad tasting monarchs. The two differences this species has is its smaller size, which is about three inches, and the fact that it has a black line across the hindwing. On Block Island, this species can be found in meadows, marsh areas, pond edges, and the wrack line.

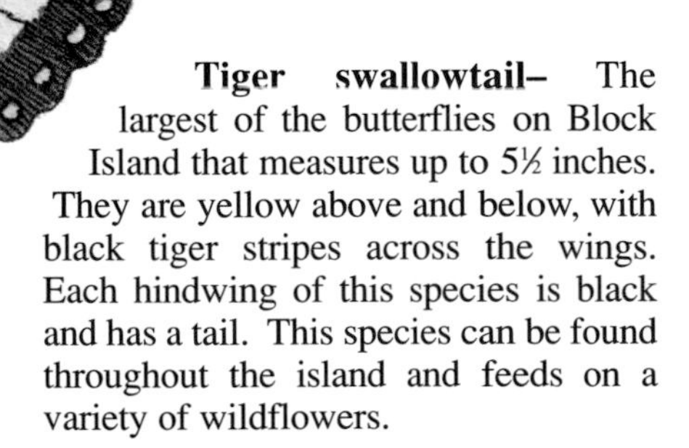

Tiger swallowtail– The largest of the butterflies on Block Island that measures up to 5½ inches. They are yellow above and below, with black tiger stripes across the wings. Each hindwing of this species is black and has a tail. This species can be found throughout the island and feeds on a variety of wildflowers.

Cabbage white butterfly–

This butterfly is quite common on Block Island, easily seen in meadows. It measures about 1½ inches and white above with charcoal tips on the forewing. Males have an additional two charcoal dots on the forewing whereas females only have one. This species is mustard yellow in color, with gray and black spots. This species is native to Eurasia and was accidentally introduced to North America in 1860.

Polyphemus moth– This is the second largest moth on Block Island, measuring 4½ inches. Wings are orange in color, with eyespots, and trimmed in black and yellow. The antennae are orange in color and look like feathers. This species is nocturnal and found in shrub habitat. It is most easily seen when attracted to porch lights.

Io moth– Named after a Greek goddess, this beautiful species is 2¾ inches long. Males of this species have a yellow forewing, whereas the female's are reddish brown. The hindwings of both are yellow, with a central black eyespot and a reddish orange band. The body of this species is yellow. This moth can be found in meadow and shrub habitats and is active only at night.

American copper butterfly– Also known as the flame copper, this species measures about one inch. Above, the forewing is a bright copper color with black spots, and the hindwing is brown with a copper-colored margin. The underside of this species is mostly gray with dark dots. This species is common on Block Island, in meadow habitats, yards and on the greenway trails.

Clearwing moth– Also known as the hummingbird moth, this species measures 1¾ inches. Its wings are reddish-brown above, and white below, with clear patches. This moth's body is thick with brown coloration toward the head, fading to red. Unlike most moths, this species is active during the day hovering at flowers like a hummingbird. It proboscis is flexible and looks a lot like a hummingbird's bill. This moth is common in gardens and meadow. It is especially common around butterfly bush.

The differences between butterflies and moths

There is no one single characteristic that separates butterflies and moths. There are four that must be evaluated before a decision is made. None of these characteristics is 100 percent true, so you must look at a variety of traits.

Butterflies are colorful, active during the day, have clubbed antennae and rest with their wings together.

Moths are active at night, more drab in color, have antennae that look like feathers and rest with their wings folded tent-like over their back.

The difference between butterflies and moths is not an exact science, but using the traits above you have the best chance to make an accurate identification.

Happy *Lepidoptera*-ing!

Block Rocks

One of the best things about going to the beach is all the amazing types of Block Rocks that can be found and examined. They come in all different sizes, shapes, and colors. Some people like to find the roundest rock, while others just want a keepsake to remember Block Island by, when they are away. Many of these rocks date back to the formation of Block Island, while others come from faraway places brought by storms and strong currents. The rocks pictured and identified on this page are examples of the many that can be found on the island beaches. How many types of Block Rocks can you find?

Vein-filled fractured rock.

Brick from a lobster pot.

Metasediment with quartz veins.

Joint plane on a biotite gneiss.

Quartzite rounded into disks.

Pink granite with mafics.

Granite vein in massive mafic gneiss.

Pink granite.

Quartzite pebble.

Vein quartz.

Autumn

Autumn is the most amazing season on Block Island even though we do not have dramatic foliage color changes like most of New England. It is a time of: beautiful weather, warm ocean water, gorgeous sunsets, tons of migrating songbirds and monarch butterflies, great saltwater fishing, and blooming wildflowers.

The weather is as good as it gets in the autumn on Block Island, with warm sunny days followed by cool nights that are great for sleeping. While there is always a risk of a hurricane (the last one of any note was Bob in 1993), we are blessed mostly with incredible weather.

The ocean is amazing in the autumn with the sun glistening on it, inviting everyone to experience its beauty. It is at its warmest (still cold by some people's standards) and great for snorkeling and, for the more adventurous, spearfishing. If you spend time in the ocean you will be rewarded by seeing tropical fish, striped bass, rock crabs, rays, and much more.

Late autumn is also a great time to head to the west side of the island and watch dramatic sunsets that fall right into the ocean. The colors are truly unbelievable with reds, purples, blues, and pinks the norm. And it is quite fun to walk out to Sandy Point and watch the sunset in the west and then the moonrise in the east.

One of Block Island's major claims to fame in the autumn is the songbird migration. This island is important as a stopover site as birds work their way south. They spend a short period of time (between two days and two weeks) resting, rehydrating and refueling in this unique place before heading south. The abundant shrub habitat that fruits in the fall is extremely important to the migrant songbirds' diet and survival.

Monarch butterflies are another species that migrates through the island on their way south to Mexico. Especially when the wind blows northwest, these fragile-looking insects can be seen throughout the island looking for food and a place to rest.

In addition to the birds and butterflies, many fish migrate though island waters during autumn. It is a great time if you enjoy fishing, and exciting if you are on the shore or out on the water and you see a feeding frenzy. Concentrated shorebird activity is the "tip off" that this is happening; with many fish coming to the surface, sucking down tons of bait fish. Watching this process gives one a serious appreciation of fish as well-designed predators.

Venturing inland, autumn is the time for vibrant wildflowers including common aster, northern blazing star, Maryland golden aster, and a number of goldenrod species. While these plants are important to wildlife like butterflies, moths, and bees, they also make the meadows of Block Island an amazing place.

For the people that live on Block Island, autumn is a wonderful season where there is actually time to enjoy it. Responsibilities slow down just enough that the island begins to regain its community feel and folks start to decompress from the active summer season.

For plants, people, and wild animals, autumn is an incredible time on Block Island, when it truly feels like paradise.

Plants and animals of September and October

As summer ebbs and turns to fall, many interesting plants and animals can be found throughout the island. For most, it is the only time of the year that they can be seen. Some of them are extremely flashy, others so drab that you can only see them if you look carefully. So this fall, keep your eyes open to see what species you can locate during this special season.

The northern blazing star is a purple wildflower that blooms throughout September. The flower heads of this state-endangered species are arranged compactly around the upper part of the central stem. They can easily be mistaken for a thistle by a casual observer. The leaves are narrow and radiate from the lower part of the stem. This creates a feathery appearance, hence the common name, gayfeather (many people on the island have varieties of this flower in their garden, and it is quite common in commercial floral arrangements). This wildflower is a primary colonizer in sandy soils (it is found in 28 separate places on the island), and it requires disturbance (either mowing or burning) to flourish.

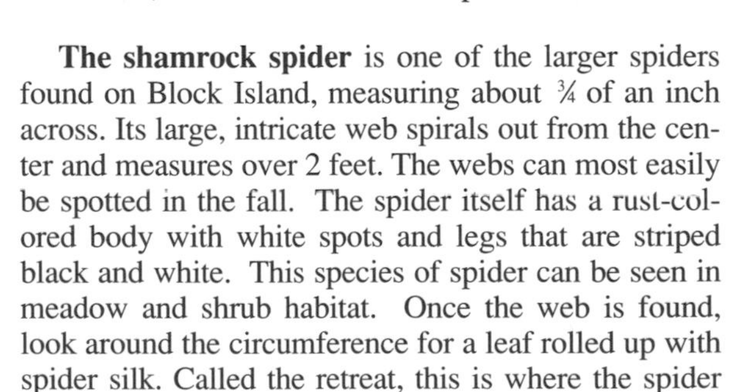

The state-endangered wildflower, northern blazing star.

The reasons for the decline of this flower, both on Block Island and in New England, are loss of grassland habitat due to overgrowth by shrubs, commercial and residential development, and deer grazing. In fact, in a study conducted at Turnip Farm Preserve, The Nature Conservancy found that 97 percent of the northern blazing star plants had been damaged in some way by the deer. Subsequently, a deer fence was erected around the patch, and the plants flourished. There are now 15,000 plants there; they form a sea of purple in the fall.

Purple needlegrass is as drab as the blazing star is flashy. This state-endangered grass species is extremely hard to detect and often blends in with the surrounding flora. Thus, you must get down low (the grass is about 10 inches tall) to find the needlegrass, which has a purple tint that bleaches out to a stark white in late fall. Then, the top part of the grass must be examined; if it looks like barbed wire, then it is the needlegrass. It is often found in clumps and occurs only in soil that is sandy and dry. The island's largest stand of purple needlegrass is near the northern blazing stars of Turnip Farm; with about 100 individuals, this population is the largest in the state. There are only three other populations of purple needlegrass known on Block Island, all in the southwestern part.

The blackpoll warbler is a long distance fall migrant.

The shamrock spider is one of the larger spiders found on Block Island, measuring about ¾ of an inch across. Its large, intricate web spirals out from the center and measures over 2 feet. The webs can most easily be spotted in the fall. The spider itself has a rust-colored body with white spots and legs that are striped black and white. This species of spider can be seen in meadow and shrub habitat. Once the web is found, look around the circumference for a leaf rolled up with spider silk. Called the retreat, this is where the spider lives. The spider attaches a signal line from the retreat to the web so vibrations are transmitted to the retreat when insect prey is caught in the web. The easiest time to find these webs are in the early morning before the dew evaporates; you'll be amazed at how many can be found.

The blackpoll warbler migrates to Block Island in the fall after spending the nesting season in the spruce-fir woods of northern New England. This time of year, the 5½-inch bird is olive-brown with black stripes on its back, white bars on its wings, a yellow throat and white belly. While these characteristics are similar to those of many other warblers that come to the island, the blackpoll has one major difference, its orange-yellow feet and legs.

This species spends time on Block Island storing up fat for its non-stop migration to the Caribbean. While the blackpoll warbler normally weighs around 10 grams, during migration it fattens up to as much as 25 grams. It is most easily seen in shrub habitat in the northern part of the island. Arrowwood, pokeweed, and elderberry make up a large part of its diet.

Meadow voles are major trailblazers on Block Island. This unique mammal is slightly larger than a mouse, with a brown back and gray stomach. It is considered a subspecies of the mainland meadow vole because it has a longer snout and a shorter tail.

It can most often be found in meadow and dune habitat. In fact, if you walk the beach early enough in the morning you can find its footprints darting in and out of the American beach grass. When in meadow areas look close to the ground and you will be able to find a meadow vole "highway" system. This species eats mostly grain and fruit. It is also a major source of food for the northern harrier and barn owl.

Monarch butterflies are common visitors to the island in the fall. They measure 3¾ inches, and have orange wings with black veins and a black edge with orange and white spots. This species is easily found in fields containing milkweed, its food plant.

Monarch butterfly

In the early fall, the monarch caterpillar, which is banded black, yellow and white, can easily be seen eating the milkweed. As it feeds, the caterpillar absorbs the toxins of the milkweed and thus becomes poisonous to predators throughout the rest of its lifecycle. When the caterpillar becomes engorged, it hangs from the milkweed in a "J" shape, and an emerald chrysalis (like a cocoon) is formed. After a period of time, the adult emerges from the chrysalis as a butterfly, and begins its migration south to Mexico. When the winds are northwest, many adult monarchs can be seen feeding throughout the island on wildflowers before continuing south.

The fall is an amazing time to see all sorts of special plants and animals. As you travel the island, see how many of them you can locate. And remember there are always new ones to be discovered. Happy exploring!

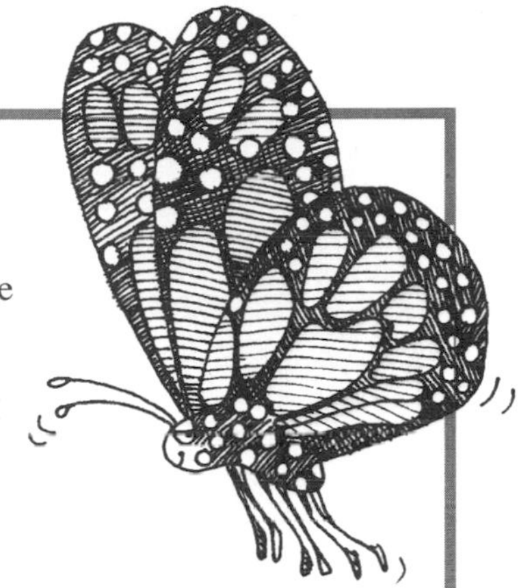

Early fall species quiz

Block Island is host to a great many plants and animals that are most easily seen in the fall. Some are easy to find and others extremely difficult. Test your knowledge below and see how much you know about Block Island's early fall species!

1) Where is the best place to see the state-endangered northern blazing star?
   - A) Rodman's Hollow
   - B) Mohegan Bluffs
   - C) Turnip Farm
   - D) Clay Head

2) What wind brings the most songbirds to Block Island in the fall?
   - A) Northwest
   - B) West
   - C) Southeast
   - D) South

3) What animal can be found eating the milkweed?
   - A) Meadow vole
   - B) Grasshopper
   - C) Song sparrow
   - D) Monarch caterpillar

4) Why are fruiting shrubs so important this time of year?
   - A) Major source of food for birds
   - B) Pretty to look at
   - C) Necessary for insect survival
   - D) None of the above

5) How many falcon species can be seen on Block Island in the fall?
   - A) One
   - B) Three
   - C) Two
   - D) None

6) What amphibian can often be seen out of the water in the fall?
   - A) Spring peeper
   - B) Green frog
   - C) Red-spotted newt
   - D) None of the above

7) What other type(s) of animals migrate through Block Island in the fall?
   - A) Bats
   - B) Saltwater fish
   - C) Dragonflies
   - D) All of the above

8) What spider species makes ornate webs in the fall?
   - A) Grass spider
   - B) Cellar spider
   - C) Shamrock spider
   - D) Daring jumping spider

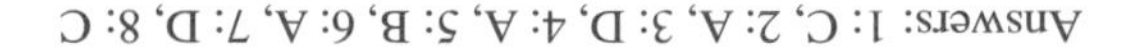
Answers: 1: C, 2: A, 3: D, 4: A, 5: B, 6: A, 7: D, 8: C

A search for rare plants

Plants, you ask? It is fall, and time for songbird migration articles; why would an ornithologist focus on plants? Well, in September of 2001, I spent a day going around with some of Rhode Island's top botanists identifying the plants (the trade slang term for this is "botanizing"), or flora, of the island.

In addition to general botanizing, the crew was assembled to search out some of Block Island's rarest plant species, some of which had not been seen in many years. This crack squad consisted of Rick Enser, Rhode Island Heritage Program; Lisa Gould, Rhode Island Natural History Survey; Annie Schmitt, Brown University; Bill Brumbeck, New England Wildflower Society; and Jerry Melaragno, Rhode Island College. Each participant came geared up for the task with a 10-power magnifier or loupe, *Newcomb's Wildflower Guide*, various other plant books, collecting bag, and field notebook.

Upon arriving, we piled into the nature bus and proceeded to Lewis Farm. The group reached the farm and spotted a merlin, a type of falcon, darting across Lewis Farm. I was feeling in my element spotting birds until everyone switched to identifying plants and using only the scientific Latin names.

The first plant we found was the yellow-flowered *Chrysopsis mariana*, or Maryland golden aster. This plant is about 1 foot high and has lance-shaped leaves. On two small hilltops there were over 150 of these state-endangered flowers. In fact, this is the only place in the state where this mid-Atlantic flower occurs. The surrounding habitat must be grassland or else it will be shaded out by encroaching shrubs.

Next, this merry band of botanizers went to Turnip Farm to look for *Aristida purpurascens*, or purple needlegrass. This grass species is extremely hard to detect; you must get eye-level with the grass (about 10 inches tall) and find one with a purple tint. Then the top part of the grass must be examined, and if it looks like barbed wire, you know it is the needlegrass. After searching for a while, we found this evasive species and eventually spotted over 100 plants.

Amongst the needlegrass was another state-endangered plant, *Liatris borealis* or northern blazing star. The Turnip Farm population of this species is the largest in the state.

During this time of year, the beginning of the Turnip Farm trail, which has over 15,000 plants, is a sea of purple blossoms.

The group then went to Dickens' Farm to investigate a species of milkweed that has never been found in the state. These plants had been flagged by Eugenia Marks of Rhode Island Audubon Society, as potentially *Asclepias purpurascens*, or purple milkweed, which would have been a new record for the state. After taking in every characteristic and consulting four different plant books, the group decided that the plant was *Asclepias incarnata*, or swamp milkweed. This distinction was made by the leaf shape and the seedpod structure.

The state-endangered Maryland golden aster.

Wash Pond was the next target area looking for *Najas guadalupensis*, or naiad, a state-endangered aquatic plant that is green in color and almost looks like algae. To me, it was hard to separate this plant from the many other green aquatic plants, but the crack team quickly located it and noted the population was doing quite well.

The washout at Sachem Pond was the next location the crew went looking for *Polygonum glaucum*, or seabeach knotweed. This low-growing nondescript state-endangered plant was at first hard to locate, but after gaining the proper search image we were able to find 42 plants. This species is a primary colonizer, which means it is the first to grow on bare sand.

We ended up at Mosquito Beach looking for a type of *Sabatia*, or marsh-pink, that had last been recorded in 1912, seen in watery depressions. After an exhaustive search, it was decided that the shrubs had probably shaded out this species a long time ago.

All in all, this was a very good day and it once again was a realization of how easy it is to take for granted all the rare plants and animals around us. It took me quite a while to decipher all of the Latin plant names but I learned a ton! Enjoy the flora of Block Island; some of it occurs nowhere else in the state!

A wildflower walk

On September 13, 2000, the third-grade class from the Block Island School went on a wildflower walk at Turnip Farm. This was the first part of a yearlong program that showed the students the diverse habitats of Block Island and its inhabitants.

It was a beautiful day, perfect for searching out wildflowers and other plants. Armed with a plant checklist for Turnip Farm, a plant book, and a plant press, we set about identifying the various plants present.

The first plant to pop up, and by far the most showy, was the state-endangered northern blazing star. This plant has spiked purple flowers, and covers the area where you enter the Turnip Farm. There are thousands of these plants in this area, making it the largest population in Rhode Island. The students learned that the white-tailed deer love to eat this plant and thus are the reason for the northern blazing star exclosure.

The third-grade in front of the northern blazing star enclosure in 2000.

The students also learned the reason for all the colorful flagging in the area; a scientist from Brown University named Ailene Kane is studying this interesting flower. The flags serve to identify individual plants. Kane can then monitor how much a plant has grown or if it's been eaten. She is looking at the life history of the plant to help us better manage for this species. From the big to-do about this plant, the third-grade understood why this beautiful flower could not be picked.

The next wildflower we saw was butter-and-eggs, which has tiny, beautiful white, orange and yellow flowers. This plant is common in areas that have been mowed and then left alone. This was one of the third-grade's favorite plants.

The students then noticed that they were walking in sandy soil and knew to look for another neat plant, the mouse-ear hawkweed. This plant has hairy leaves with a short yellow flower that is similar to a dandelion. This plant has covered many of the sandy areas at Turnip Farm. The third-grade learned that this plant is a primary colonizer, which means after an area is disturbed it is one of the first plants to come back.

As we continued we saw autumn olive, bayberry, Asiatic bittersweet, black-eyed Susan, black berry, bull thistle, daisy fleabane, honeysuckle, Japanese black pine, Japanese knotweed, lance-leaved goldenrod, low-growing goldenrod, milkweed, multiflora rose, New England aster, New York aster, northern arrowwood, panic grass, poison ivy, purple gerardia, Queen Anne's lace, rabbit-foot clover, shadbush, silver poplar, spotted knapweed, tall goldenrod, winged sumac, winterberry, and yellow hawkweed.

In total, we saw 33 species of plants. Not bad for a 1½-hour walk.

At the end of our walk we stopped again at the special blazing star and drew it in our field notebooks, along with an illustration of what the site looks like. While we were doing this, an amazing merlin (medium-sized falcon) soared right past looking for a small bird to eat.

When we returned to the classroom from our adventure we recorded more information about the walk in our notebook (date, time afield, place, weather). Each student then checked off all the plants they saw.

As always I was amazed at the knowledge these budding botanists had about plants found on Block Island!

A student sketching a northern blazing star.

Those amazing bats

In the spring, summer, and especially the fall, if you are outside at dusk in an open field or near a pond, you will almost surely see bats flying around. Bats should always be thought of as an asset for the island. None of the old wives' tales about bats are true; they will not get in your hair, or suck your blood. Bats are important because they are nature's answer to mosquito abatement. Bats love to eat mosquitoes, and help keep their population down. In addition to their usefulness to humans, bats are also extremely interesting.

Back of a silver-haired bat, note the silver tips of the fur.

Bats are the only mammals that fly. Their forelimbs are greatly modified to form wings that are very different structurally than those of birds. In bats, the fingers are greatly lengthened to support a thin skin membrane, which extends to the hind legs and tail. This thin membrane is used to gain lift, similar to the way a bird's wing feathers are used.

Bats have limited eyesight and thus must rely on echolocation. A bat emits a sound (too high-pitched for us to hear) that is echoed back like a radar beam and picked up by the bat's sensitive ears, indicating the position of obstacles to be avoided or flying insects that can be captured for food.

Bats are nocturnal, which means they are active at night. They rest during the day, hanging upside down by their feet in caves, barns, cliffs, trees, and shrubs. At dusk they emerge to feed on insects. Unlike most birds when flying, the bat is a very erratic flyer, turning and zigzagging extremely quickly, forever in the pursuit of insects.

There are about 2,000 species of bats worldwide and of these, 65 are found in the United States. It is important to note that all the species found in the United States are insectivorous (eat primarily insects). On Block Island, we have three species of bats: eastern pipistrelle, silver-haired, and the little brown bat.

The eastern pipistrelle is the smallest American bat at 3 inches. It has reddish-brown fur, brownish ears, and is a fast and highly erratic flyer. In the winter this species hibernates to survive the cold Block Island winter.

The silver-haired bat is a dark-colored bat measuring 4 inches in length, with silver-tipped fur, which is more pronounced on the back. This common bat is a slow flyer, often seen near ponds. A solitary rester, individuals hang from branches deep in the shrubs. Come fall, the silver-haired bat migrates to the middle part of the country where it continues to feed as it follows warm weather south.

The little brown bat is 3½-inches long with long narrow ears, and is brown in color. This bat rests in groups, often in barns, sheds, and other covered areas. When the cold sets in, this species hibernates like the eastern pipistrelle.

On Block Island, the silver-haired bat is most common, but all three can be observed if you look around when you are outside at night. I promise you will be amazed at how interesting bats are to watch.

Front of a silver-haired bat hanging in the shrubs.

Beetles of the Block

Beetles are insects with a hard shell that covers the wings; a line straight down the middle of the back; and chewing jaws. They come in all shapes, sizes and colors, and are found in every habitat on Block Island except the ocean. While most people on Block Island have heard about the federally endangered American burying beetle, it is only one of many interesting beetles that are found here. In fact, there are 2,074 beetle species believed to occur in Rhode Island, many of which are found on Block Island.

From 1995 to 2000 Derek Sikes, then a doctoral candidate at University of Connecticut, compiled a list of all the beetles in Rhode Island, which was recently published as the "Beetle Fauna of Rhode Island." The list was generated by three methods: a literature search of scientific journals that had Rhode Island beetle species data dating back to the late 1880s, reviewing insect collections from the state, and field collecting. Sikes did some of the field collecting himself and relied on volunteer collectors throughout the state for the rest.

On Block Island, I collected many beetles for Sikes from 1997 to 2000. There are many ways to catch beetles, which are then placed in vials containing scientific alcohol. Sweep netting is running a net through the bushes and randomly catching beetles. A black light trap can be used at night to capture beetles.

A pitfall trap is an empty coffee can buried so the lip of the can is level with the ground. The beetles fall into the trap and can't get out. A flight intercept trap is composed of a 3-by-20 foot piece of screening hung between two poles that beetles hit and then drop into a pan of water, which has some dish soap in it. The dish soap prevents the beetles from walking on the surface tension of the water.

Beetles, from left to right: Asparagus, Japanese, Tortoise and Potato.

My collecting efforts on Block Island used all these capture techniques. I found the flight intercept trap to work the best, but each type of trapping method yielded different species of beetle. I also told all of the students at the Block Island School to capture any beetles they saw that were interesting, and to bring them to me. This added exponentially to my collection efforts. For each beetle that was collected (a state permit is needed to do this) the date, location and trapping method was recorded.

Once a bunch of beetles were gathered, I sent them off to Sikes and he had the tedious task of identifying each. Over the course of the study, with the help of many volunteers, Sikes collected over 800 different species of beetles in Rhode Island; and of these, 219 were found on Block Island. In this collection were 591 species records for the state.

On Block Island, 33 beetles collected were new for Rhode Island; of these, 16 were new for New England. None of these beetles has a common name and most were small and nondescript. This is a large number of new species for a small island.

Sikes's study also found that Block Island had many beetle species that were once common on the mainland but could no longer be found there. One of the more interesting examples of this is the rhinoceros beetle. This species measures 1 inch, is very thick, black in color, with the males having a distinctive horn on its head. While this species is quite common on this island, it has not been seen in mainland Rhode Island for many years.

Block Island is nationally known for its beetle species, yet it is still hard to believe that their diversity is so high in such a small, non-tropical area. This beetle inventory is additional proof that Block Island is extremely important for its diversity of fauna. Remember, the next time you see a beetle to appreciate it because it may be unique in Rhode Island.

Did you know...

There's no such thing as a ladybug!

SEZ WHO?

According to entomologists, what we have grown up calling a "ladybug" is, in reality, a "lady beetle." Bugs are defined* as "wingless or four-winged insects with mouth parts adapted for piercing and sucking." Beetles, on the other hand, are insects "having biting mouth parts and front wings modified to form horny wing covers that overlie the membraneous rear wings when at rest." In other words... beetles munch and bugs don't!

Lady beetles consume huge numbers of plant-feeding insects—mostly aphids, small insects that suck sap from plants, killing them. Home gardeners and farmers benefit greatly from the presence of lady beetles.

Lady beetles have an interesting means of protection. Birds learn that insects that are red/orange and black, or yellow and black, usually sting (bees) or taste bad (monarch butterflies, lady beetles and others) and therefore the birds leave the lady beetles alone.

All of this may be well and good and interesting to know, but... "Lady beetle, lady beetle fly away home..." just doesn't make it!

** American Heritage Dictionary*

The best of Block Island... naturally

Everyone enjoys this lovely island for different reasons but naturally it's the plants and animals which live here that are the best of the Block. Anyone can experience this firsthand by walking the various nature trails or snorkeling in the ocean. Block Island is full of many unique plants and animals each with their own special story. The following accounts are some of the most interesting.

Butterfly-weed. Also known as orange milkweed, this plant which is 2 feet tall lives in dry, sandy meadows. The plant blooms from June to September with orange, tiny, star-like flowers. The flowers cluster at branch ends and measure approximately 2 inches across. They provide an amazing splash of color. The stem of this wildflower is hairy and its oblong leaves contain a watery juice. The seedpods are similar to common milkweed but hairier. On Block Island this plant can be found on the Fresh Swamp trail and at Lewis Farm.

White water lily. This species is identified by its large paddle-shaped leaves which float on freshwater wetlands throughout the island. The veined leaves are green above and purplish beneath. From June to September the water-lily has a white flower that measures between 3 to 5 inches with many tapering petals, which get smaller in size as it gets closer to the yellow center. What is extremely interesting about this lily is what is under the water, large tubers that in mature plants are strong enough to support a person's weight. In the past, Native Americans used these tubers for food. On Block Island one of the best places to see water-lilies is in the Murray Nature Sanctuary pond across from the Painted Rock.

White water lily.

Clay banks tiger beetle. This 0.6-inch state-endangered insect has a brick or metallic red head, center of thorax (second segment), and elytra (wing covers). The thorax is outlined in metallic green and the elytra has variable light colored markings. Block Island has the only populations of this animal in Rhode Island. As described by its name it is found where the soil is composed of clay and the topography has a slope to it. There are two known populations on Block Island, one at Mohegan Bluffs and the other at Black Rock.

Rhinoceros beetle. This is one of the larger beetle species on Block Island measuring up to an inch in length. It is all black in color with the males having a pronounced horn on its head. This scarab-shaped insect is extremely strong for its size, making it hard to hold in a closed fist. Once common throughout Rhode Island, this species is now only found on Block Island. The rhinoceros beetle is easily seen at Clay Head and Rodman's Hollow.

Barn owl. This light-colored owl has a heart-shaped face, rusty-brown back, and measures 16 inches in height. It is the largest owl living on Block Island in the summer and at night makes a raspy, hissing screech, which is truly unmistakable (unlike most owls this species does not hoot). At night this quiet hunter searches mostly for Norway rats which makeup the majority of its prey base. It is also important to note that Block Island is the only place in Rhode Island where this owl still nests. While there is always a chance when driving around at night to catch a glimpse of this majestic animal, Clay Head and Black Rock are the best places to see them with regularity.

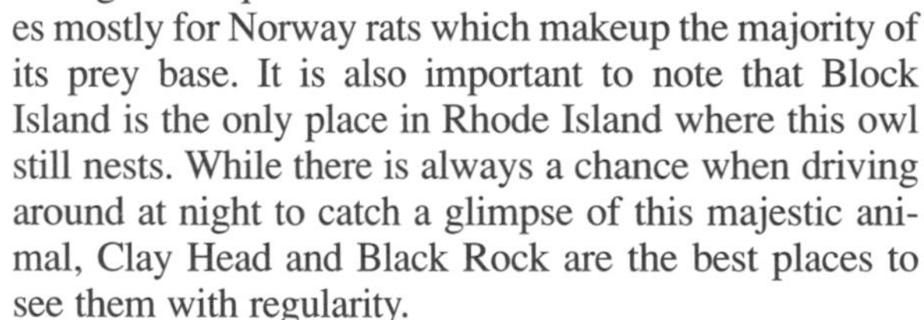

Barn Owl.

Bald eagle. Immature eagles often spend from the late spring to the early fall on Block Island feeding mostly on fish and gulls. Eagles will never nest on Block Island because there are not large enough trees to support their nests. This species is easily identified by its enormous size (8 foot wing span). The immature eagle is separated from the adult by its brown head and bill (adults have a white head and yellow bill). In fact it takes an eagle five years to have a completely white head. The rest of the immature eagle's body is brown with white on the tail. On Block Island the eagles have been very young and observers have been able to get quite close before the individual flees. Every once and a while there will be more than one eagle on the island with four being the most I have ever seen at one time. The bald eagle can be seen roosting in large trees and seen anywhere on Block Island because they are so big they soar around the whole island looking for food.

Bald eagle.

Northern lobster. The natural color of this species is greenish with blue or orange ones found very rarely. Lobsters are related to shrimp crabs and barnacles and have a hard outer shell (exoskeleton) that must be molted (shed) in order for the animal to grow. This species can grow quite large with some weighing over six pounds. A lobster eats mostly live and newly dead animal material and if close to shore feed mostly at night. They are found mostly on the ocean floor and thus crawl more than swim, using their five pairs of legs with the first set being its enlarged claws. This species is able to breath in the water using gills that are located in cavities on either side of the body. Water is pushed over the gill surface by small appendages on either side of the mouth. Lobsters mate after finishing molting and the eggs are attached to the "swimmerettes" on the underside of the female's abdomen until they hatch. This species can be seen when snorkeling in areas that have a rocky bottom.

Block Island is composed of many special plants and animals that take full advantage if this island refuge. This diversity of life is the best of Block Island, naturally.

Fall is the time for hawks and falcons

In the fall, the silhouettes of hawks and falcons migrating are a common sight throughout the island. For me it is always an amazing experience to see these birds of prey on their way south. During the 1970s and early 1980s these animals were not a common sight on the island; they were still recovering from pesticide use earlier in the century. Now that populations have recovered, seeing these amazing birds soar over the island is a real treat. Six species can be seen in the fall: the sharp-shinned hawk, Cooper's hawk, northern harrier, American kestrel, merlin, and peregrine falcon.

Except for the northern harrier and Cooper's hawk, which nest here, the remaining species migrate through. They migrate to follow their food source, which is migratory songbirds. Unlike the songbirds that migrate at night, hawks and falcons migrate during the day, often in large groups riding the thermals from the sun on their way south.

Sharp-shinned hawk

The smallest hawk that moves through Block Island is the sharp-shinned hawk. Measuring 10 to 14 inches, this bird has a slim body and tail, with short rounded wings. It is distinguishable in flight by several quick wing beats and then a glide. Adults have a dark back and a rusty-streaked breast. Immature birds have a brown back and brown-barred breast. The main source of food for this species during its trip south is small songbirds that are caught "on the wing." The sharp-shinned hawk migrates as far south as Panama.

Cooper's hawk

The Cooper's hawk is similar to the sharp-shinned hawk but larger, measuring 15 to 20 inches. This species' immature and adult plumage are also the same as the sharp-shinned's. When trying to distinguish between the two species, tail shape can be very helpful. The Cooper's hawk has a rounded tail, and the sharp-shinned has a square tail. The Cooper's hawk eats small mammals and songbirds, which are caught on the wing. This species, once rarely seen on Block Island, now nests here and is probably the most common hawk seen during its migration to the southern United States and northern Mexico.

The Cooper's hawk, a common sight during the fall on Block Island.

Northern harrier

The largest hawk on the island right now is the northern harrier, which nests here during the summer. This species measures 17 to 24 inches, with females being larger than males. They have an unmistakable white rump patch above the tail. Males are gray-backed, females are brown-backed; both have a white breast with brown streaking. Immature birds have a brown back and russet breast. Harriers glide through the air with their wings in a "V" shape. This species eats small rodents such as the white-footed mouse and meadow vole. While some harriers spend the winter on the island, most migrate as far south as Venezuela.

American kestrel

The American kestrel is the smallest falcon on the island. When trying to separate hawks and falcons on the wing, remember: all falcons have pointed wings, while hawk wings are rounded. The kestrel measures 9 to 12 inches with a reddish-brown back and tail. Males have blue wings and females brown; both sexes have a black-mustached face pattern. This species hovers with rapidly beating wings before swooping down to catch prey. It eats mostly insects and small mammals. This species migrates to northern South America.

Merlin

The merlin is a mid-sized falcon measuring 10 to 13 inches. Males have a blue back and tail, females are brown; both have a white breast with brown streaks. The merlin also has the same face pattern as the kestrel. Small birds caught in the air make up the diet of this species. In the fall this is the most common falcon on the island. It winters as far south as Mexico.

Peregrine falcon

The peregrine falcon is the largest falcon on the island, measuring 15 to 20 inches. Adults are blue-backed, with a white breast with brown streaks; immature birds are brown-backed with heavy brown streaking on the breast. Both youngsters and adults have heavy black sideburns. This bird flies quickly, flapping its wings rapidly. This species' diet is songbirds caught on the wing. It migrates as far south as Central America.

These six species are fun to watch darting around Block Island in the fall. Make sure to get out to see them before winter sets in and they are gone!

Fall bird migration

In the fall, Block Island is very important to migratory birds as a place to rest and refuel before continuing the long journey south. The migration begins about the second week of August and runs through the end of October. The migration schedule and amount of species on any given day depend on wind direction, food availability, and many other subtle factors.

The migration process begins on the nesting grounds, when the day length, which is also known as photoperiod, starts to get shorter, and the migratory birds begin to get ready for their journey south. A chemical is released in a bird's brain that causes it to continue to eat and put on the fat necessary for its long flight. This state of constant eating is called hyperphasia.

The red-eyed vireo migrates to Costa Rica.

As the night of migration departure approaches, the birds go into a state of "zugunruhe." In German, "zug" means to pull, and "ruhe" means disquiet. In the bird world, it is known as migratory restlessness. They wake up slightly after dark and are extremely active before leaving. In the fall this phenomenon only occurs when there is a north wind, so the birds can fly with the wind at their back.

Birds know the way to migrate by using a compass in their head that orients to magnetic north. In areas close to the North Pole, recent research shows that where magnetic north is obscured, migrating shorebirds navigate by the position of the sun.

In the fall on Block Island, we see the most migrants when there is a northwest wind because it pushes the birds off the mainland coast as they migrate south. It is also important to note that most of the migratory songbirds we see on the island in the fall are first-year birds that recently fledged from the nest. The reason for this is the adult birds know only to migrate when the winds are blowing from the north or northeast, which keeps them toward the coast. Young inexperienced birds will migrate on a northwest wind, pushing them off the coast, and at daybreak Block Island is the first land they see.

The migratory birds work their way south, resting at various places called stopover sites. Block Island is a major one of these for first-year migratory songbirds. Depending on weather conditions, the birds stay from one day to two weeks, resting, rehydrating and feeding. The migratory birds continue flying from one stopover site to the next until they reach their wintering grounds in the southeastern United States (short-distance migrant), or the shores of the Gulf of Mexico (long-distance migrant). The long distance migrants then fuel up one last time and fly about 20 hours across the Gulf to their final destination in Central or South America.

The mourning warbler migrates to Panama.

Generally, shorebirds are the first fall migrants arriving on Block Island in mid-August. The main reason they start early is because they have the longest distance to travel. One of the best places to see shorebirds is Andy's Way during low tide while they are feeding. If you watch from a distance, you can spot least terns, common terns, piping plovers, snowy egrets, American bitterns, ruddy turnstones and many more. Be sure to bring your bird book because many of these birds are similar in appearance.

After most of the shorebirds leave, the songbird migration begins in earnest. While it is possible to see small numbers of these birds in August (especially in fruiting black cherry trees), most of them venture through in September and early October.

Clay Head is the best place to see these migrants, which are usually in large, mixed-species flocks that move throughout the shrubs. Most migrant songbirds orient north to Clay Head before they continue on their way.

All of these birds are in their basic plumage, which is very drab so that they can blend in with the vegetation. This is why most bird books have multiple "confusing fall warbler" pages filled with illustrations of species that look almost the same. Some of the easier birds to see and identify include red-eyed vireo, Swainson's thrush, veery, black-throated green warbler, blackpoll warbler, magnolia warbler, chestnut-sided warbler, and American redstart to name a few.

Toward the end of fall migration you will see mostly short-distance migrants. These include yellow-rumped warbler, slate-colored junco, fox sparrow, ruby-crowned kinglet, and brown creeper. These species can be observed in any shrubby area, but they specifically like standing dead trees. The northern saw-whet owl is one of the final bird species that regularly migrates through Block Island. Usually, when we see this bird we know the end of migration is near.

Whether you are into birds or not, fall migration is an exciting time to be on Block Island. Each migration is different, but two things are for sure: there are always many great birds to be seen, and definitely bring a bird book because it will come in very handy.

Bird banding on Block Island

The practice of banding birds has occurred on Block Island since the early 1960s. Birds are banded for a variety of reasons, including documenting species distribution and population changes, gathering morphological data, and tracking birds from one location to another. Banding on the island has generated a wealth of information, and has documented quite a few new bird records for the region. It is hard to believe that over the years dedicated volunteers on this small island have banded over 100,000 birds representing more than 150 species.

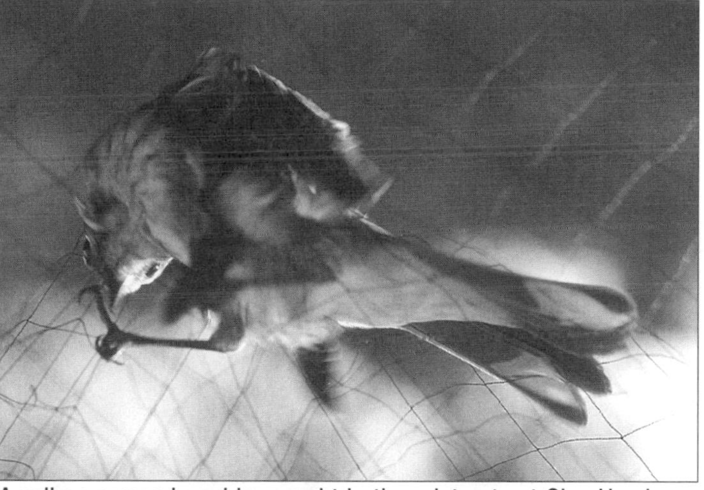

A yellow-rumped warbler caught in the mist nets at Clay Head.

In order to be a bird bander you must first apprentice for many years with a master bander. The U.S. Fish & Wildlife Service (USFWS), which is in charge of this program, licenses each master bird bander. The Bird Banding Laboratory, a division of USFWS, keeps track of all birds banded and issues the aluminum bands.

With the paperwork done, the next step is to select a site that will catch birds. On Block Island this is anywhere that has coastal shrubs. Mist nets, which are traditional Japanese hunting nets that were originally made of silk and are now made of nylon, are the standard tool for catching birds. These nets are usually 12 meters long and 3 meters high, with four pockets that trap the birds. The nets are black with a fine mesh that is hard for the birds to see. Birds fly into the net and drop into a pocket where they are trapped.

Once an hour (less if it is really hot or cold), trained banders remove all the birds from the nets (called clearing the nets). When extracting a bird, the first step is to find which side it flew in on, remove the feet next, then the wings, and finally the head. This process does not injure the bird, which is then placed in a cloth bag until it is ready to be processed.

After clearing the nets, the birds are processed, data recorded, and the birdsd are released. Each individual's species, sex, and age is determined by using a variety of books and charts. An aluminum band that has a nine-digit number that is unique to this bird, is placed on the leg. The wing is then measured with a ruler and a fat score determined. This is done by blowing back the feathers on the breast and flanks. Bird skin is translucent and thus the fat, which is yellow in color, can be seen and scored. Finally the bird is weighed and then released. The processing of a bird usually takes less than 1 minute, and the most a bird is out of its element is 1 hour from capture to release.

On Block Island, Elise Lapham has been banding at Clay Head every spring and fall since 1967. The site, which is now run by Kim Gaffett, is the third-longest continually running site on the East Coast. The Block Island Banding Station, as it is now called, has an amazing amount of information about how bird migration has changed on Block Island over the last 38 years.

Over the years there have been many other bird banders on Block Island who have banded throughout the island. When looking at all the data from all the different banders, there are two captures that stand out. The rarest bird ever banded on the island was a phenopepula, a brown cardinal-looking bird that lives in the southwestern part of the United States and does not migrate. The other extremely rare bird was a Townsend's warbler, a yellow and olive-green bird that lives on the west coast. Both of these captures were first records for New England.

Banding birds is a lot like Christmas because you never know what you are going to find when you check the nets. No matter how long you have participated in banding birds, there is always something new to experience. It is truly an excellent way to learn more about our feathered friends on Block Island.

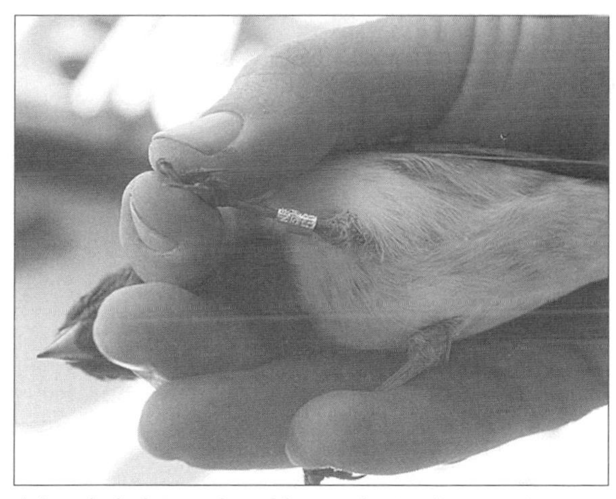

A banded slate-colored junco, just prior to release.

Avian research

There is a long history of bird research on Block Island. Research on this island has been vital to understanding the migration of birds. This knowledge led to Block Island being named one of the 500 most important bird areas in America by the American Bird Conservancy in 2002. The following is an overview of the most important bird studies conducted on Block Island.

Elizabeth Dickens started recording every bird she saw in a diary in 1911. This continued until her death in 1963, filling 11 volumes. These priceless data are now in the possession of Rhode Island Audubon. The records offer a long-term picture of the species composition of the island and how it has changed over time.

Since 1967, Elise Lapham has banded birds during spring and fall migrations on Block Island. These data give us a long-term look at how bird migration is affected by weather; how species distributions have changed over time; and provide an excellent record of different songbird species that have migrated through Block Island. In addition to this amazing amount of data, the Laphams have encouraged and supported much of the avian research that has happened in the last 38 years on the island.

Miss Elizabeth Dickens.

From 1992 to 1996, Jeffery Parrish did his doctoral research on Block Island for Brown University. His study site was in the northern part of Clay Head and focused on migratory songbird diets during fall migration. Parrish was the first to document the switch in the fall songbird diet from insects to fruit (berries). This was a landmark study that is well-known throughout the ornithological community, and documented the importance of the coastal shrub habitat for declining migratory songbirds.

In the fall of 1996 and 1997, Colleen Dwyer from Frank Moore's (a top migratory ornithologist) laboratory at the University of Southern Mississippi started her master's research at Parrish's old site. She focused on gray catbird diet and the differences between juvenile and adult birds. Dwyer also looked at the feather molting patterns of adults. This research continued to document the importance of the coastal shrubland.

Since 1998 Scott McWilliams's laboratory at the University of Rhode Island has conducted bird research at the site that Parrish started on Block Island. His first student was master's candidate Megan Whitman. She focused on the energetics of fruit for birds during migration. Doctoral candidate David Podlesak was next, with a focus on examining the chemical change that birds undergo, switching from eating insects to fruit. In 2004, doctoral candidate Susan Smith started focusing on how diet-switching and nutrient composition of foods influence fuel use in migratory birds during fall stopovers. All of these studies have proven that coastal shrubland is vital in the fall for migratory stopover locations like Block Island.

There are many other bird research projects that have been conducted on Block Island in the last 50 years. However, most of them were on a much smaller scale than the projects highlighted above. Some of these projects include: bird counts, breeding bird surveys, nesting studies, bird-banding inventories, and much more.

There is a rich history on Block Island when it comes to avian research. While much has been learned, there are still many unknowns that will be explored in the coming years. Block Island's documented importance for birds is a tribute to many people who have volunteered their time and energy to better understand our avian friends.

Dr. Jeffery Parrish.

Feathers

One of the most common things that can be found on Block Island are feathers. They can be found in all habitats, and come in all shapes, sizes and colors. Feathers are the most distinctive feature specific to birds.

It has been found through fossil records that birds started evolving from reptiles about 150 million years ago. Over time, scales on reptiles elongated and frayed, pigmentation then occurred and the modern feather was born.

Breast feather: Saw-whet owl

For all birds, feathers provide insulation essential for regulating body temperature, power for flight, and colors and patterns important for communication and camouflage. Feathers also provide other functions for many species of birds including swimming, hearing, protection, water repellence, and cleanliness.

Feathers are made mainly of keratin, an extremely long-lasting biological material that is a major component of hair, scales, claws and fingernails found on many different types of animals. However, the keratin in bird feathers is unique and found in no other type of animal.

There are four types of bird feathers, each with a specific function. The two main types of feathers are vaned and down.

Vaned feathers

Vaned feathers are the most commonly found feathers on Block Island. They are the tail, wing and body feathers of the bird and are extremely stiff. The vane is the fluffy part of the feather and the quill is the bare part of the feather. The fluffy part of the feather is held together by hooklets that connect to barbules. Essentially these parts of the feather work like Velcro, keeping the fluffy part of the feather from separating.

Down feathers

Unlike the firm vaned feathers, down feathers are soft and compactable. These feathers lie against the bird's body and help trap warm air, thus acting as insulation. In winter, birds can often be seen with their feathers puffed out; this is to increase the amount of "loft" or insulation. Of course, down is also used by humans as an excellent lightweight thermal insulator used in comforters, jackets, etc. The only problem with down is that it is not water-resistant.

There are two minor types of feathers: semiplume and filoplume.

Semiplumes

Semiplumes are intermediate in structure between down and vaned feathers. The fluffy area of the semiplume is longer than a down feather but not as tightly packed as a vaned feather. This type of feather enhances thermal insulation and the bird's aerodynamic features.

Filoplumes

Filoplumes are hair-like feathers distributed throughout the bird. They monitor the movement and position of the vaned feathers. Because they are the most sensitive of the feathers, they are most numerous near movable feathers. These feathers may also monitor airspeed.

When all the feathers described above are put together, they form the feather coat. For example, a warbler's coat has 2,000 to 4,000 feathers, whereas a tundra swan has 25,000 feathers. Although the coat covers the whole body, the feathers are not attached to the bird evenly or uniformly. Instead they are attached to the bird in dense rows called tracts.

Birds must also care for their feathers every day in order for them to remain useful. This is called preening, where they rearrange their feather coat with their bill to reposition out-of-place feathers. Birds must also remove feather parasites; this is done by foot scratching, sunning, and dust and water baths.

Finally, a bird uses a set of feathers for 6 months to 1 year depending on the species. The process of dropping feathers and growing new ones is called molting. Birds molt sequentially, meaning they drop and replace feathers in a specific order over a few weeks, enabling them to always be able to stay warm and fly.

Feathers are an important part of the bird's body but once it is no longer part of the bird it is a treasure to be discovered, studied and enjoyed up close. The nice thing about feathers like these is they will not fly away!

Parts of a vaned feather

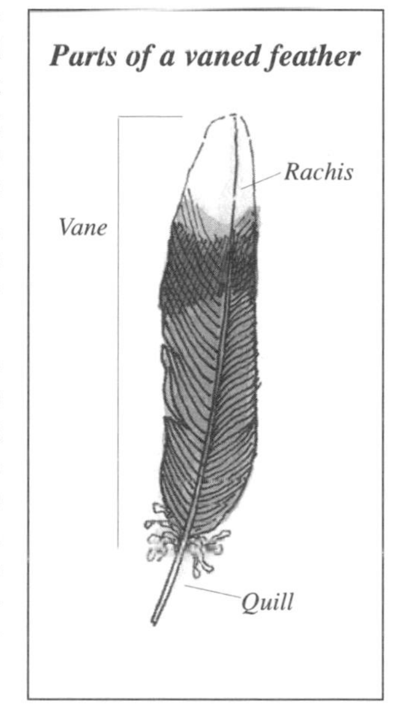

Seedpods of Block Island

With the leaves brown and many of them already on the ground as winter starts to get its grasp on Block Island, most plants become more difficult to identify. However, some become easier to identify due to the distinctiveness of their seedpods. Here are 11 species whose seeds are dispersed to new areas by wind, gravity and animals.

Buttonbush– This bush, also known as "honey-balls," is found around swamps and ponds. One of the best examples of this species grows where Mohegan Trail and Pilot Hill Road intersect. Buttonbush can reach a height of 12 feet. In late summer, it has beautiful white pincushion-like balls that become rough and brown before its seeds are dispersed.

Black swallowwort– This invasive vine is in the milkweed family and is found throughout the island on roadsides and in fields. Its seedpods are slender and smooth, ranging in length from 2 to 6 inches. If you see this species on your property, pull it before it takes over. It is best to do this before its seeds disperse.

Black swallowwort seed

Indian mallow– Also known as velvet leaf, this plant grows on roadsides and in disturbed areas. It ranges in height from 2 to 6 feet, and has a yellow flower in the summer and early fall. The seedpods are extremely interesting; each individual one looks like a star. In the fall, before its seeds drop, you can hear them rattle in the pod.

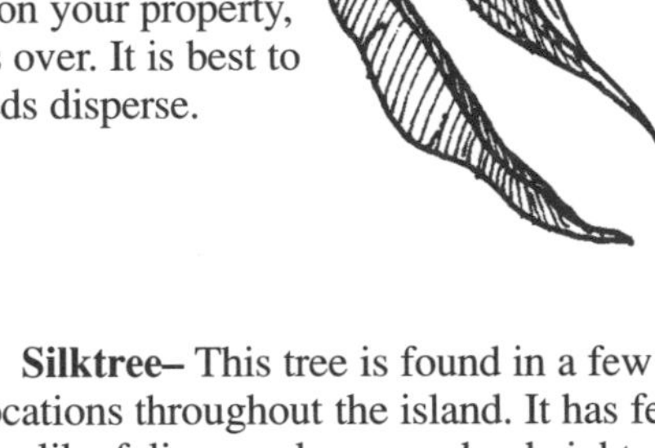

Silktree– This tree is found in a few select locations throughout the island. It has feathery fernlike foliage and can reach a height of 40 feet. In the summer, it has puff-like pink flowers, and, in the fall, its 2- to 3-inch seedpods are brown, smooth and flat. This pod is similar to a bean's seedpod.

Sea rocket– This plant, which is in the mustard family, can be found along Block Island's beaches. It is one of the first plants to disappear if there is too much human disturbance. The plant's fleshy skin repels salt, a substance that burns most plants. This species ranges in height from 6 to 12 inches. Its name comes from the fact that each of its individual seedpods looks like a rocket.

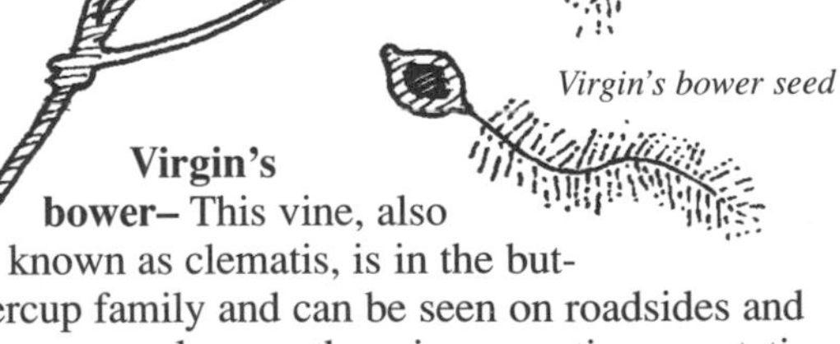

Virgin's bower seed

Virgin's bower– This vine, also known as clematis, is in the buttercup family and can be seen on roadsides and other areas as long as there is supporting vegetation for it to climb. It is probably the most distinctive seedpod on Block Island, with its cluster of feathery hairs, which is also called "old man's beard." Each cluster is about 3 inches in diameter.

Common milkweed – This native plant is poisonous to humans, but extremely important to monarch butterfly caterpillars for food. Found in dry soils, this species can be distinguished from other milkweeds by the warty appearance of the seedpod, which opens, allowing seeds to be dispersed by the wind. Please do not pick the seedpods because it is the only way we can ensure there will be milkweed in the future. This species grows up to 5 feet in height, and can be found in any meadow habitat throughout the island.

Bull thistle seed

Common milkweed seed

Bull thistle – This is an alien species, which means it is not native to the island. With spiky leaves and purple flowers, this species is unmistakable. With the flowers gone to seed, the thistle is now a favorite of the American goldfinch, which can often be seen balancing on its flimsy branches. This plant grows to 6 feet in height and its seeds are dispersed by the wind. Bull thistle is a common wildflower and can be found in any meadow on Block Island.

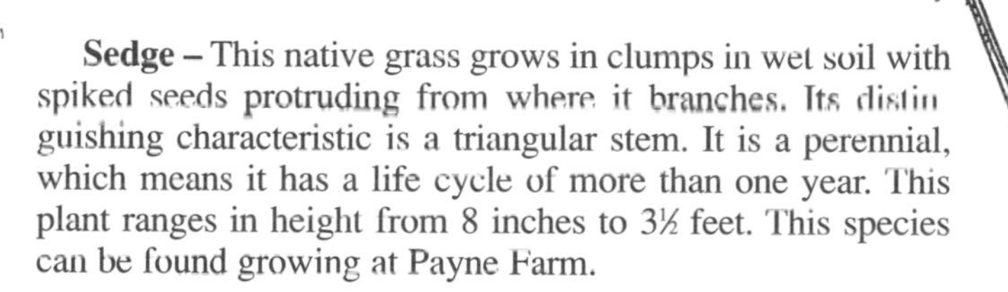

Sedge – This native grass grows in clumps in wet soil with spiked seeds protruding from where it branches. Its distinguishing characteristic is a triangular stem. It is a perennial, which means it has a life cycle of more than one year. This plant ranges in height from 8 inches to 3½ feet. This species can be found growing at Payne Farm.

Oriental chestnut – While not native to the island, some of these trees out here are over 50 years old. In the fall, they drop bright green seedpods covered with sharp spikes. Be extremely careful when picking this seed up to examine it. The nut, which looks similar to an American chestnut, is inside a protective sheath. This species ranges up to 40 feet in height. The best place to find this exotic tree is the Nathan Mott Park.

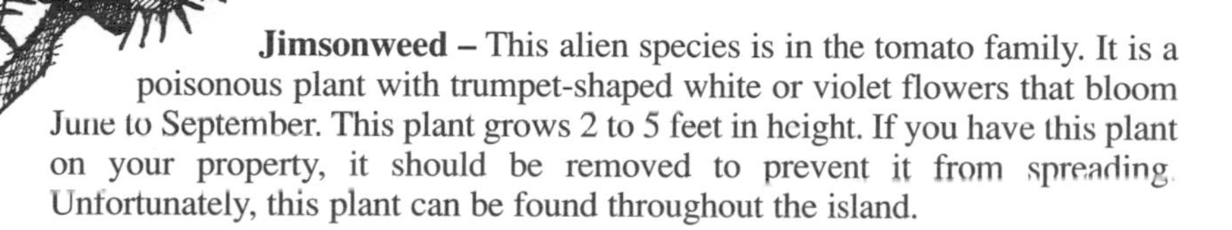

Jimsonweed – This alien species is in the tomato family. It is a poisonous plant with trumpet-shaped white or violet flowers that bloom June to September. This plant grows 2 to 5 feet in height. If you have this plant on your property, it should be removed to prevent it from spreading. Unfortunately, this plant can be found throughout the island.

While seedpods come in all shapes and sizes, the spiky ones are some of the most interesting and distinctive. In your travels around Block Island, see how many of the seedpods illustrated here you can find.

An adventure to Clay Head

There are many great adventures to experience on Block Island, but none is better than the Clay Head trails. There are approximately 12 miles of walking trails that weave around and over 150 acres in the northeastern part of the island. The area is known locally as the "Maze," but its official name is the Clay Head Preserve.

The preserve trailhead is easily reached. Off Corn Neck Road, turn right just north of the entrance to West Beach Road. There is not a street sign, but you will find a gray post there marked "Clay Head Trail." We encourage people to leave their cars here and walk, however, parking and bike racks are available less than a half mile down the dirt lane, near the fence marking the trailhead.

Walking trail systems on Block Island were born right here in the 1960s when David and Elise Lapham originally cut paths through their property to make pheasant hunting easier, and then welcomed the public to use them. The Laphams have continued to maintain the trails for the benefit of the public. If you think it is impossible to get lost on Block Island, think again. I have known many people who have become disoriented here while going for a "brief walk in the Maze."

The primary Clay Head trail is a path that runs north to south, along the Clay Head bluffs. If you feel adventurous, you can venture into the maze by turning left off the main trail, but you are on your own because there are no signs. However, some of the best nature experiences I have had on Block Island are when I do not know exactly where I am.

These trails are not shown on any map to preserve the enchantment of the area. If you become disoriented, remember that the Clay Head trail is to the east. It may take a while, but heading in that direction and listening for the sounds of the ocean will bring you to the marked path, and you can continue your walk with the confidence of knowing where you are.

Regardless of how adventurous you feel, there is a lot to see in Clay Head Preserve. At the onset, heading east from the trailhead, toward the ocean, you will see some big trees. These are sycamore maples, which mark the site of an old farmhouse. Look in the holes of the trees for nesting birds, such as the black-capped chickadee, yellow-shafted flicker, and Carolina wren.

The trail then proceeds through a meadow with open views across Clay Head Swamp to the Atlantic Ocean. Off to the south, you can see Old Harbor. The path proceeds downhill and along the edge of the swamp. Across the water are the Littlefield and Ball farms, two of the best remaining examples of the saltwater farms that once extended up and down the coast of the island.

Clay Head Swamp has only native fish, such as brown bullhead and golden shiner, which is rare for any pond in New England. As you go downhill toward the swamp, you will notice many wetland plants as you cross a bridge. In the late spring, listen for the "sweet, sweet, sweet, I'm so sweet" of the yellow warbler.

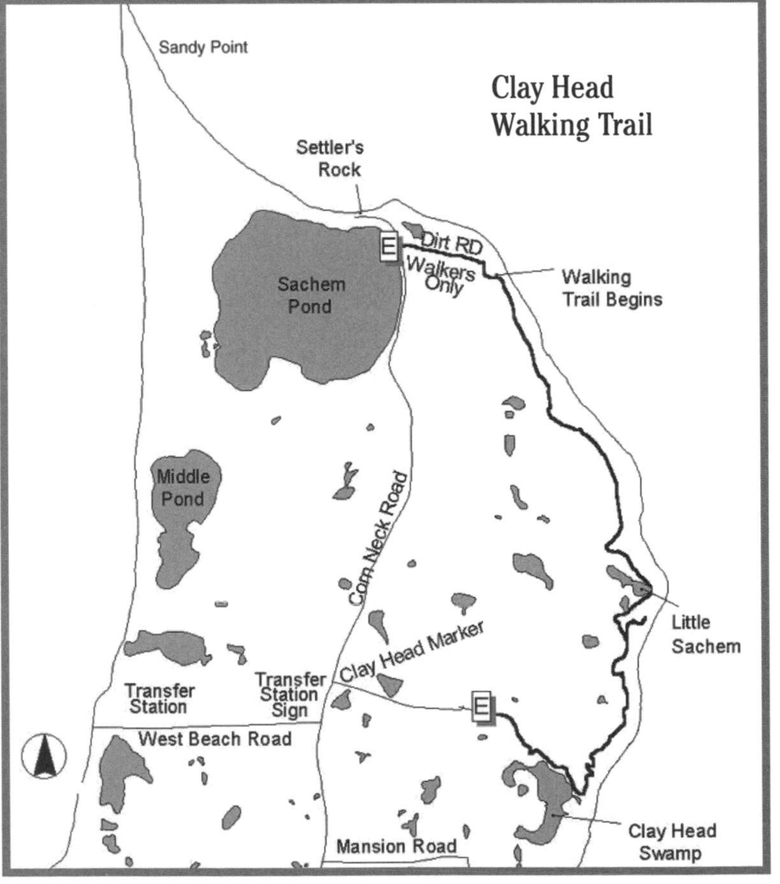

Just before the beach, the trail heads to the left and north. You might want to take a break and explore the beach. If you do, look up at the bluff and notice all the holes; these are home to bank swallows. If you are here in the summer, watch for them darting in and out of these holes in the face of the bluff.

Farther down the beach are the "Pots and Kettles." These are glacially formed underground water channels composed of rocks and sand, which have been fused by iron oxides and exposed as the bluff erodes.

From the beach, the trail climbs and then levels off, paralleling the bluff all the way until the path ends at a dirt lane, which leads back out to Corn Neck Road and beyond to Settlers' Rock and Sandy Point. Along the way are majestic views and a number of overlooks where you can see the waves crashing below. Be careful not to get too close to the bank, as the bluff is fragile and undercut, and it is a long drop to the beach.

It is important to note that the Clay Head Preserve property was permanently conserved in the late 1970s and was one of the first major land conservation projects on Block Island. Clay Head is one of the most beautiful places on the island — or anywhere, for that matter. The Laphams cannot be commended enough for their generosity, hospitality, and foresight. They gave a protective easement over this entire area, and their gift qualified the State of Rhode Island for federal matching funds used in the preservation of areas of Rodman's Hollow, Black Rock and the Mohegan Bluffs.

So remember, if you are looking for an adventure, Clay Head Preserve is the place. I promise it will be amazing!

Trees, or the lack thereof

When European settlers first came to Block Island, it was forested with large deciduous trees. The last of these native (species that grew here originally) trees were cut down by the mid-1700s. In fact, the town passed laws around 1710 to try to preserve the dwindling forests, but it was too late. From this time until the mid-1900s, Block Island's land was mostly open for pasture, hay, and crops. Since the mid-1900s many of the fields have been left fallow; shrubs have grown and are now the dominant habitat on Block Island.

When the exotic (not originally growing on Block Island) Japanese black pines began dying due to the turpentine beetle and other diseases, the question of what tree species were originally here came into prominence. In the spring of 1997, the Lapham family set up a grant for the Yale School of Forestry and Environmental Studies to explore this question.

Japanese black pines with needles and cones.

Bruce Hammond, a second-year candidate for a master's degree, was the grant recipient and his work began in the summer of 1997. His first step was to focus on what trees used to be on Block Island according to New Shoreham records, books, and other materials. He also looked at wood fragments in peat deposits. An inventory of what trees were currently on Block Island was then conducted. Finally, he looked at other native forests on Martha's Vineyard, Nantucket, and Naushon (one of the Elizabeth Islands) and designed strategies for the reintroduction of native trees to replace the dying Japanese black pines.

In his two-volume report submitted in May 1998, Hammond states that white oak, black oak, hickory, red oak, scrub oak, red cedar, beech, black gum, red maple, and sassafras were among the native trees that once covered the island. It is very likely there were more tree species but Hammond could not document them. Hammond recommends planting these trees under the dying Japanese black pines or surrounding them by shrubs as a way to protect the small saplings from salt spray and wind. He also recommends testing the soil for various readings (pH, nitrogen, drainage) to find the appropriate tree for the location.

In the winter of 1999 we started looking for places to find native saplings, and quickly found that no nursery carried high volumes of any of these native trees, and most did not carry Block Island's native trees at all. We decided more research was needed. After extensive networking we finally got in touch with tree restoration expert Tom Dilatesh. In July of 1999 we hosted Dilatesh on the island. He recommended ways of transplanting saplings from areas similar to Block Island and then raising them in a greenhouse for two years before planting. This seemed at first to be a solution but when we started looking at the amount of time and expense it did not seem to be practical. So we were back to looking for a native tree distributor.

In the spring of 2000 we were able to get red cedar, white cedar, and red oak from the Rhode Island State reforestation program (now defunct). With the help of Block Island School students these 8-inch saplings were planted at Clay Head and Nathan Mott Park.

The reason for selecting these areas was that these locations have birds that need large trees. We worry that these bird species may disappear from the island when the Japanese black pines are gone if they are not replaced with another species of tree. Mature trees also provide cover for songbirds and are important roosting spots for bald eagles, hawks, falcons and owls.

As a trial, more than 300 saplings were planted and by fall most of them had died. We hypothesized the two biggest reasons for sapling mortality were deer grazing and lack of water despite our best efforts to mitigate these issues. With only eight trees surviving after the first year and four trees as of the fall of 2004, we now know this was not the right approach. If reintroduction of native trees is attempted in the future, it must be done on a smaller scale with dedicated staff or volunteers to tend to them and ensure their survival.

Over the last eight years a great deal of important information has been researched and reported when it comes to native trees on Block Island. At The Nature Conservancy, this information is available to anyone who is thinking of planting a native tree on their property. Restoration, one native tree at a time, will benefit everyone.

Dead Japanese black pines off Cooneymus Road.

A herd of deer... a bed of clams

For every kind of animal there is a word or phrase that is used to describe a group of those animals. A herd of deer; a bed of clams; a flock of birds...

But what about a shoal? A swarm? A raft? Or even, a murder? Below are the terms used to describe various groups of animals found on Block Island. At the bottom of the page are the names of the animals. Can you match the 20 group names to the 20 animals?

You'll never guess me!

An army of ________________

A bale of ________________

A bouquet of ________________

A charm of ________________

A colony of ________________

A fall of ________________

A gaggle of ________________

A hedge of ________________

A host of ________________

A kettle of ________________

A lamentation of ________________

A murder of ________________

A murmation of ________________

A nest of ________________

A parliament of ________________

A raft of ________________

A shoal of ________________

A smack of ________________

A sord of ________________

A swarm of ________________

Ants • Bass • Bees • Caterpillars • Crows • Ducks • Geese • Goldfinches • Hawks • Herons • Jellyfish
Mallards • Owls • Pheasants • Snakes • Sparrows • Starlings • Swans • Turtles • Woodcocks • (Answers below)

A surprise of answers: An army of caterpillars; A bale of turtles; A bouquet of pheasants; A charm of goldfinches; A colony of ants; A fall of woodcocks; A gaggle of geese; A hedge of herons; A host of sparrows; A kettle of hawks; A lamentation of swans; A murder of crows; A murmation of starlings; A nest of snakes; A parliament of owls; A raft of ducks; A shoal of bass; A smack of jellyfish; A sord of mallards; A swarm of bees. **How many did you get?**

Counting: it's for the birds

Recently, dedicated ornithologists (bird nerds) encircled the island counting and identifying every avian species seen for the Veterans' Day bird count.

There are also three other counts that are done throughout the year: the Christmas, Presidents' Day, and Breeding Bird Survey. When this information is compiled and looked at over the long term, trends in populations can be seen, providing extremely valuable information.

For those of you not familiar with a bird count, here is how it works: 1) an area is selected — in this case Block Island; 2) the area is divided among the participants — six groups for this count; 3) every bird is identified and counted in one calendar day; and finally, 4) the groups get together and the list is assembled.

The 2004 Veterans' Day count was interesting because the total number of individuals was down (probably due to the high winds), but there was more diversity.

On Saturday, Nov. 6, 2004, a total of 108 species was seen, and 5,191 individuals were counted. Since 1995, the mean number of species has been 104, and the mean number of individuals 8,709. Of course when you look at these data, weather conditions must be taken into account.

Some of the interesting information from this count was the presence of a tree swallow and an eared grebe — both late for this time of year; two cave swallows — vagrants to this area; and a black guillemot — early to this area. These were all first-time records for this count.

We also had all-time highs for northern cardinals — migrating through the island for the first time; and common grackles — undergoing an island-wide population explosion.

The Veterans' Day count is a fairly new count, established in 1995. This is also true of the Presidents' Day count. In contrast, the Christmas bird count has been happening since the 1920s (with a few years missed here and there) when Elizabeth Dickens started it.

It is really interesting to see how the bird species have changed since this count was started. Most of these changes are due to habitat on Block Island shifting from grassland to shrubland.

The Breeding Bird Survey, which has been happening since 1987, is conducted in June and is performed differently. This is a point count survey, which means that there are 30 established points on the island at which an observer spends 2 minutes recording every bird seen and heard. This is done to have a continual baseline of all birds nesting on Block Island.

The four counts that are done each year help us have an accurate record of the birds that are using Block Island. We can also see how weather affects birds because we can compare the counts from Veterans' Day to Presidents' Day in the same year and see how the numbers differ.

The longer the counts are done, the more trends in bird populations can be seen, as long as habitat changes and weather are taken into account. The bird count information can also be interesting when comparing it to counts in other places. This can help prove Block Island's importance for migratory and wintering birds.

So the next time you see a bunch of ornithologists on one of these counts, remember they are more than just crazy bird fanatics — they are also gathering important information for the island that can be very helpful in the future.

The northern harrier, a species recorded on every count.

Northern saw-whet owl migration

In late October it is always exciting when the first cold front with northwest wind appears. What is so exciting about this you may ask? Well, under those conditions at this time of year, we get lots of migrating northern saw-whet owls. A similar thing happens earlier in the fall when migrating songbirds get blown off course and land here.

These cute creatures are 7 inches long with a reddish-brown back, a white belly, and reddish streaks on the breast. They prefer dense coniferous forest, so on Block Island the owls tend to be found in stands of Japanese black pine and blue spruce. The birds are strictly nocturnal (active at night). During the day they like to roost (rest) in dense evergreens, usually close to the end of the branch.

On Block Island the saw-whet owls eat mostly white-footed mice, catching them with their large talons. After the catch, the owl returns to a tree and proceeds to eat the mouse by ripping it into small chunks. Owls cannot separate the meat from the fur and bones, thus later they regurgitate a pellet, which is the undigested fur wrapped around bone, much like a cat's hairball.

Historically, ornithologists (bird experts) believed this species was relatively uncommon in southern New England, with only a few individuals present each year in Rhode Island during migration, and some years with none at all. Although approaching a saw-whet is easy because they tend to stay put, finding one is quite hard due to their stillness and camouflage. As a result, little was known about this species' numbers and distribution.

Ornithologists do not know when saw-whet owls migrate or how the population of these owls changes from year to year. In fact, very little was known about the migration ecology (how this species behaves during migration) of saw-whet owls in the Northeast until an extensive monitoring effort began in 1991. These recent efforts by biologists in a series of banding stations (New Jersey, Maryland, and Virginia) have shown saw-whet owls to be quite common (these stations captured over 4,500 saw-whets in the last 12 years).

In 1991, biologists in eastern North America established a network of saw-whet owl banding stations (OWLNET) to monitor the fall migration of this species. The stations include sites in southeastern Canada, Wisconsin, Maine, Pennsylvania, New Jersey, and Virginia. Rhode Island joined this group in 1996 with banding stations at Trustom Pond National Wildlife Refuge, Marion Eppley Wildlife Sanctuary, and a site in Richmond. In 1998, Block Island was added to the Rhode Island list of sites.

For the last seven falls on Block Island, I have set up mist nets (fine mesh nets that the birds cannot see and are captured in) in conifer stands throughout the island. Owls were attracted to the nets by the sound of a male saw-whet on the breeding grounds, played on a continuous-loop cassette tape. While the tape played, the nets were checked for birds every hour. The weather was recorded (temperature, cloud cover, wind speed) at 30-minute intervals.

On Block Island, the number of saw-whet owls caught by year is as follows: 1998: 7; 1999: 68; 2000: 25; 2001: 7; 2002: 6; 2003: 7; 2004: 10. What is the reason for this huge difference between the various years? It is hard to say because more research needs to be done in future falls, but it appears that weather and the amount of cold fronts plays a big role in saw-whet owl migration.

When an owl is captured in the mist net, the first step is to remove it. This is done with the use of a flashlight, grabbing the feet first (their talons are sharp and will break the skin), and then carefully untangling the

A saw-whet owl just prior to release.

rest of the bird, starting with the wings and finishing with the head. A U.S. Fish & Wildlife Service band is then put on the bird so we can identify the individual, and then the age and sex of the bird is ascertained using various reference books. The next step is to take morphological (body) measurements including wing length, bill length, fat percentage, flight feather molt, and weight. The bird is then released. Total time from capture to release is less than 45 minutes.

Sometimes owls previously banded on Block Island are captured again in the same mist nets a few days later. While not common, this provides valuable data as to how long these owls are staying on Block Island. So far the longest stopover period I have recorded for a saw-whet owl is eight days.

On November 10, 2004, I had a first, capturing a marked saw-whet that had been banded at another station (called a foreign band). The next day I received a call from an ornithologist who was banding saw-whets in Lookout Rock, Mass., informing me he had caught an owl that I had banded three days before. This was extremely interesting because it is the first record of an owl moving north instead of the way it is supposed to go at that time of year.

The conversation became even more intriguing when I read him the foreign band I had caught the night before and it was an owl he had banded four days earlier. Thus, on November 10th we exchanged birds.

Every saw-whet owl captured on Block Island has been a hatching-year bird (born in the year caught), and there has been a fairly even distribution between males and females. We expect first-year birds on Block Island because adult birds tend to be found more frequently inland. This is consistent with what we have documented with songbirds in the fall, because novice birds do not know the way south and get blown off course. However, it is much too early to call it a trend with saw-whet migration. It is always important to remember this is a long-term monitoring study, and we will know much more each year we do it.

A hatching year saw-whet owl.

Every fall I bring a saw-whet owl into the school and show the students. They learn about the special traits that an owl has: a heart-shaped facial disk to focus sound waves into the ears, large ears at different heights on the head to triangulate (pin-point) prey, feathers on the legs, and extra barbules (the fuzzy part of the feather) on the wing feathers to make owls silent when they fly. The students always love seeing this "cool" bird and are especially amazed at how they cannot hear it fly when it is released.

Late fall is the time to see a saw-whet owl. The best place to locate this special species is in stands of conifers, at night, using a high-powered flashlight to scan the trees. If you are lucky, there will be two yellow eyes staring back at you. The owls are very docile, so if you are quiet, they can be observed for a long time. I believe, and I hope you will agree, that this owl is truly one of the most wonderful animals found on Block Island!

Must have nature guides for Block Island:

Name and author(s)

A Field Guide to Animal Tracks
Olaus Murie
A Field Guide to the Atlantic Seashore
Kenneth Gosner
A Field Guide to the Birds (eastern)
Roger Tory Peterson
A Field Guide to the Insects
Donald Borror and Richard White
A Field Guide to Trees and Shrubs
George Petrides
Block Island Geology
Les Sirkin
Block Island Wildlife
James Kavanagh and Raymond Leung
Grasses An Identification Guide
Lauren Brown
National Audubon Society Field Guide to New England
Peter Alden and Brian Cassie
Newcomb's Wildflower Guide
Lawrence Newcomb
On This Island
Keith Lang and Scott Comings
Peterson First Guide to Butterflies and Moths
Paul Opler
Peterson First Guide to Caterpillars
Amy Wright
Peterson First Guide to Mammals
Peter Alden
Peterson First Guide to Reptiles & Amphibians
Roger Conant, Robert Stebbins and JosephCollins
Pond Life
George Reid
The Outer Lands
Dorothy Sterling
Spiders and Their Kin
Herbert Levi and Lorna Levi

"The way we were" scavenger hunt

See if you can find these natural species, which are examples of the way things were on Block Island. All of these plants and animals could be found on the island 100 years ago. How many of them can you find today? Please do not collect or disturb anything on the list.

- ☐ Horseshoe crab
- ☐ Block Island meadow vole
- ☐ Grasshopper sparrow
- ☐ Northern blazing star
- ☐ Savannah sparrow
- ☐ Barn owl
- ☐ Northern harrier
- ☐ Lily pad
- ☐ Skate egg case
- ☐ Red maple
- ☐ Moon snail
- ☐ Little bluestem
- ☐ Switch grass

Northern blazing star

Switch grass

Skate egg case

Moon snail

Block Island facts:

- The island is 7 miles long and 3 miles wide.
- The total area of the island is 6,188 acres (10 square miles).
- There are 15.8 miles of beaches on the island.
- The highest point is Beacon Hill, 211 feet above sea level.
- The lowest point is Rodman's Hollow, 20 feet above sea level.
- 42 percent of the island is conserved.
- There are about 900 year-round residents.
- The island's only town, New Shoreham, was incorporated in 1661.
- The island is 9.4 miles south of mainland Rhode Island.
- Great Salt Pond is 1,000 acres.
- Fresh Pond is the largest freshwater pond on Block Island.
- There are over 300 ponds on the island.
- Four federally endangered species are found on Block Island.
- 30 state-endangered species are found on the island.
- One freshwater aquifer supplies the whole island.
- Block Island was first "seen" by Veranzano in 1524.
- The island was named after Dutch explorer, Adrian Block.
- The island was originally richly forested.
- Archeological records indicate that the island supported a year-round Native American settlement as early as 500 B.C.
- The last Native American to die on Block Island was a full-blooded Manissea named Isaac Church, in 1886.

The way we were: from a bird's eye view

One of the major changes on Block Island in the last hundred years is the succession of the natural habitat from predominately grassland to mostly shrubland. With all the changes, some wildlife prosper and others disappear. The bird community is the best example of this changing of the guard.

Disappearing species

In the past, when Block Island was more open, there were many grassland-dependent bird species that lived and nested here. Most of them, like the upland sandpiper and vesper sparrow, are now hardly ever seen on the island. There are a few bird species, like the bobolink, which can still be seen, but only during migration. This is their story.

Upland sandpiper

The last upland sandpiper nest seen on Block Island was in the early 1990s. This species only nests in large tracts of grassland, which have for the most part disappeared from the island. This bird measures 11½ inches, and compared to other sandpipers has a short bill, small head, large eyes, thin neck and long tail.

This species will often perch on fence posts, which it uses to sing from to mark its territory. Its song is a whistled "whoooleeeeee, wheeloooooooooo." In the past, this bird was only here in the summer and migrated to Argentina for the winter. There is still a remote chance of seeing this bird during the spring and fall migration.

Vesper sparrow

This bird has also disappeared due to the loss of grassland habitat over the last 50 years. This species looks a lot like a grayish song sparrow, but instead has a distinct eye ring and a chestnut patch at the shoulder of the wing. This sparrow also has white on the outer tail feathers, which are noticeable as the bird flies.

This species used to spend the summer on Block Island and then would migrate to Central America. Again, there is a remote chance of seeing a vesper sparrow during the spring and fall migration.

Bobolink

This bird was once quite common on Block Island, but is now only seen during the spring and fall in grassland areas. It measures 7 inches in length, with the springtime male black below and mostly white above, with a brown nape. The female and autumn male are brownish with a dark striped back and head. While the springtime male is extremely easy to identify, the female is about the most nondescript songbird in North America. Historically, this species nested on the island and then migrated to the southern part of South America.

Appearing species

With the emergence of shrubs on Block Island, we now see a bunch of bird species that were not seen at the turn of the 20th century. The best examples of these "newcomers" are northern cardinal, Carolina wren, and eastern towhee.

Northern cardinal

This bird's population is inceasing as the shrub habitat on Block Island becomes denser. Each June I conduct a breeding bird survey and over the last seven years the northern cardinal has increased dramatically.

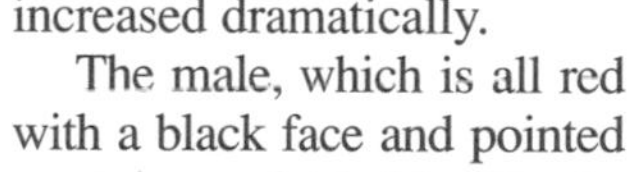

The male, which is all red with a black face and pointed crest, is unmistakable. The female is a drab buff-brown with a reddish hue on the tail and wings. Both sexes measure about 8 inches and have a large triangular orange bill. This species has a sweet-sounding "birdy, birdy, birdy" or "chew, chew, chew" song. The cardinal is a welcome addition to the island over the last century.

Carolina wren

The Carolina wren is often found nesting in garages, under decks, and in bird houses. It measures 5½ inches, is a rusty brown above with a white throat and tan belly. A defining characteristic of this species is its white eye stripe. This wren is one of the louder birds in the shrubs with a "teakettle, teakettle, teakettle, tea" song. On Block Island during non-nesting times, most flocks of birds have at least one Carolina wren in them.

Eastern towhee

The towhee has benefited from the increased shrubland because it is a species that spends a lot of time on the forest floor, kicking up leaves with its feet and looking for insects. The loud song, "drink your tea" of this species is one of the most easily recognized bird songs on Block Island.

This bird is found in shrubs and often forages on the ground, scratching with both feet. The towhee is 8½ inches long, with the males black above, rufous on the sides and white below. Females look the same except they are brown above. This species nests on the island in the summer and then most of them migrate to the southeastern United States for the winter. Each year there are always a few towhees that stick out the winter on the island.

Nature is always changing and it is amazing to think that three of the most common songbirds currently on Block Island weren't here 75 years ago. So go out and enjoy the bird species of the present because you never know when they will become just a distant memory.

The ponds of November...

Ponds follow a seasonal cycle, full in the spring, and low in the summer and early fall before starting to recharge with rainfall. Every year is different in regard to the water level in the ponds. The photos below document an extremely dry year. The one positive thing about dry years, which is drawn by old-timers from the wisdom of the years: "It won't freeze on Block Island until the ponds are full." Remember, it is the little rains that raise the pond levels. A good portion of a heavy rain does not count because it mostly runs into the ocean.

Worden's Pond, off Cooneymus Road at the big bend.

The lily pond at the Block Island Conservancy's Murray Sanctuary, across Mohegan Trail from the Painted Rock.

Vaill Pond, at the site of the former Vaill Hotel beside Mohegan Trail.

Horse Pond, at the intersection of Old Mill and Cooneymus roads.

A stroll through the Turnip Farm

Fall is the time to visit the beautiful Turnip Farm when its meadows are a sea of purple, blue, white, and yellow from its many wildflowers. This stroll with amazing panoramic views is relatively short, but connects with Nathan Mott Park and the Loffredo Loop as part of the Greenway trail system that links the Great Salt Pond with Black Rock.

The Turnip Farm parking area and trailhead are off Old Mill Road about a half a mile in from Cooneymus Road on the right. This preserve was originally owned and operated as a farm by the Mott family. There are many theories as to how it got its name but no one knows for sure.

Upon walking through the turnstile you are cast into the largest northern blazing star population in Rhode Island. This plant is described in depth on Page 86 of this book. In the western portion of the fenced enclosure the state-endangered purple needlegrass can also be found. This plant is also described on Page 86. In addition to these state-endangered plants, there are many beautiful wildflowers to be seen including butter-and-eggs, chicory, goldenrod, yarrow, mouse-ear hawkweed, and Queen Anne's lace.

While walking around the enclosure continue to look to the sky, for this is a good place to see migrating raptors as they soar around Turnip Farm looking for their next prey. In the shrubbery around the farm look for late fall songbirds, including white-crowned sparrow, white-throated sparrow, slate-colored junco, and yellow-rumped warbler.

View from one of the trails at Turnip Farm.

This open area is also a great place to see mammals like white-tailed deer, white-footed mouse, and Block Island meadow vole. These animals like areas like this one because there is a lot of food to be found and it is fairly easy to spot predators. The quieter you are, the better your chance of seeing these species.

As the trail becomes steeper, stay straight (left will take you to Dodge Cemetery), and notice how the soil becomes sandier, evidence that this is a morainal grassland. Be sure to stay on the path because there is a lot of poison ivy in this area. Many of the bushes to the left of the trail are winged sumac. This species is easily identified by the narrow "wing" that connects each leaflet (this is not a plant that will give you a rash).

Soon the trail branches to the left, which leads to the Loffredo Loop, and to the right, which ends up at Nathan Mott Park. Continuing straight you enter an area populated with common milkweed. Carefully inspecting each plant may result in finding monarch butterfly caterpillars that have black, white, and yellow horizontal striping. They are eating the milkweed and synthesizing its poison, which makes the adult monarch poisonous to predators. Please do not pick the large warty milkweed seedpods because without these the milkweed not reproduce.

The entrance to Turnip Farm off Old Mill Road.

Continuing on the hike, the trail bears left and ends at an amazing overlook. The view looks to the southwest of the island over Lewis and Dickens Farm. It is definitely one of the more spectacular views on the island. This spot is also a perfect place to watch a classic Block Island fall sunset. In addition to the wonderful flowers and scenic views at this vista, it is also an excellent place to see northern harriers and barn owls soaring over the fields looking for prey.

When finished gazing, it is time to start retracing your steps back to the trailhead. If more adventure is desired, take any one of the many trail offshoots. While this is one of the shorter Greenway segments, in the fall its beautiful wildflowers are unmatched.

Two easy-to-make birdfeeders

One of the best ways to watch birds in winter is to attract them with food. But remember, if you start feeding the birds you should continue through spring because they will depend on your feeder.

WIRE
LOTS OF PEANUT BUTTER
LOTS OF BIRDSEED
PINE CONE
STICKS FOR PERCHES
WIRE

Pine cone feeder: Find a large pine cone and two small sticks about 4 inches long. Use wire to connect the sticks in a cross pattern, then wire the cone to the sticks leaving some wire at the top as a hanger. Smother the cone in peanut butter and then roll in birdseed. Hang it out for the birds and add new peanut butter and seed as needed.

Log feeder: Find a log about 2 inches thick and 16 inches long. Nail or screw a number of plastic bottle caps to it. Add a screw-eye to the top of the log, and suspend it from a tree branch using wire or an old coat hanger. Fill each cap with a generous mixture of peanut butter and bird seed. This feeder is a good way to attract woodpeckers.

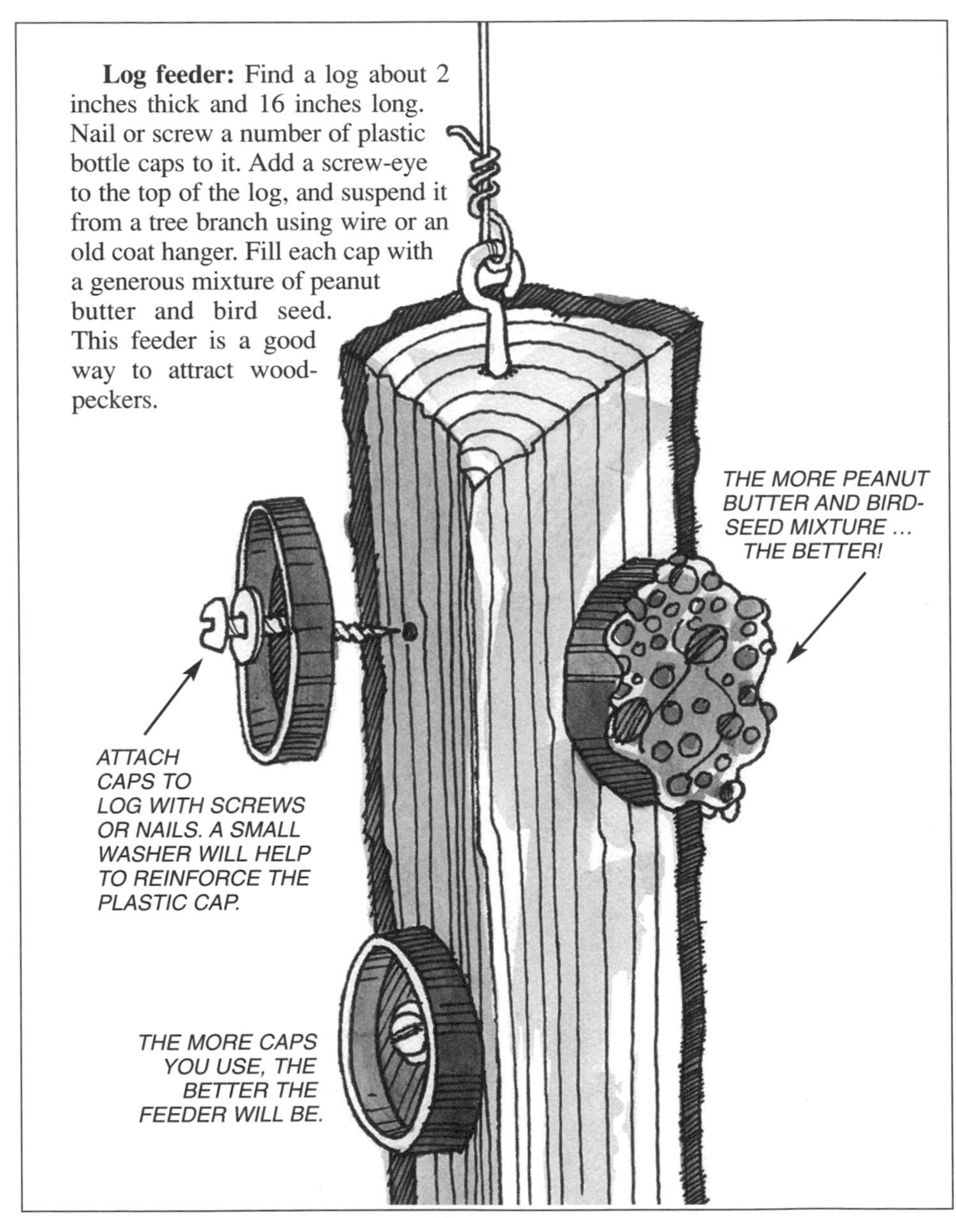

Thanksgiving is for the birds

The songbird migration is now over and our winter residents are here and feeding off the many different fruits that are still present. Some of the most common songbirds this time of year are the yellow-rumped warbler, white-throated sparrow, song sparrow, Carolina wren, black-capped chickadee and hermit thrush.

All of these birds eat the fruit you see below and could not survive on Block Island without it.

Bittersweet: This invasive plant does have one redeeming quality: it provides food for the birds. Its red center with yellow shell is unmistakable, and the birds eat it until it disappears. One of the reasons this plant is spreading so quickly is because birds spread the seeds.

Chokeberry: A fairly large berry eaten by bigger songbirds like the hermit thrush. This is not a preferred fruit, so a lot of it is left, but it too will be used as other foods vanish. This fruit disappears by the end of December.

Poison ivy: Most people don't realize that this plant has milky white berries. They have a very low protein count and thus don't rot. In late January, when the birds have exhausted all the other fruits, poison ivy berries become a mainstay of their diet. The birds then defecate the seeds which is why we have so much poison ivy.

Winterberry: This orange-red berry is found on its shrub in wet areas. The birds eat it in November, December, and January until it is all gone. Winterberry is in the holly family.

Pokeweed: This purple fruit is almost gone because it is a favorite with the birds. However, you can still find this juicy protein-filled berry in secluded spots. Look for it now because it is completely gone by December.

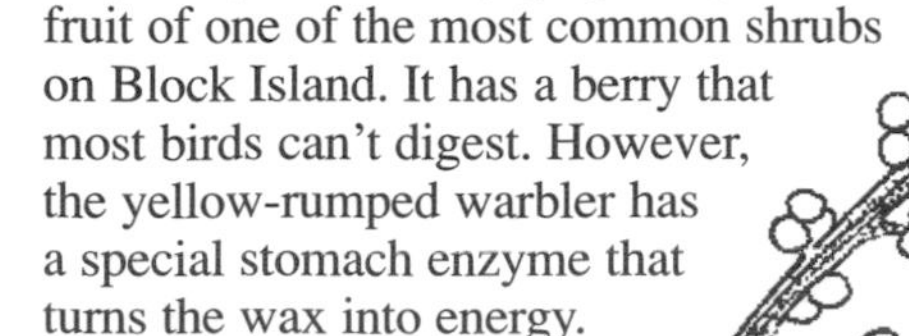

Bayberry: This waxy-gray berry is the fruit of one of the most common shrubs on Block Island. It has a berry that most birds can't digest. However, the yellow-rumped warbler has a special stomach enzyme that turns the wax into energy.

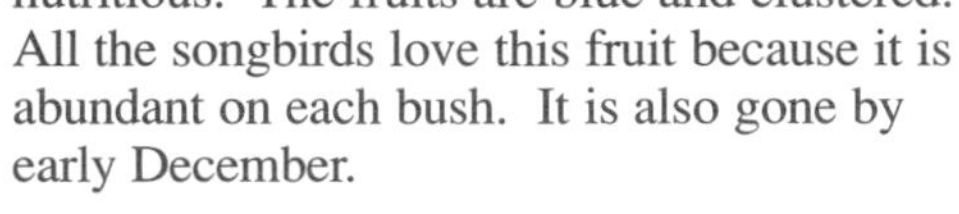

Arrowwood: This fruit is one of the most nutritious. The fruits are blue and clustered. All the songbirds love this fruit because it is abundant on each bush. It is also gone by early December.

What's for Thanksgiving dinner?

How some of Block Island's creatures spend Thanksgiving

While people in this country have a traditional Thanksgiving dinner of turkey with all the fixings, the animals of Block Island also have certain foods they eat on this day. Of course, there is a slight twist in the animal kingdom — one creature can be enjoying its Thanksgiving meal and then suddenly become the holiday meal for a larger one. This adds a whole new twist to being thankful for making it through dinner.

The following is a description of some of the meals that the most common animal species on Block Island eat on this special day.

Meadow vole

The meadow vole is the island's most interesting mammal because it is a separate subspecies from the mainland meadow vole, with a longer snout and shorter tail. This little creature is a plump mammal with short ears and beady eyes, with a body that measures 7 inches and a 2-inch-long tail. It is all brown above with a grayish underbelly. Voles are active both at night and during the day. Different types of fruit, seeds, and plant material make up the Block Island meadow vole's Thanksgiving diet.

White-throated sparrow

The white-throated sparrow is a 6-inch bird, with a black-and-white striped head and a touch of yellow around the bill. This species has an unmistakable song that sounds like a human whistle saying, "Poor old Sam Peabody, Peabody." The sparrow's Thanksgiving meal is made up of the various shrub berries that can be foraged in the winter. The two main types of fruit it eats at this time of year are winterberry and poison ivy.

Yellow-rumped warbler

Another songbird is the yellow-rumped warbler, which measures 5 inches long and has a brownish back, white-streaked breast and, most recognizable, a bright yellow rump. One of the most common songbirds, this species' loud "check" call note can often be heard in the bushes of the island at this time of year. These small birds are able to survive the harsh winters on Block Island by eating exclusively bayberry fruit, which most other animals do not eat because they are very waxy and hard to digest. However, the yellow-rumped warbler has a special enzyme in its stomach, which allows it to turn the waxy berries to energy. As you may know, wax holds a lot of energy, making the bayberry fruit a great food source for Thanksgiving and the rest of the winter for these specially adapted birds.

Norway rat

The Norway rat is the most common mammal on Block Island. Measuring 12 to 20 inches, this large rodent is brown in color with a bare, scaly tail slightly shorter in length than its body. This species spends its Thanksgiving scavenging for any type of food, plant or dead animal. Some of its favorite foods are winterberry, grass seeds and Asiatic bittersweet.

Northern harrier

The northern harrier measures 17 to 24 inches, with females being larger than males. They have an unmistakable white rump patch above the tail. Males are gray-backed and sport a white breast with brown streaking. Females are brown-backed with a white breast and brown streaking. Immature birds have a brown back and russet breast. This species' Thanksgiving meal consists of small rodents, like the white-footed mouse, and small birds, like the yellow-rumped warbler.

Barn owl

One of the most elusive animals on Block Island is the barn owl. This light-colored owl has a heart-shaped face, rusty-brown back, and measures 16 inches long. Keep your ear out for its raspy, hissing screech, which is truly unmistakable. This animal is nocturnal, so it will be celebrating its Thanksgiving at night, searching the fields for rodents — especially the Norway rat described above — a favorite holiday delicacy.

As you can see, the animals above have different Thanksgiving meals. However, all are thankful when they get to eat, and are not eaten.

Mistaken identity: meet the muskrat

Driving around Block Island, I am distressed when I see dead muskrats on the side of the road. People confuse the muskrat with the Norway rat, and deliberately try to run over this larger, slower-moving species. But the muskrat plays an important role in Block Island's ecosystem.

Muskrats are most often found in or near ponds, marshes or wetlands, and are designed for semi-aquatic life. They are classified as rodents because of four incisor teeth in the front of their mouths. Like the teeth of other rodents, the upper and lower incisors overlap, so they self-sharpen when they are used. This animal weighs between 2 and 4 pounds, with a body 10 to 14 inches in length and an 8- to 11-inch furless tail. The color of its coat ranges from silvery brown to dark brown, with a lighter-colored belly. The coat consists of soft, dense underfur and long, coarse, shiny guard hairs that keep the animal dry when in the water.

To aid in swimming, the muskrat has large, webbed hind feet and a long, vertically flattened tail, which is used like a rudder. They can swim at speeds of up to 3 miles per hour, and can even swim backwards. This amazing animal can also stay submerged for up to 15 minutes.

Muskrats are herbivorous, feeding on aquatic plants such as the roots and stems of cattails, lilies, sedges, and grasses. Folds of skin behind its front teeth allow a submerged muskrat to cut vegetation without getting water in its mouth. This animal collects vegetation during the summer months and stores it for winter use. The muskrat diet of aquatic plants helps keep wetlands from filling in with vegetation. According to the Rhode Island Natural Heritage Program, this animal was introduced to Block Island to help keep the ponds clean of cattails and other vegetation.

Muskrats are very territorial. The male of the species marks its territory with a "scent post," a mat of cut sedge leaves mixed with mud, where the animal leaves its musky secretion. This is done to keep other muskrats out of its territory. In fact, when the muskrat population becomes too dense, they will fight to the death.

Muskrats make elaborate homes in an underground den, or they build a conical lodge that can rise up to 3 feet in height. In either case, their homes are equipped with an underwater entrance, various passages and a nest chamber. They are active throughout the year, but are affected by the cold and spend long periods of time in their dens. The home range of a pair is within 200 yards of its den, although the young may travel several miles over land searching for an appropriate habitat and mate.

This species is a prolific mammal, with adult muskrats having up to five litters in one year. Normally in northeastern states, muskrats average between two and three litters a year with five or six kits (young) per litter. Female muskrats reach sexual maturity at 10 months, have a gestation period of 28 days, and raise the kits for one month before they leave the lodge.

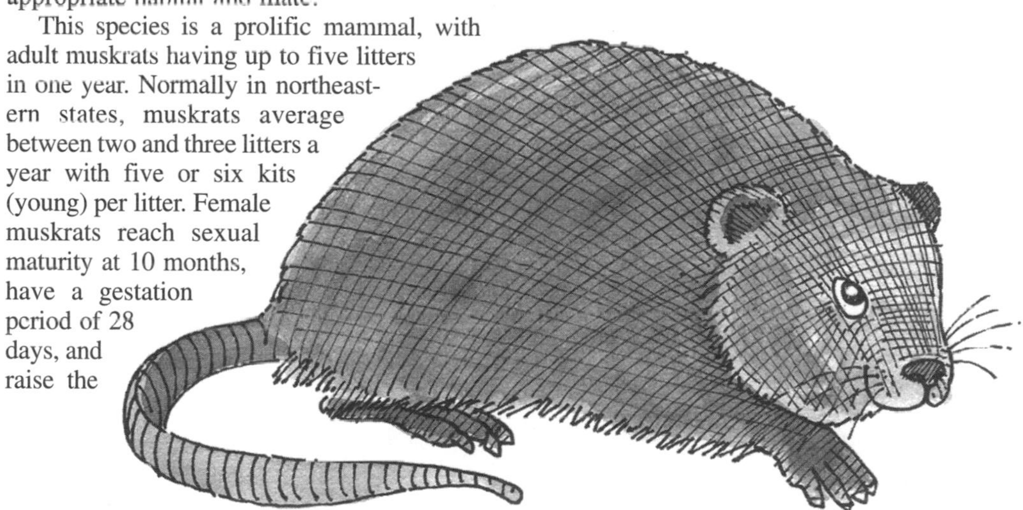

In addition to keeping the wetlands from filling in, muskrats are a source of food. Smaller muskrats are eaten by barn owls and northern harriers, while adults provide food for large raptors such as the bald eagle.

So the next time you see a large rodent on the road with a tail as long as its body, remember, it's a muskrat — and you should let it be because it is beneficial to the Block Island ecosystem.

All you need to know about seals

Seals use Block Island's beaches for rest stops from November to May. While they may seem cute and approachable, it is best to give them plenty of space, for both your sake and theirs.

The seals need to rest and can become aggressive if approached, and if provoked can give a nasty infectious bite. So always enjoy watching them from a distance.

Observers can spot four different species here: harbor seals, a common visitor; gray seals, which are less common; harp seals, which are uncommon; and hooded seals, which are rare.

Seals like to rest on rocks or beaches, a practice called "hauling out." When people walking on the beaches come into contact with resting seals, they often wonder what to do. In most cases, the answer is to give them a wide berth. Stay at least 50 yards away, and restrain your pets. The seals will not be able to rest if they are continually approached, and their body rhythms may be seriously disturbed. And do not worry if you see a small seal pup alone, resting after a long swim, even if it is not moving and appears dry — they sometimes sleep for long periods of time.

A pair of harbor seals "hauled out" on a rock.

You know you are getting too close if the seals are all looking at you, if they start to make more noise, lift their heads to look at you, or start to move back into the water.

Seals are protected by the Federal Marine Mammal Protection Act, which states it is illegal to touch, feed, or otherwise harass seals. Individuals may be fined up to $20,000 for violating this law.

Never get in the water with seals. They are big animals and if threatened can become aggressive.

Limit your viewing time to 30 minutes.

Call the Mystic Aquarium at 860-572-5955, extension 107, or The Nature Conservancy at 466-2129, if you see any of the following things: the seal is bleeding profusely (not just a little cut but a serious gash); is entangled in rope, fishing gear, or other foreign objects; remains "hauled out" in the same place for 24 hours; or is dead.

Using the rules above, enjoy observing seals and call only in the above cases. These special marine mammals deserve our respect and care.

Seals in bad weather

A common question I get, when leading seal programs for the Block Island School, is where do seals go when the weather is bad? This is an appropriate question with the stormy weather we regularly get throughout the winter. The short answer is just because the weather is bad to us, it is not bad for them.

When seals are swimming in the water the weather going on above them does affect them. However, with turbulent water, not all seals use the same strategy for riding out what we consider to be bad weather. If the waves are large and the wind strong, seals may move further offshore, to the lee side of the island or into sheltered areas like Cormorant Cove.

One circumstance where poor weather directly affects seals is when it is stormy and the waves are too big for the seals to "haul out" (climb up and rest on rocks) without getting knocked off, such as by St. Andrew's Parish Center on Spring Street. In this case they either stay in the area and do not haul out, or they go to a place where there is less disturbance for them.

One of the reasons you may see seals swimming in areas where they cannot haul out is that there might be better opportunities to feed than when it is calm. The reason for this is that in the murky water, the seals can sneak up on prey before they are seen. On calm days, when the water is clear, it is easy for prey to see the seals coming, so it may make more sense energetically to haul out and rest.

Just remember: the next time the weather is horrible, try and be more like a seal and not let it bother you!

Winter

Winter is the harshest time to be on Block Island, with high winds and cold temperatures commonplace. However, there is also a lot of beauty and wildlife to be found if you are willing to brave the weather and get out to look around.

Visibility is never clearer than it is in the winter. There is a lot happening out on the ocean, and this is the time to see it: from whales, porpoises, and dolphins frolicking in the distant cold sea waters to a wide assortment of sea ducks and seals near the shore.

On really cold days there is the amazing sea smoke, a fog that rises off the ocean when the air is much colder than the water. It is on these days that Block Island feels like a mystical place; at least until you go outside where you are quickly brought back to the reality of bone-chilling temperatures.

Winter is also the time for spectacular surf and no-boat days. When the wind howls all night, which is fairly often during this time of year, it is quite a bit of fun (unless you were supposed to leave on this day) to go around to different spots on the island and check out the size of the waves.

While most of the vegetation this time of year is dormant, it also means better views into the wilds that are Block Island. It is always amazing what you can see and how different things look once the leaves drop. In fact, this is the best time to find bird nests (of course, no longer in use) on the island.

Winter is also the only time to see snowy owls, majestic animals that only visit once every few years. Believe it or not, there are actually quite a few birds (both songbirds and ducks) that spend only the winter here before heading north for the rest of the year.

For people who live on Block Island this is the time of year to catch up with friends, decompress from last summer, and prepare for the next one. Recreation is also a large part of the winter when the ponds are frozen, with ice-skating and ice-boating common activities.

While winter is always difficult with the short days, high winds, and frigid temperatures, it is also when it is easiest to find the spirit that is Block Island. That is why when asked how long you have lived here, most people answer by stating how many winters they have done.

As hard as winters can be, there are always a few sunny days that are warm for the season sprinkled in, when Block Island is as beautiful as it ever gets. It is during these times that animals are extremely active, the beaches are full of shells to be combed through, and you truly feel like you are in god's country.

Spending the whole winter on Block Island is an acquired taste and obviously not for everyone; but if you have not had at least a short experience with this place in the winter, I recommend it. I promise it is something that you will remember for both its beauty and brutality for a long time.

A Christmas visit to the Hodge Preserve

In between all of the festivities around Christmas it is great to get outside and take a hike with your family. In my mind the Hodge Family Wildlife Preserve is the place, located on the left-hand side of Corn Neck Road north of the Transfer Station. This hike with gentle slopes has something to offer for everyone, from dramatic views to excellent birdwatching.

The 24.8-acre Hodge property was conserved in 2002 by the Block Island Land Trust, Block Island Conservancy, Town of New Shoreham, and The Nature Conservancy at a cost of $8.5 million. While this was a substantial amount of money for conservation to come up with, and in fact much money is still owed on the property, once you walk it, I am sure you will agree it was worth it.

The trailhead on this property begins at the northern end of the parking lot, which was once a barnyard. In fact, there was a barn where the Phragmities (tall grass) is now, which blew down many years ago during a storm.

As you start the walk, the trail meanders through meadow habitat comprised of goldenrod, milkweed, aster, butter-and-eggs, and many other wildflowers. Before the trail turns to the right be sure to notice the cleared area with a big tree in it. This is where the Hodge family's house once stood. This house burned in the early 1970s and was never rebuilt. When conservation bought the property we removed what was left of the house because it was a safety hazard. Be sure to look at the view from here because it is truly spectacular.

Continuing down the trail, be sure to stay on the path through this section because there is lots of poison ivy. While no one likes this plant, its fruit is very important to the birds of Block Island as their main food throughout the winter. Bearing left at the large shadbush, the trail starts toward Middle Pond.

The trail then goes through coastal shrub habitat, which is also very important to the birds of Block Island. Be sure to look for winterberry, which is in the holly family and makes me think of Christmas. After walking for a few minutes, there is a spur trail to the right. This is definitely worth it because it has the most dramatic views of the property.

After turning on to the spur, the trail goes through what is the largest common milkweed field in the preserve. In the fall there will be lots of monarch butterflies, but right now everything is dormant. Soon a stonewall is reached where beautiful views of Sachem Pond, Sandy Point, and the North Light can be seen. While this is the boundary of the property, this view will never change because the next lot, called the Breed land, is owned by the Town of New Shoreham.

Continue to hike on the spur and soon it will link up with the main trail to Middle Pond. Take time to look to the left because there are wonderful views of the Niles Swamp, named after one of the island's original families. After a little ways the trail branches, with each offshoot ending up in the same place after a short distance, and after an equal distance the trail dead-ends at Middle Pond. This is one of the larger coastal ponds on the island and is extremely important in the wintertime for ducks.

Some of the more common species this time of year are the bufflehead, common goldeneye, ruddy duck, and American black duck, to name a few. The technical term for a group of ducks when on the water is raft. See how many different types of ducks you can spot.

After inspecting the pond, it is time to turn around and start the journey back to the trailhead.

Although you are mostly walking on the same trail, you will notice new things because of your different perspective. If you have not already, you are sure to notice the many bluebird boxes throughout the preserve. These were built and installed by Kim Gaffett and George Dodge in the spring of 2004. While none were used by bluebirds, they were used by many different species that summer including eastern kingbird, Carolina wren, and black-capped chickadee.

The walk back to the trailhead is faster if you do not take the spur trail, and after a little hike the parking lot is reached. To walk all the trails on the Hodge property takes about an hour, which is a perfect amount of time for a hike during the winter on Block Island. For those people who like the cold this is a great place to take a sunset jaunt.

During Christmas do not forget to get outside and work off some of the holiday calories while experiencing one of Block Island's most incredible places, the Hodge Family Wildlife Preserve. I hope to see you there!

The Christmas Bird Count

Since 1999, Block Island School students have assisted with the Christmas Bird Count. They have braved many cold windy days to be a part of this important island tradition, and have added much enthusiasm to it.

Nationally, the Christmas Bird Count began in 1900 with 27 participants recording data in 25 different locations. In 2004, there were more than 50,000 people participating at over 1,000 sites. The information recorded gives scientists broad data to see trends in bird populations.

On Block Island, Elizabeth Dickens started the Christmas Bird Count in the 1920s, and local school children have participated in many of them. Currently, Block Island's Christmas Bird Count is one of three that occur in Rhode Island. The goal of each count is to see how many bird species and individuals can be found in a given day for a specific area. For each count there are different parties that search throughout the island for bird species both common and unique, recording each of them. Since 1999, the Block Island School students, their teachers, and I have comprised one party and our search area is around the school.

The following results from Jan. 9, 2004, are an excellent example of a typical Christmas Bird Count for the Block Island School party.

Due to the extreme cold, much of the birdwatching was from the nature van, which worked surprisingly well. The first grade participated in the count right after the school day began. Soon after we started, a flock of 20 Canada geese flew past the van. Excitedly we recorded the data on our field checklist. We also got an amazing look at a northern mockingbird eating multiflora rosehips. These birds barely moved, allowing each student a chance to practice with their binoculars. Most of the birds we saw were puffed up, which allows the birds to keep more heat close to their bodies.

The preschool was next, searching high and low for new species. After a while we found a flock of white-throated sparrows. Eight of these beautiful birds were foraging on the ground, and the students were lucky to see these birds up close. We also enjoyed seeing a mourning dove patiently sitting on a phone wire.

Although it was still cold outside, the sun was now getting higher in the sky, and the birds seemed more active. At Sands Pond with the third grade we saw common goldeneyes, buffleheads, and mallards. The students also learned that a group of ducks on a pond is called a raft of ducks.

The sixth and seventh grades also spent time at Sands Pond. Both groups saw many herring and great black-backed gulls, and a large raft of mallards. It was definitely becoming apparent that on this day it was a lot easier to see waterfowl on the non-iced-over ponds than songbirds that were mostly hunkered down in the bushes.

At Payne Farm with students from the high school we found very little in the way of birds. However, a few American crows popped up, along with a couple of yellow-rumped warblers. We definitely had to work very hard to find any birds to record.

At the end of the school day, the fifth grade and their kindergarten friends walked down Payne Road looking for any avian creatures. A beautiful male northern cardinal was spotted along with a Cooper's hawk soaring and a pair of black-capped chickadees chattering.

The end tally for this very cold and windy day, combining all the school groups, was a hard-earned 31 species and 478 different individuals. The following species were seen: great cormorant, Canada goose, American black duck, mallard, common goldeneye, bufflehead, red-breasted merganser, northern harrier, Cooper's hawk, ring-necked pheasant, herring gull, great black-backed gull, sanderling, mourning dove, northern flicker, blue jay, American crow, fish crow, black-capped chickadee, Carolina wren, hermit thrush, American robin, northern mockingbird, European starling, yellow-rumped warbler, northern cardinal, song sparrow, white-throated sparrow, slate-colored junco, house finch, and house sparrow.

An average Block Island Christmas Bird Count when all the parties' results are tallied, is between 90 and 100 different bird species. For the results of any of the recent Block Island counts, check out the birdsource.org web site.

Since 1999, over 100 different Block Island School students have participated in the Christmas Bird Count. Each got a chance to observe birds and be a part of an on going scientific study. Hopefully, it is something they will always remember.

The twelve species of Christmas: Part 1

It being the holiday season, most plants have lost their leaves and many of the animals have headed south, but there are still a lot of plants and animals to observe and enjoy. This holiday season, take a walk outside and see how many of these 12 species of Christmas you can find!

Harbor seals.

A number of these species can be seen only on Block Island in the winter. For instance, one of our favorite winter residents, the **harbor seal**, has just returned. This marine mammal is between 5 and 6 feet in length, and weighs up to 220 pounds. It is light gray to brown in color, with darker blotches. This time of year, 60 percent of its body is fat in order to keep it warm in the cold waters. The best places on Block Island to see these special creatures are the rocks below St. Andrew's Parish Center and Cormorant Cove. Please remember not to get too close or you will disturb seals when they are "hauled out" (resting on the beach or rocks).

The **white-tailed deer** is another animal that can easily be spotted on Block Island. Although they are the bane of many people's existence because they damage gardens and host the ticks that carry Lyme disease, this large mammal is still fun to watch. When a deer is scared, notice how it raises and wags its tail. This is to warn other deer in the area of danger. It is also fun when you come across bucks to see how many points they have on their antlers.

White-tailed deer.

Another bird seen more frequently in recent years is the **red-breasted nuthatch**. This small songbird has a slate-blue back and a reddish breast with an upturned bill, and it likes the habitat provided by the large pine trees on the island. Because of its nasally "yank, yank, yank" call and the fact that it runs down trees headfirst, it is easy to distinguish in the field.

Red-breasted nuthatch.

The brilliant red of the male **northern cardinal** also brightens up the drab wintertime shrub habitat. This bird has a large, orange, conical beak, a black face and a pointed crest. The cardinal's beak allows it to eat seeds that most other birds cannot crack. In recent years this species has become quite common on the island.

The **red cedar** is the closest thing to a Christmas tree among the island's trees and shrubs, but do not cut this tree down because it provides optimum cover for songbirds from hawks and other predators. The fact that this tree does not lose its needles makes its green color stand out among the gray and dormant shrubs. Next time you go for a walk in the winter, see how many cedars you can find.

Red cedar.

Little bluestem, a native grass, has turned a nice golden brown for the winter. Even though this species is now dormant, it is important for shelter for many of the island's mice and voles. This grass can be seen in areas where there is sandy soil and on morainal grasslands (hilltops in the southwestern part of the island). If you look underneath the grass you can see the little trails created by the small mammals.

Winterberry.

One of the animals making these trails in the little bluestem is the **Block Island meadow vole**. This animal is slightly larger than a mouse, with a brown back and a gray stomach. It is considered a subspecies because it has a longer snout and a shorter tail than the mainland meadow vole. In the winter this animal eats grass seeds and berries and is a source of food for barn owls and northern harriers (marsh hawks).

One of the most festive plants this time of year is the **winterberry**, which is in the holly family. Its bright red berries are unmistakable. This shrub is very important to birds and rodents as a source of food during the lean winter months. This shrub is often seen surrounding ponds and wetlands.

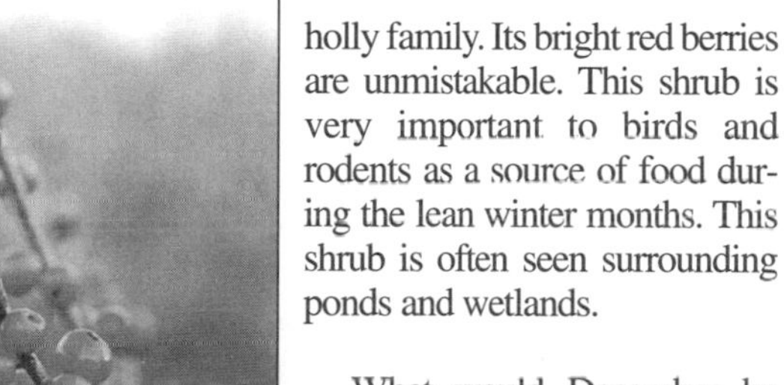

Snowy owl.

What would December be without snow! Three animals on this list have this cold white stuff in their name. The first is the **snow bunting**, a 6-inch member of the finch family that has white on the breast and brown on its back. No other songbird has so much white on it. Often found in flocks that flush from the ground on the way out to Sandy Point or Hippocampus (Beane Point), this is one of the most beautiful birds that you can see in the winter.

The **snowy owl** is unmistakable, a large white bird with bright yellow eyes. This majestic animal is often seen on the tops of open hills or dunes.

Another large white bird is the **snow goose**, which is all white in color except for black at the tip of the wings. These birds are often seen in V-formation flying over the island. Sometimes they set down in grassy areas and you can then see their pink bills and feet.

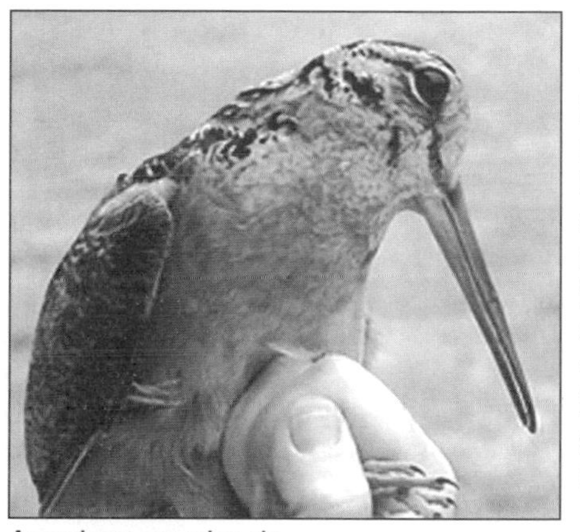

American woodcock.

Finally, the plump **American woodcock** can often be scared up in December. This rotund, almost neckless brown bird with a long bill and eyes that look like they are about to pop out can often be found in wet grassy areas. This incredible creature can make special movements with its bill, which it uses to probe for worms in the mud. Often the only way to see it is to step close to it so that it flushes into the air.

These 12 species are just a few of the many special plants and animals to be seen in winter. One way that you can give a gift back to wildlife this holiday season is to manage your property to provide food and shelter for them in the future. If you have shrubs, it is good to leave them, and if you have open grassy areas away from your house, please wait to mow them until spring because they provide good cover.

Should you have any further questions about how to better manage your property for wildlife, call me at The Nature Conservancy, 466-2129.

Please note:

Whereas there are pear trees on Block Island, there are no partridges. And, although there are turtles, there are no turtle doves.

The twelve species of Christmas: Part 2

Christmas is a time to be thankful for the world around you. I find this is especially true in regard to the plants and animals that brighten up our days and help make the winter more bearable. For them it is an extremely tough time of year with harsh weather and reduced amounts of food available. When you start to look it is amazing how many species are here in the winter; these are 12 of their stories.

The gray seal, the second most common seal on Block Island, appears in December. This marine mammal is between 7 and 8 feet in length ,and weighs up to 800 pounds. It is easy to distinguish from other seals by its large head (when compared to body) and nostrils that are shaped like a "W." Unlike the harbor seal, this species mostly hauls out on the beach. The best places on Block Island to see this cool creature are Crescent Beach, Cow Cove and Cormorant Cove. Most of the gray seals that visit Block Island are young, have just swum a great distance, and need to rest. Make sure not to disturb this species by observing from a distance

Gray seal.

Another mammal, although terrestrial, is the **white-footed mouse**. It is 7 inches long with a 3-inch tail, and reddish-brown above with white undersides and feet. This rodent eats mostly seeds and nuts, caching them in piles throughout its home range. This hearty soul is active at night throughout the winter except in extremely harsh weather. It is also an important food source for the wintertime raptors of Block Island.

Switch grass.

Switch grass, a native species, is a favorite hiding spot of the white-footed mouse. This 3-foot grass is found in areas with sandy soil, and is dormant this time of year. It is light-brown in color and usually found in clumps. Further investigation at the base of this species can illuminate a network of rodent trails that are used all winter.

Another plant that is important in the winter months is **bayberry**. This coastal shrub can reach 15 feet in height, and is identified this time of year by its gray waxy berries. These berries are extremely important to the yellow-rumped warbler, which has a special enzyme in its stomach to digest the wax of the berry and turn it into energy. As a wintertime project you can pick the berries and boil off the wax and make candles. It takes about 9 pounds of berries to make one bayberry candle.

Bayberry.

One of the rarest plants on Block Island is the native type of **Phragmites.** Most people know the exotic form of the tall reedy grass that can be found at the entrance to Mosquito Beach, but there is also a native form that was just rediscovered on the island in 2002 (the last island record was from the 1880s). This species is only found in a few places in New England, with two populations being found on Block Island (near the road into the Sullivan House and on the old Ocean View property).

Native Phragmites.

A common sight on Block Island, this time of year, is the **slate-colored junco**. This 6-inch bird has a dark gray back with a white breast. Its most distinguishing characteristics are a pink bill and white outer tail feathers that are flashed while feeding. This bird eats mostly seeds, and can be seen at birdfeeders and in almost any songbird flock in the winter.

Another bird found in the shrublands is the **fox sparrow.** This 7 1/2 inch sparrow has a streaked breast and a bright rufous tail, which becomes obvious when the bird flies. This flash of red when the bird flies is reminiscent of a fox's tail, hence the name. This species is only found on Block Island in the winter searching for berries and seeds.

Often found foraging with the slate-colored junco is the **white-throated sparrow.** This species spends from

White-throated sparrow.

late fall to early spring on Block Island. It measures 7 inches, is brown above, white below, with yellow nares (area at the base of the upper part of the bill) and a striped head. Often heard in the winter is this species' distinctive song, "poor old Sam Peabody, Peabody," which sounds like a human whistling.

Another seed-eating bird is the **downy woodpecker.** This species is the smallest woodpecker on Block Island with a white back, white-spotted black wings, and a red nape. This woodpecker lives on the island all year and is often found where there is standing deadwood or a birdfeeder.

Downy woodpecker.

One of the larger birds on Block Island is the **ring-necked pheasant,** which was introduced in the 1920s. This unmistakable species is originally from Asia and has now become naturalized on the island. Interestingly, the island is one of the few places in New England where the population is self-sustaining and no new individuals have to be released for hunting. The main food for the pheasant in early winter is Asiatic bittersweet, a favorite food from the land where the species originated.

Dovekie.

With some luck, the **dovekie** can be seen from the beach floating out in the ocean. This chubby 8-inch bird has a black bill, head, and back with a white breast and throat. It is definitely one of the wintertime birds that is most difficult to see. It is easiest to locate the species after a storm when they come closer to shore for shelter.

A common bird species on the beach during this time of year is the **sanderling**. This 8-inch sandpiper has a gray back and white breast and is fairly nondescript. However, its behavior of repeatedly following retreating waves and then running away from impending surf makes identification quite easy. Sanderlings are often found in groups of 10 or more making their way up and down the beach.

These 12 species are examples of the many species that can be seen on Block Island during this time of year. Remember, Christmas is a wonderful time to explore the island and enjoy nature's gifts. Do not forget to make your own list of Christmas species.*

** Note: Flying and/or red-nosed reindeer don't count.*

Make your own list here:

Wintertime treasures

One of the positive things about the stark winter landscape, with the brush mostly barren of leaves, is finding treasures that wwere hidden during the more verdant months: bird nests. These nests, inhabited last summer but empty now, come in all shapes, sizes and locations. As soon as the leaves disappear, they magically begin to appear.

Because much of Block Island's vegetation is so dense, nobody has ever done a nest-searching study to establish a complete list of summer-breeding birds. Instead, avian researchers have relied on singing males in the early summer to establish this list, which continues to be revised each year.

Wintertime, when it is long past most birds' breeding season, is the best time to find these delicate structures. The time and energy spent by one or both parents to build a nest and the longevity of the nests is truly amazing.

Upon finding a nest, five basic questions will help birders identify the species that constructed it. Ask yourself what type of habitat the nest is in; how high off the ground it is; how big the nest is; what type of nest it is; and what materials were used to construct it.

Learning to identify bird nests is similar to beginning birding; learn the common species first, and over time you will pick up the rarer birds as you see them. Below you will find the answers to the five basic questions to help identify some of Block Island's most common songbird nests. For more advanced nest identification, use the *Peterson Field Guide to Eastern Birds' Nests*.

Gray catbird

This species typically nests in dense thickets, shrubs, or marshy areas 3 to 10 feet above the ground. The nest's outside diameter is around 14 inches, and its height is about 9 inches. It is a sizeable nest with a bulky foundation and cup-shaped with an open top. It is constructed using twigs, grapevines, grasses and leaves, and the interior is lined with roots. The pair builds the nest, but the female does most of the work.

American robin

The robin nests in barns, houses, shrubs, garden edges or thickets and rarely nests on the ground. The nest's outside diameter measures 7 inches; its height, 3 inches. It is a deeply cupped nest made of grasses and plant stalks, which are woven into wet mud at the base (used to adhere the nest to the tree limb or ledge). The female builds the nest on her own.

Common yellowthroat

Thickets, swamps, shrubs, or hedgerows are where this bird typically nests. The nest is located anywhere from ground level to 3 feet above, and has a 4-inch outside diameter and thickness. This nest is bulky and significantly anchored to abutting vegetation. It is made of weedy stems, ferns, bark, leaves and lined with fine grasses or roots. This cupped nest is built solely by the female and often takes only two days.

Northern cardinal

The cardinal nests in stands of trees, gardens, thickets, or shrub edges and ranges in height from 3 to 20 feet above the ground. The outside diameter of the nest is about 10 inches, with a thickness of 8 inches. It is flimsily constructed with twigs, leaves, bark, grasses and lined with hair. This cup-like nest is constructed in three to nine days by the female with the occasional assistance of the male.

Eastern towhee

This species builds its nest in brushy fields, thickets, shrub edges, or hedgerows, and the nest is usually 2 to 5 feet above the ground. The outside diameter of the nest is 5 inches, with a thickness of 4 inches. This well-built nest is composed of leaves, bark, twigs, and lined with fine grasses or pine needles. The female builds this cupped nest in about five days.

Song sparrow

This species is the most common nesting songbird on Block Island and can be found throughout the island. Nests range in height from just off the ground to 12 feet and have an outside diameter of 5 to 9 inches, with a thickness of 5 inches. It is constructed of grasses, leaves and bark and lined with roots or hair. The cup-shaped nest is built by the female in five to 10 days.

While the nests described above are the most common, there are still many other types of nests to be found around the island. It is unbelievable how many can be located once you start looking. Each nest is unique, a true wintertime treasure!

Gray catbird's nest

Meet the yellow-rumped warbler

While I was staring out my window trying to decide what aspect of Block Island's flora or fauna to write about for this section of the book, a flock of yellow-rumped warblers flew into a bayberry bush and started devouring the berries, oblivious to everything else around them except for the waxy, blue-gray berries. Though tiny — the yellow-rumped warbler measures only 5 inches long and weighs about 10 grams — and common to Block Island, these winter residents are amazing and well worth a page all to themselves.

Most recognizable by its bright yellow rump, this warbler has a trill-like mating song that rises in pitch, then falls off. The rest of the year it relies on a loud "check" call that can often be heard coming out of island bushes during the fall and winter.

In the spring, the yellow-rumped warbler leaves Block Island, flying to northern New England to nest in conifer and mixed forest stands. They return to the shelter of the island's thickets in the fall as they migrate south to Panama. Block Island's bayberry shrubs are such a good food source that many of them stay on for the winter.

The yellow-rumped warbler.

The yellow-rumped warbler has a predilection for bayberries, the fruit of the shrub that covers the island with dense thickets. Most other animals find the waxy fruit difficult to digest, but the fortunate warbler has an enzyme in its stomach that enables the bird to digest it.

Wax is an ideal food source for surviving the winter because it holds a lot of energy. Bayberry supports a large population of these warblers. In fact, a recent bird count found more than 800 overwintering warblers, each one itself contributing to the process that makes the bayberry so common here: propagation by air-borne consumers. Bayberry seeds are dispersed when the yellow-rumped warblers excrete them as they flit from bush to bush in search of food or shelter.

This time of the year, the yellow-rumped warblers travel in flocks for protection from predators like the northern harrier, Cooper's hawk, and feral cats. Thanks to this flocking behavior, they are very easy to see. One moment there may be no activity on a bayberry bush, and the next it is swarming with birds. Once the warblers find a fruit-covered bush they will stay there until they eat all the food or are scared away, making it very easy to observe this species' behavior.

It is easy to encourage the yellow-rumped warblers on your property. Just stop mowing — the bayberry will fill in and draw them like a magnet. Try allowing some bushes to grow near a window of your house to get the best opportunities for viewing.

Although it is a common bird, we are extremely lucky to have the cheery yellow-rumped warbler on Block Island to brighten our winters! It is an ingenious species that has figured out a way to survive here during the harshest months of the year.

Snowy owl blessings

Snowy owls do not bless Block Island with their presence every winter. When they do appear it is usually starting around Thanksgiving, and they can be spotted throughout the island from Rodman's Hollow to Sandy Point. Their island-wide activity allows many lucky people a chance to see this amazing bird. Anyone who has seen this species in the past is usually thrilled and awed by an encounter.

The snowy owl, *Nyctea scandiaca*, is an unmistakable large white owl measuring 23 inches, with a rounded head and bright yellow eyes. Dark bars and spots on the white feathers are more common of females and young birds. This animal has large talons (claws) that it uses to kill its prey, and feathers covering its legs so that it can keep warm in the cold climate in which it lives. It is the largest owl on Block Island and can easily be distinguished from the wintertime white-plumaged barn owl by eye color (barn owls have dark eyes) and size (barn owls measure 16 inches).

The presence of snowy owls on Block Island depends on the lemming population on the open tundra of Canada and Alaska. For some unknown reason the lemming population crashes about every four years. When this happens the owls wander south to find food. Block Island is on their path and a few owls stop here and feed for the winter. Normally when there are multiple reports on Block Island there are also many throughout the Northeast. Some adventurous snowy owls will go as far south as Alabama and Oklahoma.

During a lemming crash the snowy owl, which eats almost exclusively lemmings, expands its diet to include other rodents, birds, fish, and marine invertebrates. The owls must not only migrate, but also will not breed in years when the lemmings have crashed. In years where the lemming population is thriving, the female owl lays more eggs and may have multiple broods.

On Block Island you can see the snowy owl perched on a stump, rock, or on the ground in the sand dunes or fields looking for its next meal. This species rarely perches in trees. A snowy owl can be seen flying or perching at any time during the day. They can most often be seen where there is food. Thus the area from Settlers' Rock to Sandy Point and on the beach below Clay Head tend to be great spots to see this incredible bird because there are lots of birds and rodents to eat. Other places where snowy owls have been seen in the past are West Beach, Andy's Way, Charlestown Beach, the airport, Mohegan Bluffs, and Lewis-Dickens Farm.

Just because you go to these spots does not mean you are going to see the bird. You must put your time in — the more effort spent exploring beach and grassland habitat, the better your chance of catching a glimpse of this bird. If you are blessed by seeing one, quietly observe its activities but do not get too close.

Of the many species of birds that I have seen on Block Island, very few measure up to the snowy owl's combination of size and beauty. Hopefully you are lucky enough to see one some winter when they are here. Remember that if you miss it, the wait will be a few years until your next opportunity to view this bird on Block Island.

The amazing snowy owl.

Snow days: how the animals weather a storm

When it snows prolific amounts, as it does in the winter, it is always a challenging time for the animals that are active all winter.

During an actual snowstorm, animals are hunkered down, and do not eat much of anything. Afterward they become more active, as they tackle the difficulties of finding food. While they are out and about during this period of activity, it is a good time to observe them.

The snow, of course, makes it much easier to see footprints and identify the creatures that are coming and going. For example, in my yard alone there have been tracks from the white-tailed deer, Block Island meadow vole, Norway rat, and white-footed mouse, not to mention many different songbird tracks.

If you follow the tracks, you may be lucky enough to see the animals that made them. Other times it is just a confusing maze of footprints. After one storm, I was able to follow some of the rodent tracks back to dens where rodents had recently excavated the snow from the entrance to their home.

For many animals, the usual pattern of foraging changes after a snowstorm. Instead of their normal routine, they seek out areas that don't have a lot of snow. These areas become 'oases' where animals can find food. While these oases can be anywhere, chances are they are in more exposed areas where the snow has been blown away. Usually if you find a drift, nearby you will find a bare spot or oasis.

These areas are often densely packed with many different species around the clock. In the daytime, an observer might see all sorts of different birds including the white-throated sparrow, song sparrow, northern cardinal, yellow-rumped warbler, and ring-necked pheasant. At night, the visitors include most of Block Island's mammals.

The animals' behavior while foraging after a storm demonstrates just how hungry they are after not eating much while the heavens opened — and the longer the storm, the more desperate they are for food. Often, they are more worried about finding food than they are about the threat of predators, and an observer can walk pretty much right up to them without them paying any attention.

But that is not to say that getting too close is a good idea. The animals do not have any energy to spare on activities that are not vital to their survival, including avoiding you. So an important rule when watching animals foraging after a storm is to make sure to give them space.

In the cold morning that follows a snowstorm, you will find that most birds are puffed up. By doing this birds increase the loft (thickness) of their down feathers, helping them hold in more heat.

In addition to increasing loft, birds often spend time on the south side of houses, where temperatures are slightly higher, to cut down on the energy they spend staying warm. There, they tend to probe around looking for food in shingles and on windowsills.

It's vital to remember that if you have feeders around your house, you must continue to fill them. The birds in your area will have come to depend on this food source. I recommend filling your feeders before a storm comes and then keeping a close eye on it while there is snow cover. Chances are that during periods like these, the feeder will have to be refilled more often.

The Block Island meadow vole, white-footed mouse, house mouse and Norway rat have a similar diet to birds at this time of year, comprised mostly of seeds, berries, and the occasional invertebrate. White-tailed deer continue to search for red cedar and other conifers, rose hips, and other foliage. In fact, the deer actually benefit from the snow because it lowers branches they normally could not reach. It also weighs down garden netting, allowing them greater access to the food in your garden.

Snowstorms often negatively alter the daily routine for humans and animals alike; but they can also provide a unique opportunity to observe the many species that brave it through the rough Block Island winter.

Meadow vole runs through dunes and fields

Have you ever seen a meadow vole on Block Island? This small animal is the island's most interesting mammal because it is a separate subspecies from the mainland meadow vole. This rodent is often seen running through meadows and dunes. When taking a closer look in these habitats, one can often find a "runway system," which is made by the vole clipping vegetation along the sides of its passage.

The meadow vole is a plump mammal with short ears and beady eyes and a body that measures 7 inches, plus a 2-inch-long tail. Its longer snout and shorter tail distinguishes it from the mainland meadow vole. It is all brown in the summer; in the winter the underbelly becomes grayish. When walking the beach look for its hindprint, which measures 5/8 of an inch and displays five wildly splayed toes. This animal is active both at night and during the day.

Different types of fruit, seed, and plant material make up the Block Island meadow vole's diet. It is also an important food source for the state endangered northern harrier and barn owl, as well as for other raptors.

The Block Island meadow vole is one of the most prolific mammals. A vole has from six to 17 litters a year, consisting of three to 10 young. The number of litters and young depend on the temperature and how much food is available. Nest areas are usually found in grass clumps, under boards, or in thickets. In the winter when it is too cold to nest, the vole looks for food using the runway system, or goes underground in harsh weather. If it snows, the vole will make a new runway system so it can forage.

A separate species?

In 1998, The Nature Conservancy and the University of Rhode Island decided to undertake a study to see whether the Block Island meadow vole was a separate species from the voles on the mainland. Two factors already supported this notion: 1) the Block Island meadow vole population had been isolated from the mainland population for over 6,000 years; 2) the Block Island meadow vole was physically different from the mainland meadow vole.

With Professor Tom Husband, a study was designed to compare the DNA of the two subspecies. On Block Island and in South County voles were captured and blood samples taken. With the help of his graduate students, Dr. Husband ran the samples through his laboratory and compared the two.

Unfortunately the results were not conclusive, but there is some evidence that the Block Island meadow vole is a separate species. To answer this question definitively, more research must be completed.

Whether the Block Island meadow vole is a separate species or subspecies, it is a unique animal. If you are interested in encouraging this species on your property, it is easy: just mow once a year in the spring, which will turn the habitat into a meadow. Some of the vole's favorite plants on the island are switch grass, little bluestem, and American beach grass.

Although a rodent, the Block Island meadow vole is another animal that is special to the island. So remember, the next time you are on the beach or in a meadow, look for this plump creature. If you do not like little furry animals, at least look for their runway system, which is really neat!

The formation of Block Island

One look at the rolling topography of the island, and its glacial history becomes apparent. This is seen under the ground as well, with the dramatic changes in soil from sand to gravel to clay all occurring in a small area. For those interested in a more in-depth description of the glacial history of Block Island, I recommend Les Sirkin's *Block Island Geology*, from which most of the information on this page is derived.

Block Island was formed over a 200,000-year period, a short amount of time when looking at glacial history, which mostly deals with time periods in millions of years. During the formation of this island there were two glaciers that slowly moved material composed of sand, gravel, clay and rocks like an avalanche in slow motion, advancing a few feet or less each year. The first glacial period lasted 60,000 years, and deposited material from the northeastern part of the country as it started to recede around where Block Island and other Elizabethan Islands are now located.

After the first glacier receded from the Block Island area there was a 65,000-year period where the climate was warm, then a 30,000-year period of cold, and an 8,000-year period of warm. The second glacier, coming from parts northwest of eastern Connecticut, reached Block Island 22,000 years ago. As it started to recede, leaving material in the same area as the first glacier, Block Island was formed. The ice melting at uneven rates, stacking of glacial material, and pieces of ice breaking off and forming holes, led to the rolling topography that is now found throughout the island.

Block Island became free of the glacier 20,000 years ago. At this point much of the sea water was still frozen in the glacier, and the ocean was miles away from the raised land that was to become Block Island. This area that would eventually become the island was really a pile of discarded material, which was surrounded by sand plains. During this time animals were able to freely move between what was to become Block Island and the mainland.

About 12,000 years ago with the drainage of the glacial lakes, Block Island became the first of the Elizabethan Islands to be isolated from the mainland. However, during this time, Block Island was actually two islands composed of a north part and south part that were much larger than they are today. Around 10,000 years ago a sand bar connected the north and south parts. This connection of two pieces of glacial till by a sand bar is called a tombolo.

Block Island's species diversity is much lower than the other Elizabethan Islands when it comes to amphibians, reptiles, and mammals, because it was isolated from the mainland when it was still too cold for these animals to survive. The native amphibians, reptiles, and mammals on Block Island may be subspecies, or separate species, because they have been isolated from mainland populations for well over 8,000 years.

Eventually due to sea level rise and wind and wave erosion, Block Island will become significantly smaller, revert back to being two islands, and eventually disappear in the extreme future. Of course this will not be a problem for countless generations. A positive way to look at this is that eventually everyone will have waterfront property.

Block Island is a heap of sand, clay, gravel, rocks, and soil deposited from the melting of two glaciers. Geologically speaking, the island was formed very rapidly. It is hard to believe that something this perfect, and enjoyed by so many, could have been created so quickly.

Stonewalls

Block Island has hundreds of miles of stonewalls that are found throughout the island. One look at the stonewall map that was made in the late 1880s shockingly demonstrates how they cover the island. What is even more amazing is that they were built by hand and with the help of oxen. The plethora of stones on the island were used to make walls to delineate property lines and livestock fields, and thus helped ease the shortage of wood after trees on the island were harvested.

Stonewalls are an important part of Block Island's heritage and if they are on a property boundary they are illegal to destroy. Hopefully in the near future the Town of New Shoreham will make it illegal to destroy any stonewall on Block Island.

While many stonewalls remain exposed, there are still more that lie hidden in the shrubs. All of these walls are important habitat for many different types of wildlife found on Block Island. Under the rocks it is easy to find garter snakes, daring jumping spiders, centipedes, millipedes, isopods (sow bugs), snails, earthworms, white-footed mice, and trapdoor spiders to name a few. Without this tremendous amount of habitat available throughout the whole island many of these animals would be a lot less common, and some possibly not here at all.

Birds love to forage around stonewalls because there is always a high density of insects around them. For birds, insects are like power bars offering an energy boost with minimal labor. Certain bird species like the Carolina wren make their nest in the cracks of those walls covered with shrubs, which offer a tremendous amount of protection from predators. As chicks fledge the nest, stonewalls offer many wonderful hiding spots for them to rest and wait for their parents to return with food.

On cold days, stonewalls that face south trap the heat and are important refuges for animals trying to keep warm. When the rocks heat up in the sun, dragonflies, damselflies, and other insects can often be observed on rocks, warming themselves for the coming day. These areas, specifically called microhabitats, are small areas where the conditions are different than the rest of the ecosystem. Plants grow in these areas like they would in a greenhouse. It is usually in these microhabitats that you see the first plants leaf out, start to grow and bloom, and also see the last plants go dormant in the autumn.

When I lead nature trips for students, they always gravitate to the walls because there is so much to see in a compact area. Kids are especially amazed on chilly days when the cold-blooded animals are moving slowly and are easy to catch. They also enjoy the soft feel of the green moss that is found on the north side of the walls, and the rough texture of the green-gray lichen. Stonewalls covered with lichen are a good thing to see because they are an air pollution indicator species, disappearing when the air quality is poor.

Stonewalls are found on almost every property on Block Island. In addition to being a visually pleasing tie to the past of the island, they are important for much of the flora and fauna of the island. Stonewalls are more than a pile of rocks; they are habitat.

Ecological changes in the last century

There have been profound ecological changes on Block Island in the last century. The change in land use from agriculture to vacant land has had a significant impact on the plants, animals, and habitats of the island in particular. Other changes have occured due to the natural ebb and flow of species in their environment.

At the beginning of the 20th century, Block Island was made up almost entirely of grassland. As agriculture declined, fields were "let go" in the 1950s and the encroachment of shrubs began (bayberry, arrowwood, shadbush). This gradual change from one habitat (grassland) to another (shrubs) is called succession. The growth of shrubs actually improved conditions for a number of animal species, and allowed birds that had disappeared after the forest was eliminated to nest here again. In the latter part of the century the bushes became quite large, covering stonewalls and ponds. The reason why the shrubs are so large is because there are no canopy trees, such as oaks, to shade them out and stunt their growth (the settlers wiped out virtually all tree species by 1750). In fact, we may have the largest shads in the world!

With the significant transformation in habitat on Block Island, the nesting bird species have changed. Two grassland bird species, the upland sandpiper and vesper sparrow are now gone. The grasshopper sparrow was one of the most common birds on the island, but there are now just two nesting pairs left. In contrast, we have seen shrub-nesting species like the gray catbird, eastern towhee, and song sparrow become the most common birds on the island.

In the third quarter of this century we saw the disappearance of migrating hawks, falcons and eagles on Block Island in the spring and fall due to DDT use throughout the United States. Now, at the beginning of a new century, these raptors are back in extremely high numbers. In the last few years, it is quite common in the spring and fall to see Cooper's hawk, peregrine falcon, and bald eagle.

Not only have native species changed on the island in the last century, but we have seen the introduction of numerous animal and plant species. In the 1920s the ring-necked pheasant was introduced and has been a part of the Block Island ecosystem ever since. In fact, it appears that the pheasant is at an all-time high in numbers (based on bird counts). We think this may be due to the excellent winter food supply and cover provided by shrubs and vines, especially the Asiatic bittersweet and winterberry. In the 1960s, the white-tailed deer was introduced, which has had numerous impacts on both the human and natural community.

There has also been the introduction of fast-growing exotic plant species like Asiatic bittersweet, multiflora rose, black swallowwort and autumn olive. These plants are now widespread throughout the island and are continuing to take over in many areas. Non-encroaching exotic plants have also been introduced like Japanese black pine, rosa rugosa and sycamore maple. These plants have stayed in the areas they were planted, and have become important to birds for nesting habitat and cover.

As with anything living, there are constant changes in the Block Island ecosystems. It will be very interesting to see what happens to the plants and animals in this new century.

Block Island circa. 1880.

Block Island today.

Block Island Cetaceans

What is a Cetacean? It is a member of the scientific order of the same name, which includes porpoises, dolphins, and whales. These species, known as marine mammals, are warm-blooded, breathe through lungs, bear live young and nurse them, and have hair (generally a few strands). On Block Island it is possible to see 10 of the 81 total Cetaceans in the world. This is their story.

The harbor porpoise is a small, stocky animal that is mostly found in coastal waters. It is brown or dark gray above, changing to a lighter gray on the flanks, and has a triangular-shaped dorsal fin. This porpoise can grow to 6½ feet, and weigh up to 200 pounds. Its prey of choice is herring, mackerel, sardines, and squid. This porpoise can be seen on Block Island in any season, and is the most common cetacean around the island in the winter. Often, in the winter, you can see this species south of the Old Harbor breakwater as you leave on the ferry.

The common dolphin gets it is name because it is the most-seen cetacean and was recorded often in history and literature. It is easily distinguished from other dolphins by a well-defined beak and a complex yellow, tan and gray crisscross pattern. The mouth of this species contains 160 to 200 razor-sharp teeth. This dolphin can reach up to 8½ feet in length, and weigh up to 300 pounds. The main prey for this species are squid and small fish. The common dolphin can be seen in Block Island waters during any season.

The striped dolphin was first recorded by the ancient Greeks, who drew many pictures of them. This acrobatic species has a slender body, a long, sharply defined beak, and a curved dorsal (middle fin on back). It also has two black stripes on each flank; one that runs from the eye to the flipper, and another spanning from the eye to the base of the tail. Like the common dolphin, this species has between 160 and 200 teeth. It can reach a length of 8 feet, and weigh up to 330 pounds. Similar to the common dolphin, this species eats mostly squid and small fish. Interestingly, this species does not associate with other dolphin species. The striped dolphin can be seen around Block Island during any season.

Atlantic white-sided dolphin.

The bottlenose dolphin is the largest of the beaked dolphins. This species became the face for all dolphins with the popular "Flipper" television series. This dolphin is distinguished by its gray above and white below color pattern, medium-sized thick snout, and sickle-shaped dorsal fin. This species can grow to 9 feet, and weigh up to 550 pounds. There are two types of this species; the coastal type that is smaller, and the offshore type that is larger. The diet of this species consists of squid, fish, and crustaceans. The bottlenose dolphin is only seen around Block Island is the summer and early fall months when the ocean temperature is warm.

Harbor porpoise.

The Atlantic white-sided dolphin is black on its back, with dark gray flanks and a long white oval blaze below the dorsal fin (fin on back). Above the blaze, there is a yellowish-tan band. This animal has a white belly with a black ring around the eyes. Its body is stocky and torpedo-shaped. The Atlantic white-sided dolphin can reach 9 feet in length and weigh up to 800 pounds. A varied diet composed of squid, herring, smelt, shrimp, and other small fish make up this animal's prey base. The Atlantic white-sided dolphin can be seen around the island during any season.

The long-finned pilot whale, which is in the dolphin family, has a distinct rounded head with a very slight beak, and is all black to coal gray in color with a white anchor-shaped patch on its belly. This species can reach up to 20 feet in length, with a weight of 3 tons.

It eats mostly squid and other small fish, and has only 40 to 48 teeth compared to120 in most other dolphin species. The pilot whale is a common sight around Block Island during any season.

The finback whale is long, sleek, and streamlined with a V-shaped head, which is flat on top. There is a series of 50 to 100 grooves on the underside of its body that extend from under the lower jaw to the navel. This whale is light gray to brownish-black on its back and sides, with white on the underside of its body, flippers, and fluke. Its most unusual characteristic is the asymmetrical coloring of the lower jaw, which is creamy yellow on the right side and mottled black on the left side.

This species is the second-largest cetacean, reaching a length of 78 feet, and a weight of 70 tons. The finback whale is nicknamed the "greyhound of the sea" because it can swim up to 23 miles per hour. This species is a baleen whale, which means that during feeding large volumes of water and food are taken into the mouth, and the grooves in the throat expand. As the mouth closes, water is expelled through the baleen plates, which trap the food near the tongue to be swallowed. The preferred food of this species is krill (shrimp-like crustaceans) and small fish, which it eats up to 2 tons of each day. Summer is the best season to see this whale in Block Island waters.

The blue whale is the largest mammal, and possibly the largest animal, to ever inhabit the earth. Its blue-gray body is long and streamlined, with a very broad and flat head that is almost U-shaped. There are 55 to 68 grooves extending from the lower jaw to near the navel. This species reaches 80 feet in length, and 125 tons in weight. If not for the buoyancy of the saltwater, this animal would be crushed under its own weight. This species is also a baleen whale, eating exclusively krill. Researchers believe that an individual blue whale eats up to 40 million krill a day. Summer is the best time to see this species around Block Island.

The humpback whale gets its name from the motion it makes before it dives. This species ranges from white to gray to black in color, with 14 to 35 throat grooves that run from the chin to the navel. In addition to being quite acrobatic, this species also sings amazing songs. It grows to 52 feet in length, with a weight of 50 tons. Also a baleen whale, this species eats mostly krill, plankton and small fish. This species tends to be found on the surface of the ocean, and can be observed around Block Island during any season.

The northern right whale is the most endangered of the Cetaceans, with only 400 individuals remaining in the world. They were named by whalers who considered them the "right" whales to hunt because they were rich in blubber and easy to catch. This whale has a bow-shaped lower jaw, a head that is hairier than most whales (300 hairs found on the tip of the lower jaw and 100 on the upper jaw), and callosities (a series of growths) found in the head region. It is usually black to dark gray in color with white and brown splotches. The northern right whale has large flippers and no dorsal fin or throat grooves. It grows up to 50 feet in length, with a weight of 120,000 pounds. This species is a skimmer baleen whale, which filter feeds by slowly swimming with its mouth open, constantly eating plankton and tiny crustaceans. Although extremely rare, the northern right whale can be found in any season around Block Island.

While it takes some luck to see any one of the Cetaceans, these species can be spotted anywhere around the island. The best vantage points are at Black Rock, Pebble Beach, Mohegan Bluffs, and from the Block Island ferry. I hope you get an opportunity to observe these rare creatures that are the largest and most intriguing of Block Island's marine animals.

Stranded pilot whale at Cow Cove.

Block Island seals

In the winter Block Island is an excellent place for observing seals. Each year they return in large numbers from their summering grounds up north. The best places to observe seals are Cormorant Cove, behind St. Andrew's Parish Center, and off Clay Head. Other places that you may find them if you are lucky are Sandy Point, Grove Point, Beane Point - Hippocampus, West Beach, Dicken's Point, Graces Cove, and Dory's Cove. Basically, if you are near the ocean, keep your eyes peeled for seal heads popping out of the water.

Seals visit us here frequently from November to May. On Block Island there are four possible species of seals that can be found on the beaches, rocks, and in the water: harbor, gray, hooded, and harp seals. Of these, the harbor seal is by far the most common, but it is always possible to see one of the other three species. While around the island these seal species eat a variety of food including sand eel, herring, squid, and skate.

A pair of harbor seals "hauled out" on a rock.

The harbor seal is between 4½ and 6 feet long, and weighs from 175 to 250 pounds. Generally, males are bigger than females. This seal has a short muzzle, its nostrils form a broad "V," and its coat is light gray, tan to brown, or black with fine dark spotting on its back.

The gray seal is between 7 and 8 feet long, and weighs up to 800 pounds. This species has a long snout, its nostrils resemble a "W," and its coat is dark brown, gray, or black.

A gray seal.

A hooded seal.

The hooded seal is between 7 and 9 feet long, and can weigh up to 880 pounds. Its nostril area appears flattened, and males have a hood. The coat has distinct, irregular, black patches that cover the animal.

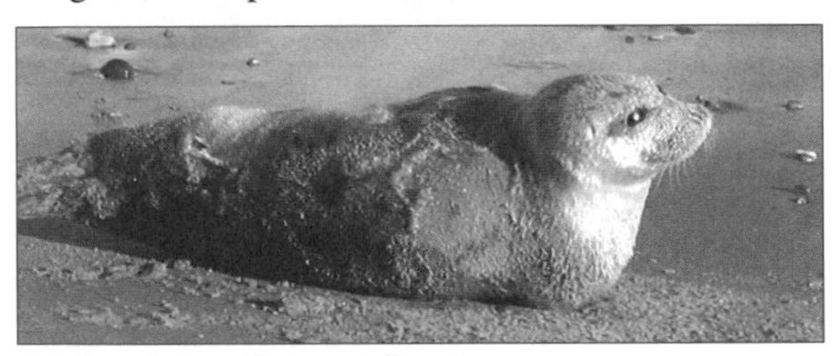

A harp seal on Crescent Beach.

The harp seal is 6 feet in length, and can weigh 400 pounds. It has a dog-like muzzle, and its head and chest are darker than its tan body.

It is important when watching seals to remember to never to get too close or harass the animals, especially the young ones you might find on sandy beaches. The youngsters, or pups, have just left their mothers and are on their own for the first time, needing to rest and feed undisturbed.

It is also a good idea to keep dogs away from seals. In fact, seals are federally protected under the Marine Mammal Protection Act, which states that it is illegal to kill, approach, or interfere with them in any way. If cornered, seals can give a nasty, infectious bite even though they may look cute and cuddly.

If you observe seals on the beach or on the rocks, they are "hauling out," something they do on a daily basis. It does not mean they are ill or injured. However, there are four reasons you should call for help: if a seal remains "hauled out" in the same place for more than 24 hours; is entangled; has a deep gash and is bleeding profusely (seals often have a little blood around the mouth from playing and this is not a reason to call); or is so thin you can see its bones.

Another reason to call for help is if you find a recently deceased seal washed up on the beach. The seal will be taken to Mystic Aquarium for a necropsy (an animal autopsy) to figure out itscause of death.

In addition to dealing with seal strandings, The Nature Conservancy has been working with the Graduate School of Oceanography at the University of Rhode Island to monitor the seal population on Block Island from October to May. Twice a month on days with the lowest tides, I count the number of seals that appear within an hour of low tide at each major seal haul-out location.

Since 1998, I have conducted the monitoring study. Over time we will be able to determine if the population of seals is increasing or decreasing. Each year of the study so far, there have been more seals than the previous years. Each winter, I take out all the classes in the Block Island School to participate in this interesting long-term study.

Observing seals is one of those special Block Island experiences that can only be done in the winter!

A winter bird walk

On Friday, Feb. 4, 2000, I took the Block Island School kindergarten on a wintertime bird walk down Payne Road. It was sunny but cold, with some snow on the ground, a perfect day for seeing our feathered friends. When I arrived at the classroom, the students were getting ready for the elements with boots, hats, and mittens, and discussing the various birds that they might see.

We left the school armed with binoculars, a bird book, and an inland wintertime bird checklist composed of 24 species. Excitement peaked when the first bird was spotted flying overhead. It was a large bird with black wings and a yellow bill. One student shouted, "it's a gull," and all the students agreed. After looking it up in the book, the students discovered that the bird was a great black-backed gull.

After hearing some birds in the bushes, we decided to try and "pish" (an alarm call sound that the birds come and investigate) them out. It worked, and three small birds with yellow rumps and white tail spots popped up. One of the students said, "it's a warbler," but none of the students knew which one. So we went to the book and quickly found that it was a yellow-rumped warbler. The kindergarteners then learned that these small birds are able to live on Block Island in the winter because they are able to turn waxy bayberry fruit into energy.

Luckily, in our travels down the road we were able to come upon a flock of birds moving around in a couple of Japanese black pines. There were birds moving everywhere, and we were quickly able to hear black-capped chickadee ("chickadee-dee-dee-dee"), red-breasted nuthatch (a nasal "yank, yank, yank"), and white-throated sparrow (a whistle "poor old Sam Peabody"). The students with their good eyes also picked out a slate-colored junco with its pink bill and white in the tail, and a blue jay.

Carolina wren.

On the return stroll to the school we heard the most joyous sound: "teakettle, teakettle, teakettle, tea." From previous bird trips the students knew immediately that this loud songster was a Carolina wren. Even on this cold day hearing this song made us think of spring.

After returning to the classroom we excitedly tallied the birds that we saw. We observed a total of 16 species of birds. This is a great number of species to be seen on a cold day in February. The young ornithologists who took part in this trip were Sam Spier, Theo Mott, Kyle Schwarzer, Cody Nicastro, Olivia Mattyasovszky, Tyler Nelson and Michaela Wilson.

If you have any questions about any of the birds observed, do not hesitate to ask any of these budding ornithologists! Special thanks goes to their teacher, Debbie Hart, for skillfully keeping the students focused.

Take a wintertime walk on Block Island and, you will see a bunch of birds.

Wintertime Birds Checklist

- common loon
- Canada goose
- mallard
- common goldeneye
- bufflehead
- red-breasted merganser
- northern harrier
- ring-necked pheasant
- sanderling
- great black-backed gull
- herring gull
- common murre
- mourning dove
- downy woodpecker
- blue jay
- American crow
- black-capped chickadee
- Carolina wren
- northern mockingbird
- American robin
- hermit thrush
- yellow-rumped warbler
- northern cardinal
- eastern meadowlark
- slate-colored junco
- song sparrow
- white-throated sparrow
- house finch

Nature's Valentine's Day

With Valentine's Day right around the corner, it seems appropriate to write about some of the more interesting mating rituals of Block Island's wild animals. Granted, these animals do not celebrate a certain day, but instead base their mating cycle on day length, weather, and food availability. Each species of animal has its own special way of "getting in the mood," and often the ritual helps make sure that the reproductive process has the greatest chance of success.

The courtship display of the **American woodcock** can be seen between dusk and dawn, especially during the full moon, in late winter and early spring. This bird is probably one of the funniest-looking animals on Block Island. An unmistakable 11-inch plump bird, with bulging eyes and an extremely long bill, it can be found throughout the island, especially near places that have open fields, mud or shallow standing water. The woodcock, using its unusually long beak, probes in the mud for earthworms and other delicious invertebrates, eating more than its weight every day.

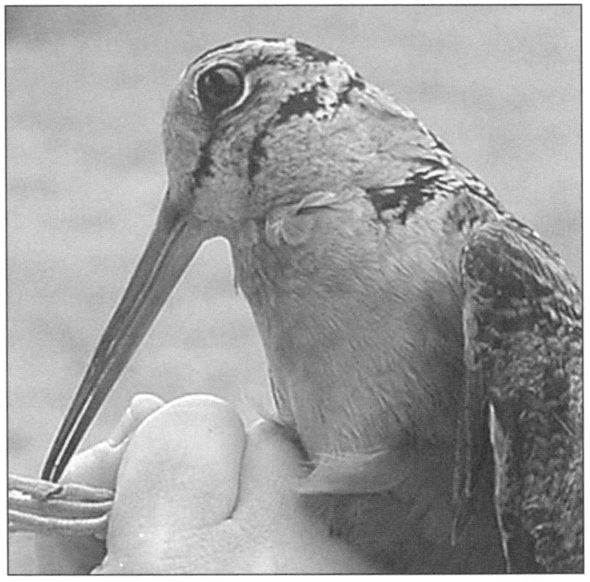
American woodcock.

As dusk descends, the male, with his wings whistling (the outer wing feathers are modified with a small gap between feathers to produce the sound), flies in widening spirals rising up to 100 feet, circles his highest point, and zigzags to earth like a falling leaf. When he reaches the ground he releases a nasal "peent." This display is repeated many times. It is truly amazing to watch.

The red-winged blackbird returns in the early spring. The male of this species is glossy black with a red wing patch (also called an epaulette) tinged with yellow, and the female is streaked brown and looks like a large sparrow. Both measure 7 inches in length, with the male having a "kon-la-reee" song.

The male red-wing begins to set up a territory to impress as many females as possible. They are polygynous, which means one male mates with two or more females.

The size of the male's territory depends on the amount of red in the epaulette. As they sing, the males flash their red wing patch. The larger the red epaulette, the more dominant the male, and the more attractive it is to the females. Also the more dominant the male, the larger the territory, and thus the more females, it can accommodate on its staked claim.

The muskrat is a 25-inch-long rodent with brown fur, a silver belly, and a long scaly, naked tail. This mostly aquatic species should never be confused with the smaller, often-hated Norway rat. In fact, this animal was introduced on Block Island to help keep the ponds clean of cattails and other vegetation.

A muskrat pair uses aquatic plants in marshy areas to build a complicated conical home that can rise up to 3 feet in height, with the entrance under water, various passages and a nest chamber. In these homes, the muskrat pair raises two litters of two to nine young. The male of this species marks its territory with a "scent post," a mat of cut sedge leaves mixed with mud on which he leaves his musky secretion. This is done to keep other muskrats out of his territory.

In March, the male **barn owl** begins its mating ritual by clapping its wings together in a courtship flight near a potential nesting site (on Block Island, near the top part of a bluff where a rock has fallen out creating a small cavern). He then lands and stiffly presents a rodent to the female near the nesting cavity. Mating follows.

Barn owl.

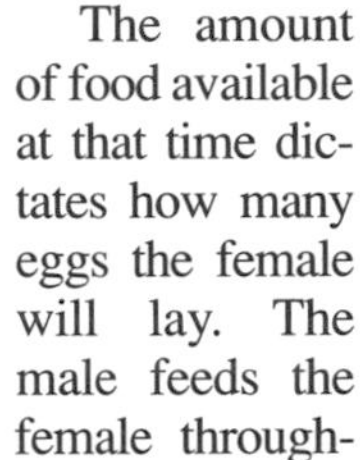

The amount of food available at that time dictates how many eggs the female will lay. The male feeds the female throughout incubation of the eggs by returning to the nest with both birds and rodents. Once the eggs hatch, both the male and female feed the chicks until they can fly and feed on their own.

In April, a courting male **northern harrier** (marsh hawk) can be seen doing his amazing sky dance, which consists of a series of dives from a near stall with some barrel-rolls in multiple U-shaped loops. The male does this to "win" over a female who is holding a territory with a nest (on Block Island, usually a small grassland

Northern harrier and chicks.

gap surrounded by shrubs).

Once they mate, the female incubates the eggs and chicks while the male feeds her. The male hunts for rodents and birds and then swoops by the nest and drops the recently caught food. Sometimes the transfer occurs in the air, called a prey pass.

In late May or early June, the male **marsh wren** will build up to 30 nests on his established territory (on Block Island, in reedy marsh grass). When a female approaches, he takes a position slightly above the female and fluffs his breast while flapping partially folded wings. The male then takes the female to inspect each nest, and if she find one that she likes then they will mate.

Marsh wren.

He feeds the female mostly aquatic insects while she incubates the eggs. Once the eggs hatch, both the male and female feed the chicks until they are fully fledged.

In late June, the **American burying beetle** is prowling the grasslands of Block Island for rotting carcasses or carrion on which to begin its mating ritual. The beetles prefer one that weighs between 100 and 200 grams, usually a pheasant chick or rat.

American burying beetle.

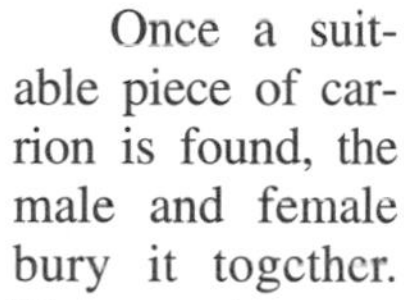

Once a suitable piece of carrion is found, the male and female bury it together. They create a cavern around the item with a mating chamber off to the side. They then pluck the feathers or fur from the body and coat the body with secretions to keep it from rotting further.

After mating, the female lays the eggs on the dead animal. When the larvae hatch, they eat the carrion for a little more than a week, and then crawl into the soil to pupate (develop into adults). The newly mature adults emerge from the soil 45 to 60 days after the parents initially bury the carcass.

While this is an account of some of the more interesting mating rituals of wildlife on Block Island, it is important to note that each species is unique in the way it approaches reproduction.

So as Valentine's Day passes, remember to keep an eye out for the unique fauna of Block Island celebrating the spirit of the day during the coming spring.

Animal Personals

Below are personal "advertisements" for animal species on Block Island searching for mates. To test your knowledge of each animal's life history, the species name has been left blank for you to fill in (answers at the bottom).

1) Single male ____________ looking for mate to help in search for carrion and perhaps to bury it.

2) Single female ____________ looking for partner to hunt for delicious Norway rats, and to share a cozy oceanfront home.

3) Single male ___________ searching for that special someone to enjoy pond-side lodge. Must be a vegetarian.

4) Single female ___________ related to royalty, seeking hard working drone to gather pollen, and perhaps share a hive.

5) Single male ___________ looking for someone to help search for early-morning worms with. Must be the nesting sort.

6) Often-widowed female ___________ searching for someone to worship with and catch insects.

7) Single male ___________ looking for that special someone to croak at and jump around the trees with.

8) Single female __________ searching for colorful partner who enjoys sunning on rocks and swimming in ponds.

Answers: 1) American burying beetle; 2) barn owl; 3) muskrat; 4) honey bee; 5) American robin; 6) praying mantis; 7) spring peeper; 8) painted turtle.

Building Bird Boxes

A great solution to the winter doldrums on Block Island is building bird nest boxes. Below are two different plans, one for American kestrels and one for eastern bluebirds (also good for tree swallows and Carolina wrens). Currently neither of these bird species nest on Block Island, but by building them a place to live there is a chance they will become summer residents. Be sure to get these boxes out by early April and watch what happens.

Kestrel Nest Box Plans

Align the sides 4" from the top edge of the back

Ventilation holes

Front

3" diameter hole

11 1/2" From the bottom edge.

Materials

Lumber: One 1" x 10" x 8' (#2 white pine or cedar)
1 1/2" galvanized nail or screws.
Two 2" non-removable hinges

25" | 17" | 16" | 16" | 13" | 8"

9 1/2" | Back | Side | Side | Front | Top | Floor

16" | 17"

Construction:

1. Mark and cut out the pieces as shown.
2. Cut a 3" diameter entrance hole in the front piece, 11 1/2" from the bottom edge.
3. Drill three 1/4" holes near the top edge of both side pieces.
4. Align the two side pieces 4" from the top of the back piece. The longer end of the side piece should be against the back. Attach these to the back with 3 nails per side. (See diagram for illustration)
5. Insert the floor into the bottom of the box. Nail to the side pieces.
6. Attach the door to the front of the box nailing into side pieces.
7. Finally attach the roof using two hinges, for easy cleaning access.
8. Place 2-3" of sawdust on the bottom of the box.
9. The box should be firmly attached to a support structure, such as a tree or post, 10 to 30 feet above the ground in an open area.

Bluebird Nest Box Plan

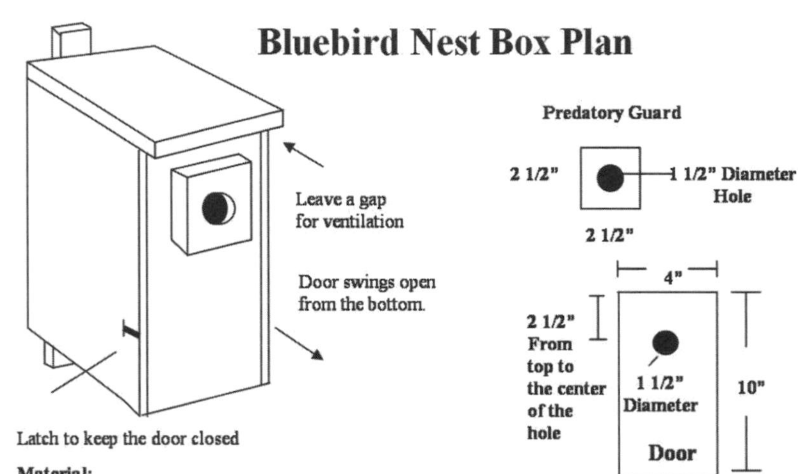

Material:

Lumber: One 1"x 6" x 6' (#2 white pine recommended) You will have 16" left over which can be used for a predator guard and bracket for the back to help hang the box to a post.
1 1/4" galvanized nails or screws. If you uses screw I recommend pre-drilling the holes.

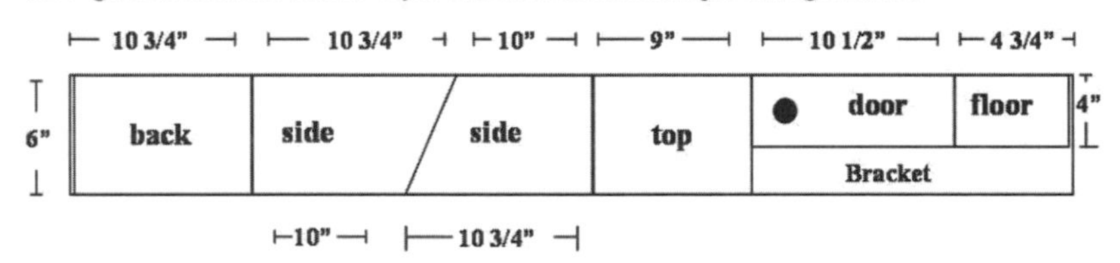

Construction:

1. Mark and cut out the pieces as shown.
2. Cut a 1 1/2" diameter hole in the door, 2 1/2" inches from the top. See diagram.
3. In a 2 1/2" x 2 1/2 piece of wood, cut a 1 1/2" diameter hole in the center. This is the predatory guard. This piece will lay over the hole in the door. Pre-drill two holes before attaching it to the door.
4. Take the two side pieces and line up the angles so both pieces slope downward toward you. Next take the back piece and place it between the sides against the highest angle. Nail the sides into the back 3 times on each side.
5. Take your top, align one of the 6" edges with the back piece. Your top should slope downward. You will leave a 2" overhang in the front. Nail into the side pieces.
6. Insert your floor into the bottom of the box. Nail to the side pieces.
7. Finally take your door and place it in the front of your box. **Do Not** place the top of the door against the roof, leave a 1/4" gap for ventilation (see diagram.) This will also leave you approximately 1" overhang on the bottom. This will assist you in opening the box. **Only use two nails to secure the door.** One on each side of the predatory guard. This allows you to swing the door open and closed for cleaning. To secure the box closed, drill a hole from the side of the box into the door. Make sure the hole is large enough to remove the nail but snug enough to keep it closed. This is your latch.
8. Nail the bracket to the back of the box, centering it. Make sure you have an overhang on both the top and bottom. This will help you attach you box to a post.
9. Place the box on a fence post 4-6 feet up, in an open area.

The Great Bird Rescue

On Wednesday, Feb. 23, 2000, Heather Sniffen and her daughter Cailin brought a sea bird called a common murre to the office. They had recovered it at Cormorant Cove. The bird was still very active but could not fly because it was covered in black motor oil. This individual had swum through some oil floating in the ocean.

The common murre is a beautiful bird that is found off the coast of Block Island in the winter. This species is a diving bird that eats fish. It is 17 inches in length, with a large, slender pointed bill. Its body is dark gray above and white below, with one white stripe on each wing. This bird looks a lot like a penguin, but with much larger wings.

Upon initial evaluation at The Nature Conservancy office, it was quite obvious that the bird was covered in oil and had ingested the oil by trying to preen (clean) its feathers. After the evaluation, a call was placed to veterinarian/bird rehabilitator, Dr. Bird (yes, that is her real name). A plan was then formulated to evacuate the bird off the island and start its rehabilitation.

The last boat for the day had already left, so flying the bird off was the only option. One quick call to New England Airlines and the bird was booked to go on the next plane to Westerly where one of Dr. Bird's rehabilitators would meet it. The oily bird was placed in a cardboard box and sent off on the plane.

Rehabilitator Vivian Lee met the murre in Westerly and immediately jumped to action. She filled a tub with hot water at precisely 104 degrees Fahrenheit, added Ivory Soap, and placed the unhappy bird in it. The black oil started to come off the feathers. The water was drained and the process repeated. Finally, the bird was placed in a clean rinse to remove the soap.

Deciding the wash and rinse cycle was traumatic enough for this poor bird, Mrs. Lee placed it in a cage for the night. The next morning it was time to remove the oil inside the bird. The bird was fed a solution of Pepto-Bismol and water, and this cleared out the internal oil.

The murre, now clean, needed to regain its strength. Mrs. Lee purchased live minnows and placed them in the tub (now with cold water) with the bird. The bird went crazy plucking one minnow after another.

Feeding time was twice daily for the next 10 days, and the bird quickly regained all the weight it lost. Three days before the bird was slated to return to Block Island, Mrs. Lee placed the bird (in a cage) outside for the night, so that it could get used to the cold. A day before the return, the bird was placed in a tub of salt water; this is done to reactivate the bird's salt gland. The salt gland is very important for birds that live in the ocean because it is their way of excreting salt from the sea water they ingest.

With the salt gland operational, the bird was now ready for the trip back to Block Island. The common murre returned to Block Island on March 6th on the 11 o'clock ferry in a vented travel kennel. The release site was the East Beach by the Town Beach Pavilion. The Block Island kindergarten came along to share in this special occasion.

After a brief presentation to the young ornithologists, the door to the kennel was opened The bird bolted out of the kennel and then paused as if taking its bearings. This gave each student time to observe the movement and behavior of this special bird. After a few minutes, the bird ran about 100 feet in an awkward way (murres have a big body and small wings), then became airborne and flew about 50 feet, and landed in the ocean. The murre took a long-awaited saltwater bath, and started diving to look for fish.

Excited by a job well done, Mrs. Lee returned to the mainland. The students went back to class and wrote a journal entry about witnessing this special bird returning to the wild. The kindergartners also wrote a story about the bird called "The Smallest Classmate." As the kindergarten class will attest to, this is truly an extraordinary bird because very few individuals survive being covered with oil.

If you want to see this amazing species in the wild the best place is out in the ocean off Grove Point, but make sure to bring your binoculars because the murres are always quite far offshore!

Presidents' Day Bird Count

On Saturday, March 1, 2004, the Presidents' Day Bird Count finally took place after two weather-related postponements. Eight bird observers, including me, spent the day searching Block Island, recording the numbers of species seen and total individuals counted. The Block Island Presidents' Day Bird Count has been done every year since 1996.

A typical bird count is conducted in a designated area (in this case a 10-mile circle centered on Block Island), for a certain period of time (24 hours), by groups of birders called "parties." Each party is given a specific location within the designated area to record the numbers of species and individuals seen or heard. At the end of the time period, all the parties get back together and a master list is assembled.

The master list from a well-executed bird count is an excellent record of a species' presence and density for a given day. If a count is done annually, it can start to show trends in bird populations. Both nationally and locally, certain counts like the Christmas Bird Count have been occurring for more than 60 years.

On Block Island, there are three major counts a year: Veterans' Day, Christmas and Presidents' Day. In addition to these, a point count survey is done of breeding birds in June.

The counts, the survey, and the spring and fall migration bird-banding data from the Block Island banding station at Clay Head combine to create a very accurate portrait of bird species distribution on the island each year. The yearly portraits of Block Island birds can then be compared to show population trends for each species over time.

I picked up seven observers at the ferry at 8 a.m. after they had a productive ferry ride — i.e., there was good birding all the way across. In fact, they saw a northern fulmar, the second record of this species in the Block Island Sound. Parties covered the southwestern part of the island, the southeast, the north end, Clay Head, the island interior, and a seabird watch stationed at Grove Point.

Clay Head Preserve was my section to observe. The sunny day with little wind was perfect for recording the maximum number of species and individuals. I started at the Clay Head parking lot and walked north on the bluff trail, then went inland and zigzagged back to where I began. It took me a total of four hours, and I covered five miles of walking trails.

The highlights were a barn owl being mobbed by American crows in a Japanese pine stand, and a sharp-shinned hawk bathing itself in a recently melted puddle. I definitely recorded lower numbers of songbirds because of the harsh winter, and less waterfowl because the wetlands at Clay Head were iced over.

The parties met up again at 5 p.m. at the boat, and the Presidents' Day count coordinator collected each party's data before hopping on the ferry. From these data, a master list was made, which tallied 79 species and 5,327 individuals. In 2003, we saw 72 species and 7,049 individuals.

Bird counts are extremely fun to participate in, and are also important because they document long-term population trends. The more years this count is done, the more significant the data. Thus, I look forward to doing the Presidents' Day Bird Count for years to come.

Barn owls

Results for each Presidents' Day Count

Year	Species	Individuals
1996	67	5,237
1997	66	3,490
1998	78	5,614
1999	74	6,089
2000	78	4,336
2001	78	8,176
2002	82	6,047
2003	72	7,049
2004	79	5,327
2005	75	3,980

Wintertime beachcombing

We are often blessed during the winter with some nice weather that is perfect for wintertime beachcombing. Crescent Beach is full of sand in the winter, instead of rocks, and there are many shells, birds, and seals to be seen. The sandy condition of the beach makes it easier to walk and more attractive to many of the rare beach species.

When you walk Crescent Beach, it is easy to find crab legs along with the shells of quahogs, blue mussels, and common slippers. However, in winter there are greater numbers of some of the harder to find things on the beach. Let me tell you about sand dollars, false angel wings, and channeled whelk shells, three of the more interesting finds on the beach. If you are lucky enough to come across these, please leave them for other people to see.

The sand dollar, when it is alive, is a flat animal with a felt like coating of fine spines that are brownish in color (in many ways similar to a sea urchin). These neat animals shuffle through loose sand feeding on microorganisms, with flounders and other bottom feeders in turn eating them. On the beach, the sand dollar is brown to white in color (depending how long the sun has bleached it), with a five-petaled pattern of tiny holes. This animal can grow up to three inches in diameter.

The false angel wing grows up to 2 inches, and is a bivalve, which means there are two shells (or valves) connected by a hinge. Like other bivalves, it lives by pumping saltwater into its shell and then extracting both oxygen and food from the water. This animal also bores into peat or stiff mud, creating holes that are perfectly round and appear as if they were done with a hand drill (this can be seen on any peat clump found near the saltwater). On the beach, the false angel wing's beautiful shell is white and often very brittle. This animal gets its name because its shell looks like the shell of another bivalve called, angel wing, both of these shells, when held vertically, look like the wing of an angel.

The channeled whelk is the largest sea snail on this coast, growing up to 7 inches. They feed mainly on bivalves, which they attack by inserting part of their body between the prey's valves, and then using their shell as a hammer to create an opening. On the beach, these large bluish-white shells are easy to spot, but it is hard to find a whole one. The whelk's amber-colored strings of egg capsules can also be found on the beach.

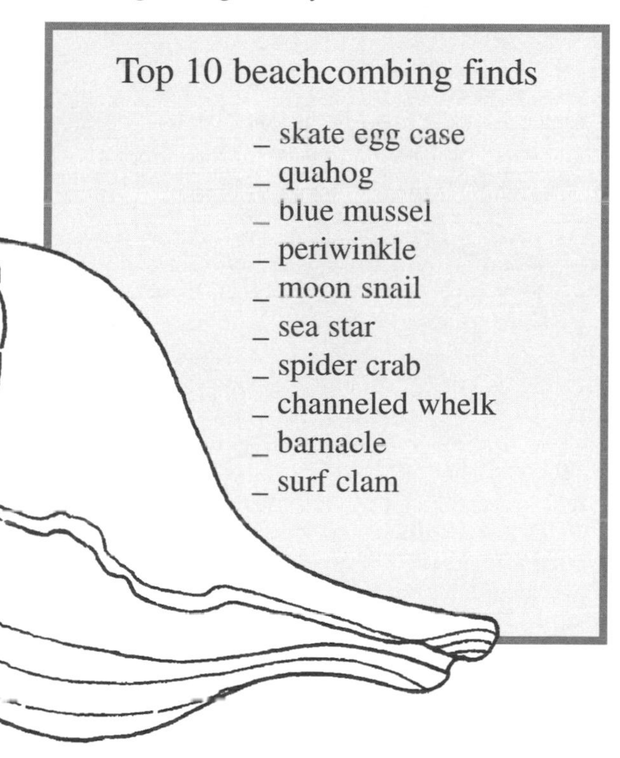

What else? While you are beachcombing, in addition to the remains of organisms, you will also come across animals that are alive, such as birds and seals. The most common bird species to be seen on the beach are herring (gray wings) and great black-backed gulls (black wings). With luck you will also spot little birds running near the water's edge. These are sanderlings.

If it is low tide you may see harbor seals (fine spots on back) hauled out on the rocks, or the rarer harp seals (large brown blotches) on the beach. This is a perfectly normal place for the seals to rest. Make sure to give them a wide berth. If they make noise or raise their heads, you are too close.

In the winter exploring, Crescent Beach is very rewarding and a great way to avoid cabin fever!

Top 10 beachcombing finds

_ skate egg case
_ quahog
_ blue mussel
_ periwinkle
_ moon snail
_ sea star
_ spider crab
_ channeled whelk
_ barnacle
_ surf clam

Wintertime bird foraging

Recently, I was asked the question: "When I watch my birdfeeder, why are certain birds always on the ground, while others aggressively protect their spot on the feeder?"

As I thought about it, I realized that the reasons behind this observation help illustrate how songbirds forage on Block Island throughout the winter. (When we use the word foraging in reference to birds, it means looking for food.)

White-throated sparrow.

During non-breeding times (fall and winter), a bird's two main goals are food and protection from predation. All birds have what's called a search image — an ability to pick out the food they normally eat from a confusing environment. Over time, each species of bird develops certain behaviors around its interactions with other species and the environment.

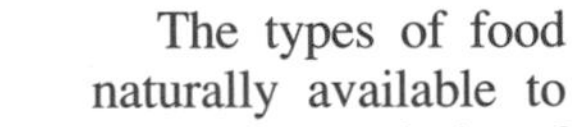

The types of food naturally available to songbirds on Block Island in the winter are fruits of winterberry, poison ivy and bayberry; seeds from thistle, goldenrod or other wildflowers, grasses and pines; and on warm days, the occasional arthropod (insects, spiders, etc.). If you want to attract wintertime birds to your property, encourage these native plants.

When a feeder is introduced to an area it gives seed-eating birds the opportunity to find a lot of food using very little energy. The birds come to rely on the feeder, and this is why you should never stop refilling a feeder in the winter.

Black-capped chickadee.

Some birds, such as mourning doves, northern juncos, and white-throated sparrows, look for their food on the ground. Others, like the brown creeper, red-breasted nuthatch, and downy woodpecker, probe the bark of trees and shrubs for their food. Finally, the majority of songbirds, including yellow-rumped warblers, northern cardinals, and black-capped chickadees, feed in the shrubs and trees at different heights off the ground.

Feeders enhance competitive behavior, such as birds chasing each other from the food. This helps to account for the normal scene at a feeder on Block Island, with the ground-foraging species below and the rest of the species competing for spots at the feeder. When space becomes limited, less aggressive birds such as song sparrows and nuthatches are kicked out by northern cardinals and black-capped chickadees.

While these aggressive interactions happen often at feeders, in the wild, where winter food sources are much less concentrated, birds look to forage together for protection. Little energy is wasted on competitive behavior because the food is so spread out.

Mixed-species flocks move throughout the island foraging for fruit, seeds, and the occasional insect. Specific species fill different height strata, from the ground to the canopy. The more birds that are feeding together, the better the chance that one will sight a hawk or other predator and sound the alarm. If you pay attention while you walk you will see these flocks of birds, mostly made up of white-throated sparrows, yellow-rumped warblers, and dark-eyed juncos, with the occasional black-capped chickadee, northern cardinal, song sparrow, or hermit thrush.

So the next time you take a walk or are watching the feeder, as well as identifying birds, try to observe their behavior. I am sure you will be amazed!

Feeder Checklist

— downy woodpecker
— mourning dove
— blue jay
— black-capped chickadee
— Carolina wren
— northern cardinal
— slate-colored junco
— song sparrow
— white-throated sparrow
— house finch

Feeding the birds of winter

One of the most common questions I am asked is, "What can I do to help birds survive the winter?" The answer is actually quite simple: feed the birds in your area. While this will greatly help Block Island's avian inhabitants, it will also provide you enjoyment throughout the slow winter months.

Most people know that they must keep a feeder filled or dependant birds may starve. Recent research has also shown that feeders sometimes can be the source of disease for birds that visit them. With little effort, it is easy to maintain a clean feeding area that is beneficial for birds. Adhere to the following tips and techniques for ways to help birds and enhance your feeder experience.

It starts with a healthy feeder area

Always hang feeders in shrubs or trees that obscure views from raptors hunting above. Only birds that feel safe will visit a feeder. If you desire to use a window feeder, start with feeding birds in the shrubs; and as they become used to it, move it closer to the house.

Before refilling a seed feeder always be sure to dislodge any seed that has become compacted. Also make sure that all remaining seed is dry. Any wet clumps of seeds should be removed.

Try to remove all hulls from feeder daily.

Once every few weeks, clean feeders with a weak bleach solution (one cap full of bleach to a gallon of warm water). Rinse with clean water and then let feeders dry before replacing seed.

In order to keep rodents, insects, and moisture out, keep seed in an airtight container like a garbage can or large Tupperware container.

Only use platform feeders when the weather is dry to keep the seed from spoiling. In bad weather feed birds from covered feeders that keep the seed from getting wet.

If you feed with shelled sunflower hearts, place them in a covered feeder to avoid the weather ruining them.

To make the feeding area less attractive to rodents, only place enough seed for the birds to use by dark.

If you see a sick or dead bird in your feeding area ,call The Nature Conservancy (466-2129) for advice on dealing with this situation.

If you have problems with birds running into your windows, either move the feeding area farther away from the house, or make sure that birds cannot see the outside through your house.

Remember, birds depend on your feeder in the winter. So make sure to have a feeding plan if you are going to be away for part of the winter.

Seedy tips:

The most common seed that is used in feeders is the black-oil sunflower because the majority of feeder species are able to remove its thin shell and access its large seed.

If your goal is to attract a diverse group of birds, you are going to need a variety of seeds, which need to be dispersed in appropriate feeders. Place sunflower seeds in tube, hopper or platform feeders; thistle in tube feeders; suet in suet cages; and mixed seeds on platform feeders.

To encourage northern cardinals, black-capped chickadees, and red-breasted nuthatches, use thick-shelled, gray-striped sunflower seed. Safflower seed will exclusively attract northern cardinals.

Make sure not to place wild-bird mixes in tube feeders because birds will remove all the contents just to pick out the sunflower seeds. This leads to more seed on the ground, which can attract rodents.

To attract timid birds like sparrows and juncos, place a small brush pile close to the feeder to give them cover.

The more natural your feeding area is (branches to perch on, shrubs to hide in), the more comfortable birds will feel, which will lead to more feeder participants.

For the serious feeder of birds:

Driving around the island in the winter you will notice good amounts of roadkill (usually birds and Norway rats). Using gloves, collect a recently dead animal and place carefully in a Ziploc bag for transport. Once at home, place the roadkill out in an open area, attaching it with wire to the top of a fence post or tree limb. This odd practice will be appreciated by American and fish crows, and with any luck a northern shrike. For obvious reasons this experiment should only be conducted in the winter.

Winter is a brutal time on Block Island for all animals, especially birds, but by using the suggestions above you will safely make their lives a little easier. Happy feeding!

Red-bellied woodpecker.

The daffodils seem to know that spring is coming, as Old Man Winter delivers one last half-hearted snowfall. The days lengthen and warm; the snow melts for a final time; the red-winged blackbirds return; the peepers are active; and Block Island starts to come alive and embrace the promise of the new season.

It is not yet spring, but it is no longer winter. The daffodils know it… and the snow does too.

Acknowledgements:

There are many people Bruce and I would like to thank for their help in making this project happen. For something that has been more than two years in the making, it is always risky to start acknowledging people, because somebody will undoubtedly be forgotten. So in advance, thank you to everyone who has helped with this book in any way, shape or form. However, without the following people this book could not have happened.

First we would like to thank Keith Lang for his excellent introduction. It does a wonderful job of setting the tone for the pages that follow. It always amazes me how Keith can turn a brief conversation into a wonderful written piece.

Any writer will tell you they are only as good as their editor, and I was lucky enough to have three of them. Suzanne Notler and Charlotte Herring made excellent suggestions, corrections and additions to the first few drafts of the book. Betsy Littlefield did an amazing job on the final edit! At first I was nervous at the seemingly endless number of red marks on each page after Betsy read it, but I soon realized that this book was much better because of them.

John Foster deserves a big thank-you for his work on the final touches to Bruce's wonderful layout work. John's ability to put the final touches on the project, run it through the "Foster-izer" and get it ready for the printer, was a huge timesaver and much appreciated.

Nothing is worse than having a great idea for a section, only to realize that there is no photo to complement it. And also realizing that it will be impossible to wait until the next time the season comes around to take it. The following people or organizations were more than willing to share their amazing photos to solve this problem: Shannon Cotter, Geoffrey Dennis, Olya Evanitsky, John Foster, John Fournier, Kim Gaffett, Andrea Kozol, Keith Lang, Emily Lindquist, Fran Migliaccio, Mystic Aquarium, Suzanne Nolter, The Nature Conservancy, Mike Tucker, Peter Voskamp, and Kevin Weaver. Each of these photos was a total lifesaver, and this book has benefited from their valuable addition.

Other folks helped a ton on specific pages of the book. Big thank-yous go to: Laura Smith, who shared her design for eastern bluebird and American kestrel nesting boxes; Shai Mitra, who contributed Veterans' Day Bird Count totals; and Robert Thorson, who identified all the rocks in the Block Rocks section by email. The willingness of each to share their expertise in a timely manner, was much valued.

It is also important that I acknowledge the students at the Block Island School for their wonderful questions, that keep me researching and learning new things about the nature of Block Island. Most significantly, their love of, and interest in, the natural world gives me tremendous inspiration and hope!

Last, and most important, Bruce and I would like to thank our better halves, Peggy Montgomery and Suzanne Nolter, for their patient support and understanding. In the last year, this book has taken a significant amount of time to complete. And without their encouragement, I am sure we would still be working on it!

—SBC

Photography and illustration credits

Royal Bruce Montgomery: Cover, 3, 7, 9, 14 (bird feet), 15, 19, 20, 23, 25, 26, 27 (photo), 31, 32 (illustrations), 33, 35, 39, 40 (beach), 41 (dead pines), 42, 44, 48-53, 55-59, 61, 64-66, 67 (illustrations), 68 (meadow and sign), 69 (shrubs), 72-75, 78, 79 (all except water lily and golden aster), 80, 81, 84, 85, 87 (illustration), 91, 92 (eagle), 95, 97-99, 101, 102, 104 (owl on right), 106 (snail, egg case, and gull), 107, 108, 110-113, 115, 119 (winterberry), 120 (bayberry), 122, 125 (ducks), 126, 128, 139, 143, 148, back cover.

Scott Comings: 10 (robin), 11, 12, 16, 18, 21, 29, 30, 32 (photo), 34, 40 (blazing star and swamp), 41 (grassland and grosbeak), 45 (goldfinch), 54, 62, 63, 67 (newt), 70 (sign), 71, 76, 77, 79 (golden aster), 82, 83, 86, 88-90, 94, 96 (Dr. Parrish), 100, 103, 104 (owl on left), 105, 106 (blazing star), 116, 117, 118 (nuthatch and cedar), 119 (woodcock), 120 (phragmitics), 121 (sparrow), 123, 127, 129 (shrubs), 132 (hooded seal), 133, 134 (woodcock), 135 (wren), 137, 140.

Comings Family Block Island Collection .... 129 (old photo)
Shannon Cotter 36
Geoffrey Dennis .... 10 (Blackbird)
Olya Evanitsky 118
John Foster .... 45 (oystercatcher)
John Fournier .... 10 (oystercatcher), 43, 135 (harrier)
Kim Gaffett .... 87 (photo), 93, 121 (woodpecker and dovekie)
Holiday Magazine .... 96 (Miss. Dickens)
Andrea Kozol .... 38, 135 (beetle)
Keith Lang .... 24, 70 (view)
Emily Lindquist .... 114, 118 (seals), 132 (harbor seals), inside back cover
Fran Migliaccio 141
Mystic Aquarium .... 13, 60, 120 (seal), 130, 132 (gray and harp seals)
The Nature Conservancy 131
Suzanne Nolter .... 17, 68 (stairs), 69 (view), 79 (water lily), 92 (water lily), 106 (switch grass), 109, 120 (switch grass)
Laura Smith 136
Mike Tucker .... 92 (owl), 119 (owl), 134 (owl)
Peter Voskamp .... 125 (deer)
Kevin Weaver 37
E. L. Youmans .... 14 (swift), 22, 27 (crab), 28, 46, 124, 138

Index

Species, Places, People